THE KICKS SERIES, VOLUME 5

Stealth Kicks

The Forgotten Art of Ghost Kicking

He will not know what hit him:
Feint Kicks based on Misdirection and Dissimulation

from Karate, Kung Fu, Krav Maga, Tae Kwon Do, MMA, Muay Thai, Capoeira and more

By

Marc De Bremaeker

Fons Sapientiae Publishing

Stealth Kicks – The Forgotten Art of Ghost Kicking. Published in 2015 by Fons Sapientiae Publishing, Cambridge, United Kingdom

Please note that the publisher and author of this instructional book are NOT RESPONSIBLE in any manner whatsoever for any injury that may result from practicing the techniques and/or following the instructions given within. Physical and Martial Arts Training can be dangerous, -both to you and others-, if not practiced safely. If you are in doubt as how to proceed or whether your practice is safe, consult with an accredited coach, physical trainer or a trained Martial Art teacher before beginning. Since the physical activities described maybe too strenuous in nature for some readers, it is essential that a physician be consulted prior to any type of training.

martialartkicks@gmail.com

ISBN: 978-0-9934964-9-3

Recommended reading, by the same author:

"Ground Kicks-Advanced Martial Arts Kicks for Goundfighting" (2015)
"Stop Kicks-Jamming, Obstructing, Stopping, Impaling, Cutting and Preemptive Kicks" (2014)
"Low kicks-Advanced Martial Arts Kicks for Attacking the Lower Gates" (2013)
"Plyo-Flex-Plyometrics and Flexibility Training for Explosive Martial Arts Kicks" (2013)
"The Essential Book of Martial Arts Kicks" (2010) by Tuttle Publishing
"Le Grand Livre des Coups de Pied" (2016) by Budo Edition (In French)

Dedication

To the Miracle of New Life, and more particularly
to my beautiful second grandson,

Elliot Chance Yiu Jao De Bremaeker

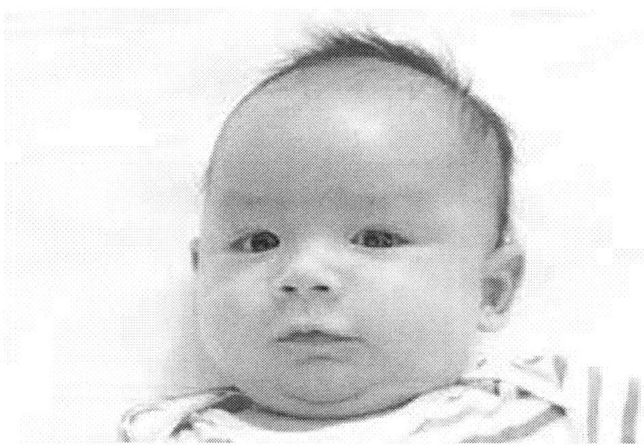

包耀祖

G-d Bless Him

Dear Reader,

In this day and age, the life of a serious author has become quite difficult. The proliferation of books and the explosion of internet content has made it nearly impossible to promote work based on extensive research and requiring complex lay-out. Please enjoy this book. Once you are finished, I would ask kindly that you take a few short minutes to give your honest opinion. A unbiased Amazon review, of even a few words only, would be highly appreciated and encouraging.

Thank You,

Marc

No act of kindness, no matter how small, is ever wasted.
~Aesop

ACKNOWLEDGEMENTS

Without the active support of my wife and life companion, ***Aviva Giveoni***, this book would not have come to life. Being an athlete in her own right, she understands the meaning of hard work and dedication.

Sensei Sydney Faige in action

Among many teachers and heads and shoulders above, my late Sensei, -***Sidney (Shlomo) Faige***-, should be mentioned with longing thankfulness. Sensei Faige founded the Shi-Heun style of Karate.

Roy and Marc

Special Thanks to my life-long friend and training partner, ***Roy Faige***, for his help and support. Roy is now heading the Shi Heun school is also my co-author of *The Essential Book of Martial Arts Kicks*. His influence and advice is felt in nearly every page of this work and the previous books in the series.

Dotan De Bremaeker

Thank you to ***Ziv Faige, Gil Faige, Shay Levy, Dotan De Bremaeker, Nimrod De Bremaeker and Itay Leibovitch*** who helped by painstakingly posing for some of the photographs.

Most photographs have been taken by the author and Aviva Giveoni. But special thanks have to be extended to talented ***Grace Wong*** for some long sessions. Thank you also to professional photographer ***Guli Cohen***: some of the photographs in this book have been extracted from the photo sessions he gracefully did for previous volumes.

The drawings in this book are mine. Everything that I have learned about line art, I have done so from professional Illustrator ***Shahar Navot***, who illustrated *The Essential Book of Martial Arts Kicks.* Thanks Shahar!

All war is deception.
~Sun Tzu

CONTENTS

PART TWO GHOST KICKS

PART THREE NEAR-FEINT KICKS

Foreword to the "Kicks" Series

A goal is not always meant to be reached, it often serves simply as something to aim at.
~Bruce Lee

The 'Foreword' and 'General Introduction' are very similar to those of the previous book in the 'Kicks' series. In order to spare a near re-read to our faithful readers of 'Low Kicks', 'Stop Kicks' and 'Ground Kicks', we invite you to go directly to the 'Introduction to Stealth Kicks' on page 18.

My Martial Arts career started with Judo at age 6. Judo was pretty new Fifty years ago, and a bit mystical in the Western World. A mysterious Oriental Art teaching how to use one's opponent's strength against him was a pretty attractive proposition for a wimpy kid. And the decorum and costume trappings made it a unique selling proposition. That is, until the Kung Fu craze of the Seventies, starring Bruce Lee, and then others.

In my opinion, what fascinated the Western masses, and the teen-ager I was then, was mostly the fantastic kicking maneuvers in the spectacular fights of those Kung-Fu movies. The bulk of the fight scenes were based on spectacular exchanges, the likes of which we had never seen before. What was new and revolutionary back then, may seem banal and common to today's younger reader. But we had been raised in the era of boxing and we had been conditioned by the fair-play of *Queensburry's* rules: we had no idea one could fight *like that*!

It was also the first time that the general public in Europe and America had seen a well-rounded Martial Art in action: punching, but also striking, kicking, throwing down, grappling, locking... It comprised all fighting disciplines in seamless aggregation. Wow! Judo was great, but I now wanted to *kick* like Bruce Lee. I therefore took up *Shotokan Karate*. 'Shotokan-ryu' is not the most impressive kicking style, but it was then the most developed Kicking Art outside of Asia and the only one available to me. It is as well and I certainly do not regret it. Though it is not an art known for extravagant kicks, Shotokan is very well organized didactically. It also emphasizes tradition, hard training, focus (*Zanshin*) and mastery of basic work. In all athletic endeavors, the continuous drilling of basic work at all levels of proficiency is the only real secret to success.

Shotokan Karate drills and low training stances definitely fit this bill.
So, during the whole of my career, I kept practicing Shotokan Karate, or a Shotokan-derived style at all times. I also kept at Judo, my first love. But in parallel, I started to explore other Arts a few years at the time, as opportunities and geography allowed. During my long Martial Arts career, I also did practice assiduously Karatedo from the *Kyokushinkai*, *Shotokai*, *Wadoryu* and *Sankukai* schools. I also trained for long stints of *TaeKwonDo*, *Muay Thai*, *Krav Maga*, *Capoeira*, *Savate-Boxe Française*, two styles of traditional *Ju-Jitsu* and some soft styles *of Kung Fu*. This search is where I developed my individual methods and my own understanding of the Art of Kicking and its place in complex fighting. It also provided the basis on which to build my own personal research. Of course, this is strongly accented towards the type of maneuvers and training that favor my personal physiology and personality, but I have tried very hard to keep an open mind, among others through coaching.

Sometimes during this maybe too eclectic career, my travels took me to the ***Shi-Heun*** School of the late *Sensei Sidney Faige*, mentioned in the Acknowledgements. The *Shi-Heun* style is *Shotokan*-derived and mixed with *Judo* practice. It emphasizes extreme conditioning, total fighting under several realistic rules sets and the personal quest for what works best for oneself. And its self-defense training is based on no-nonsense *Krav Maga*. As this was only the early Eighties, this was definitely a prophetic ancestor of today's phenomena of Mixed Martial Arts of 'UFC' fame. The free-fighting rules in the *Dojo* were 'all-out' and 'to-the-ground', but this did not hinder the success of the School's students in more traditional tournaments under milder rules. The direct disciples of *Sensei Faige* did indeed roam the tournament scene undefeated for years.

Sensei Sidney Faige

In these days, points tournament fighting was mainly WUKO (World Union of Karate Organizations), with some notable exceptions like *Kyokushinkai* and *Semi-contact Karate* bouts. Unfortunately, WUKO generally (boringly) consisted in two competitors safely jumping up-and-down and waiting for the other to initiate a move, in order to stop-reverse-punch him to the body.

Sensei Faige with the winning Israeli National Team; the author and Roy Faige are on the right

When my name was called up in these events, there was usually some spontaneous applause from the spectators; they knew they were going to see, finally, some kicking. I apologize if it sounds like boasting; the point I am trying to make is that Karate fans of these times came to see kicking and rich fighting moves, and not some unrealistic form of boxing. And this is not to denigrate *Karatedo*, but more the castrating effect of unintelligent rules sets.

Marc and Roy facing off at the finals of a 1987 Points Tournament

Marc, kicking in point tournament

It is my strong belief that Kicking is what made the Oriental Martial arts so appealing. As I have already mentioned in articles and previous books, I do firmly argue that ***kicking is more effective than punching.*** This usually causes many to stand up, disagree and maybe want to *punch* me. This is an old debate, still raging, and I respectfully ask to be allowed to complete the sentence. I strongly believe that kicking is more effective than punching, but proficiency takes much more time and work. When presented this way, I do hope that this opinion is more acceptable to most. Let me detail my position briefly.

Kicking is more efficient than punching:

1. Because of the longer range

2. Because the muscles of the leg are much bigger and powerful than those of the arms

3. Because kicking targets, unlike punching targets, go from head all the way down to toes

4. Because kicks are less expected and therefore more surprising than punches, especially at shorter ranges

I readily admit that the opponents of my position do have valid arguments. They will point out that kicks are inherently slower than punches and can be easily jammed because they start from longer ranges. They will also point out that kicking often opens the groin, while forgetting that so does punching usually as well. It is my experience that, ***- after a lot of dedicated and intelligent work-,*** many kicks can be *as swift as punches and can be delivered at all ranges and from all positions.*

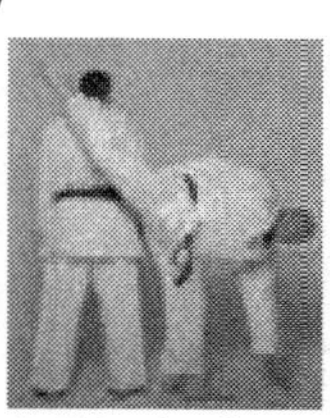

One needs to drill kicks from very close ranges as well

During all my training years, I invested a lot of time, personal drilling and original research into Kicking Arts from all over the world. I experimented with all training tips gathered and I endeavored to try all mastered new kick variations in actual free-fighting and competitive tournaments. Here is the place to note that this is *not* about a huge number of different techniques; it is about finding the best possible techniques suited to one's specific strength, physiology and affinities (Once you have found your few techniques and the best way to drill them, then you focus on fast and perfect execution from all ranges and positions). During my quest in the realm of kicking, I slowly developed a personal kicking style based on my personal history and mindset. I researched most of the available literature, but very few treatises were actually *dedicated* to kicking. The few works I found about kicking were generally very good, but usually style-restricted and unorganized. I never found the kind of book that I would have liked to have at the start of my Martial arts career. And so I decided to write it myself and share my global view of the subject. To the best of my knowledge, there has never been an attempt to compile and organize all the different Kick types and variation in such a way that it could serve as a reference work and the basis for exploration for the kick-lover. I did try to start this potentially huge work, probably imperfectly, with a series of Books I chose to name the 'Kicks series'. A global overview of Basic Kicks was presented in **'The Essential Book of Martial Arts Kicks'** (Tuttle). Its success lead me to follow with the important lower gates attacks in **'Low Kicks'**, and then **'Stop Kicks'** about preempting, jamming, impaling, obstructing and 'cutting' Kicks. As a sign of these MMA times, the series was naturally enriched by **'Ground Kicks'**. We are now continuing this work with this present volume, **'Stealth Kicks',** covering misdirection and dissimulation while kicking; and we hope that all this work will be built upon by others in the future. As mentioned and underlined many times, kicking proficiency requires a lot of serious drilling. I have therefore also published a work about the basic general drills that will help you reach higher levels of proficiency. As in all athletic endeavors, it is the basic drills that will build the strong foundation needed; and it is to those basic drills that the truly good athlete will come back for further progress again and again. **'Plyo-Flex Training for Explosive Martial Arts Kicks and Other Performance Sports'** does present those general, basic but so-important exercises that one should regularly practice for continuous improvement of kicking proficiency.

And now last, but certainly not least: it is important to underline that my strong views do not try in any way or form to denigrate the Punching Arts. My personal philosophy is that Martial arts are a whole with a world of possible emphasis. A complete Martial artist should be proficient in punching, kicking, moving, throwing, grappling, evading and more.

But every Artist will have his own preferences and particular skills in his own way to look at the Martial Arts as a whole. And here must I add the obvious: *there is no kicking mastery* without punching proficiency! Even for a dedicated kicker, punching will be needed for closing the gap, feinting, setting up a kick, following it up and much more... This will be made abundantly clear from most of the applications presented in this volume, just as it is clear from all my previous work.
It must be said that Punching is sometimes the best or the only answer in some situations. I have known and met some extraordinary Punching Artists using kicks only as feints or set-ups. On the other hand, great kickers like legendary *Bill 'Superfoot' Wallace* were extremely skilled punchers and working hard at it, as I personally experienced in a few seminars. Kick and Punch, Punch and Kick: well-rounded is the secret.
And this leads me naturally to my last point. I would not want my books and my views to be misunderstood as an appeal to always kick when fighting, and especially not as an appeal to always high-kick. The best kicker in the world should not execute a high Kick, *just because he can*. A Kick should only be delivered *because and when it is suitable* to a specific situation! Obvious maybe, but certainly worth reminding. In someone else's words:

Take things as they are. Punch when you have to punch. Kick when you have to kick.
~Bruce Lee

General Introduction: The 'Kicks' Series

This book is not a "How to" book for the beginner, but, hopefully, a reference work for the experienced Martial Artist. It presupposes the knowledge of stances, footwork, and concepts of centerline, guards, distance, evasions and more. It also expects from the reader a good technical level in his chosen Martial style, including kicking. As this work is building upon the *Essential* basic level towards more sophisticated kicking maneuvers, all *Essential Kicks* are considered mastered from the author's point of view. The reader is invited to consult previous work already mentioned above. This book is intended as a tool for self-exploration and research about kicking outside experienced Artists' specific style. Therefore, the description of the different kicks is very short and typical examples are only briefly explained. The author relies more on photos and illustrations to exemplify his point. Let the reader try it and adapt it to his liking and morphology.

The author tends to prefer drawings over photographs to be able to underline salient points sometimes hidden in photos.

The experienced trainee will probably notice quickly that the basic background of the author is Japanese *Karate*. This cannot be avoided but was not deliberate. This book aspires to be as "style-less" as possible, as its purpose is to bridge across the different schools on the basis of common immutable principles. The author's philosophy is that Martial Arts are an interconnected whole, where styles are just interpretations of some principles and their adaptation to certain sets of strategies, rules, cultural constraints, or morphologies. It is one and same thing, although it may seem different from different angles. In the pictures and illustrations, the reader can see technical differences and adaptations from different styles. This is done on purpose to underscore the style-less philosophy of the treatise. Sometimes the foot of the standing leg is flat on the floor, as required in traditional Japanese styles, and sometimes the heel is up as in certain deliveries of Korean arts. It should be clear that the biomechanical principles are identical for trained artists and the small differences of emphasis are meaningless. It is more important for a trainee to adapt the technique to his morphology and preferences, once it is well mastered. This book definitely does not pretend to present an axiomatic way to kick! In the same vein, arms during kicking are sometimes close to the body in hermetic guard and sometimes loose and counterbalancing the kicking move. Hands can be open, or fists tight.

Like in previous efforts, it has proved very difficult to name and organize the kicks into and within groups. The author has given the techniques descriptive names in English, whenever possible commonly used names. But the more complex, exotic and hybrid kicks have sometimes either several different appellations in use or none, while being difficult to describe. The names the author has chosen could certainly be disputed and improved upon by some. For the most basic kicks common to all styles, we have added the respective original foreign names. The author apologizes in advance to the purists of all styles: It is clear that the description of a technique cannot be in all details valid for all styles (For example, the basic Front Kick is taught differently in *Shotokan* karate than in *TaeKwonDo)*. The original foreign names in Japanese, Korean, Chinese or Portuguese are just there as an indication for further research by the reader. It should also be noted that some techniques have different names in different schools of the same Art! For the more complex or exotic kicks, we have purposely omitted original names. Only when a kick is especially typical of a certain style, did we mention it, as a tribute to the specific school. The author also apologizes for his arbitrary transcription of foreign names, as purists could dispute the way it was done.

The kicks presented in this volume are tagged "Advanced". This does not necessarily mean that they are more difficult to execute than the *Essential* basic kicks. On the contrary. Besides being a requisite of some form of classification, it mainly means that the principles behind the "basic" kicks should be first thoroughly mastered. A *Front Stop Kick* is relatively easy to perform and slightly different than a regular Front Kick. But for maximum power, it is important to follow the same principles of a basic Front Kick, with chambering, kicking through and chamber back. And the principles of the leg development stay the same for the more difficult Flying Front Kick. And even if a Low Front kick seems easy to perform, it will be done so under the same principles already mastered for maximum speed and power. A typical Feint Kick, the Roundhouse-chambered Front Kick is slightly tricky to master, but it is more a question of hip flexibility and acquaintance drilling: the principles behind the power of what is ultimately a Front Kick stay the same. Once the principles behind the basic Front Kick are mastered, all other "Advanced" kicks will be faster and more powerful. **This is all about mastering the basics and principles first**, and only later trying out variations in all kinds of situations, fancier or not. This is, by the way, true for any other physical activity. But because Advanced Kicks are more a variation on the theme of their underlying basic kicks, they will be presented in all their complexity by many variations in specific applications.
This volume will not detail *Essential* basic kicks. If needed for the clarity of the narrative, some of them will be very briefly illustrated as a reminder.

This volume deals with ***Ghost and Feint Kicks*** only, as a variation of all six basic categories of Essential Kicks presented in previous work (Front, Side, Back, Roundhouse, Hook and Crescent Kicks). Further volumes are in preparation to present the spectacular Flying kicks, the complex Multiple kicks, the surprising Suicide kicks and the devastating Joint kicks.

Some Advanced Kicks have been omitted, as the author felt he had to draw the line somewhere. Again the decision was arbitrary, and could be considered as open for discussion. First have been omitted the whole range of nuances of a given kicks: As already mentioned, the same basic kicks are delivered in slightly different ways in all different styles and schools. The small differences come from the different emphasis of each style, and do not alter the basic principles. The author therefore described the kicks in the way his own experience dictates as best, and each reader can adapt it to his own personality. Many possible variations are presented for completeness in the applications though.

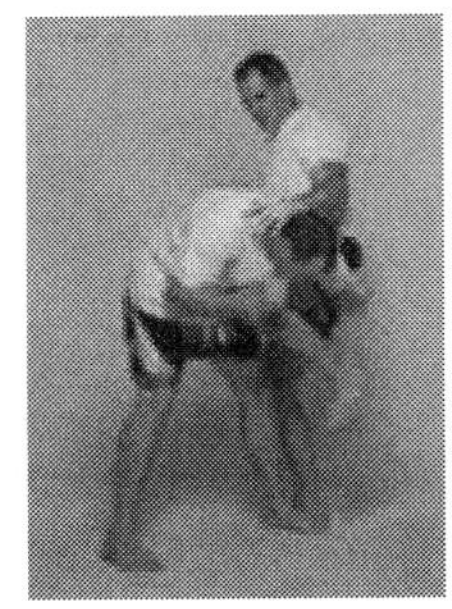
Knee Strike

Secondly, hybrid kicks variations have been omitted, as the infinite number of intermediate possible deliveries in between two kicks would make this endeavor ridiculous. For example, many possible kicks as hybrids of Front and Roundhouse Kicks exist, each one with different levels of emphasis on the "front" side and the "roundhouse" side. In this specific book about Feint Kicks of all types, it is even truer: there are a great number of deliveries possibilities to execute a Roundhouse-chambered Front Kick, as the length and depth of the feinting part of the kick is highly dependent on the circumstances and the reaction of the opponent.
Kicks combinations, and kick-punch combinations are infinite in numbers and will not be presented as such; *but feint-kicking with the purpose of setting up punches will be briefly hinted at.* Knee strikes, although very effective and versatile, will not be presented; for the purpose of this work, they will not be considered as kicks.

The remaining ***Feint Kicks and Ghost Kicks***, which will be presented in this work, will be so, generally, in a set descriptive way: After a brief ***general*** introduction and the ***description*** of the kick (mainly by illustrations), the main ***key points*** to remember for a good execution will be noted. Please remember that the book is intended for conversant martial artists. The relevant ***targets*** to be kicked in most applications will be mentioned, although only general targets will be mentioned: The specific and precise vulnerable points are out of the scope of this volume. Examples of ***typical application*** will then be detailed and illustrated.

The typical application will generally be, unless irrelevant, a detailed use or set up of the given kick in a tournament-type situation. This will generally be a movements combination based on alternating different attack angles or/and levels (For example: hi-lo-hi, or/and outside/inside/outside), or the Progressive Indirect Attack principle as it is called by Jeet Kune Do artists. The tactical principle involved will not be detailed or presented systematically though, as it is beyond the scope of this volume. Of course, those applications will also usually be relevant to real life situation, and training work. Whenever possible, ***specific training*** tips to improve the given kick will be detailed. The specific training section will be brief and will only deal with the very specific characteristics of the kick and the ways to perfect them; general kick training guidelines are outside the scope of this book. The training of a Feint Kick is generally also the drilling of the corresponding Essential basic kicks, before the fusion of the two into the feinting version. Back to basics then! Last, and in order to widen the scope of applications, an additional example of the use of the kick will be presented, generally more suitable to a ***self-defense*** or mixed martial arts application.
And now, let us go to STEALTH KICKS...

Victorious warriors win first and then go to war, while defeated warriors go to war first and then seek to win
~Sun Tzu

Introduction to Stealth Kicking: Feint Kicks and Ghost Kicks

There are three kinds of fighters: the aggressive fighter who charges in blindly trying to get the upper hand, the defensive fighter who blocks and evades until his opponent is tired, and then the most dangerous type of fighter, the one who waits for his opponent to make a mistake
~Aaron B. Powell

Stealth: The act of moving, proceeding, or acting in a covert way; the quality or characteristic of being furtive or covert; a secret, quiet, and clever way of moving or behaving; the state of being furtive or unobtrusive...

These several definitions of the word *Stealth* do give a clear idea of what we were intending to talk about when we did title this book: Stealth Kicks.
Furtive, covert, clever...

But under the title ***Stealth Kicks***, we have grouped two different categories of sneaky kicking maneuvers: the *Feint Kicks* and the *Ghost Kicks*. Both categories are based on treachery and misdirection; they are therefore both tactical variations of Basic Kicks, and it is why they are presented together. Both categories are highly sophisticated kicking variations, preferring brain power over brute force: you trick your opponent in order to have your kick reach him. Both *Feint Kicks and Ghost Kicks* were an important part of older Arts, but their practice has been a bit forgotten along the rise the sporting versions of Martial practice. Mastering Stealth Kicking takes assiduous and time-consuming specific training, and the executions are often incompatible with the various rules of sport competition. But, for the well-rounded Martial Artist, Stealth Kicking is an important tool and, most probably, the most intelligent way to approach applied kicking.
The difference between the two types of Stealth Kicking is quite simple. Examples will be given in the respective introductions coming later in the text, but in brief:

- ***Feint Kicks*** are based on *misdirection*: your starting action will cause your opponent to mis-react in a way that will uncover and open the real ultimate target of your technique.
- ***Ghost Kicks*** are based on *dissimulation*: you deliver kicking techniques that your opponent will have the utmost difficulty to see coming, as their trajectory will be outside of his field of vision.

There is, in the author's opinion, no higher level of kicking that Stealth Kicking. In the Arts of War, surprise and deception are the most valuable attributes to any encounter. But mastery of Stealth Kicking requires a lot of training, purposeful free-fighting, experimentation and the development of intuitive fighting: not all techniques do apply to all situations and to all opponents. And moreover, the opponent must often be first conditioned to one way of reacting, before the feinting technique can work. A simple example: a high Roundhouse Kick starting as a Front Kick-feint will have a higher success chance if the opponent is first attacked with convincing and same-looking Front Kicks. One must also remember that the susceptibility to Feints can vary enormously from one Artist to another: this is a question of a particular personality or mindset, a question of fighting style and a question of proficiency. For instance: a strong but inexperienced Artist could not "see" the intended Feint, or a head-strong Stop-fighter could not care and plunge forward regardless of the feint.
Keep in mind that there are no set rules, but the incremental building of intelligent intuitive fighting. But, in the end, the mastery of Stealth Kicking will certainly justify the long and hard work invested in it.

First, the reader is invited to try to execute the kicks presented here in the spirit in which they are presented. The reader is supposed to be a practicing Martial Artist and will have no problem to execute the techniques presented, as they are combinations and/or variations of regular basic techniques. In fact, sometimes, it is nearly only the mindset that differentiates the Stealth Kick from its underlying basic kick.
The reader should then try to drill the applications presented, both in the *Applications* and in the *Self-defense* sections. Some of those combinations may seem far-fetched or inappropriate to some readers, because it does not align with their style, because the way free-fighting is regulated in their art/sport or because they do not "believe" in it. The author begs you to drill these applications anyway: the body should be subjected to all possible situations and ways to fight, even if the specific technique would not be used willfully by the trainee. Just like mental intuition is in fact based on a long experience at the subconscious level, real fighting is done automatically by your body and by your *unconscious* mind, based on all the experience gathered in training. You

never know when your body will decide in the fight that a certain "new" reaction is the right thing to do. You can plan a general tactic before a fight, but once in the fire of the action, it is your unconscious that will react: if you would have to think about your reaction to a specific strike, you would be in serious trouble. Therefore you must feed "data" to your body and mind, by drilling time and again all sorts of combinations, techniques, reactions, positioning, and more.

I can illustrate this with a personal anecdote that I already mentioned in my previous book about *Stop Kicks.* It is relevant here as well, as my delivery of the Stop Hook Kick is highly based on Stealth principles, as will be explained in the Ghost Kicks section: What would become my favorite stop-kicking technique, - the 'timing' Hook Stop Kick-, just appeared suddenly of its own volition in my free-fighting practice. I had drilled it in training, but along with many other Stop Kicks, and I had not felt any special affinity for it before. I had drilled it under the Stealth trajectory I had been introduced to, but I definitely preferred the Stealth version of the Roundhouse Kick. In fact, I used to Roundhouse stop-kick my opponents most of the time, as a favorite technique everybody knew about. But I kept drilling all sorts of kicks, including the famous Stealth-trajectory Hook Stop Kick. And both my body and mind did probably identify this particular kick as most suitable to my morphology and personality, and un-holstered it at the right moment in a no-thinking sparring situation. Needless to say that, from then on, I did give it particular attention and further training. It became my most natural and potent competing weapon. My regular opponents knew it was coming, but could not stop or avoid it. The point is: Try everything and drill it hard; your body and mind will do the rest.

And try not to judge other styles and other ways of fighting than your own school: you can never really know. Not everything in your style or not everything working for you is necessarily the best for others. Among the comments I received after the publication of *The Essential Book of Martial Arts Kicks*, was from a reader that did not agree to the use of a Drop Kick presented as an application against a mugger in the Self-Defense section. Why go to the ground against a mugger? Although I personally would not use this particular technique, it is certainly valid if used by some artists like Capoeira practitioners, MMA ground fighters, some Indonesian stylists and many more. You could find yourself on the ground by accident too! I have had the greatest difficulty in handling ground fighters myself, and I would not be quick to judge any technique. I advise the reader to keep things in perspective, to be respectful of the emphasis of other styles and to try everything. And to keep an open mind...Hubris has caused many downfalls...

With this in mind, the reader is invited to start his journey in Stealth Kicking with the more traditional and better-known *Feint Kicks*.

PART ONE

FEINT KICKS

PART ONE FEINT KICKS

INTRODUCTION TO FEINT KICKS

Feint is a French term that entered English via the discipline of Fencing. Feints are maneuvers designed to *distract or mislead*, done by giving the impression that a certain technique will take place, while in fact another, or sometimes none at all, will. It generally is a feigned attack designed to draw a defensive action *away* from the intended target. Other definitions are: a *deceptive* action calculated to *divert* attention from one's real purpose; a *mock* blow or attack on or toward one part in order to distract attention from the point one really intends to attack; a quick movement that you make to *trick* an opponent

Feint Kicks, unlike the *Ghost Kicks* that will be presented later, are intended to be detected by the opponent and to cause a reaction! This is the big difference between the two categories of Stealth Kicks. In fact, Feint Kicks even need sometimes to have exaggerated starts, in order to make sure a reaction is provoked.
This book is not about feinting, it is about Feint Kicks. In fact some Feint Kicks can be executed after a feint in order to make them more realistic. A feint is a move, -generally at the start of an offensive combination -, that distracts or misdirects the opponent in order to allow you to close the distance to your opponent in the safest possible way before you start the actual technique you intended from the beginning. The simplest example is the banal Jab-high feint that prepares a following mid-level Front Kick; and we have presented below the corresponding traditional Karate combination with a full-stepped *high* lunge punch-opening to divert attention from the real coming Front Kick (*lo*) and the (*hi*) Jab follow-up.

Opening high punch-feint to prepare the mid-level Penetrating Front Kick; capped with a high jab follow-up

The principles of feinting are, of course, well-known by the experienced Artist and do not need deeper analysis here; they are not relevant to this book and will be analyzed in detail in a future volume about tactical considerations. Two further very simple examples are presented on the next page.

Throwing your keys towards an aggressor's face is practical feint that will have him react and open his mid-section to a powerful kick. And a high palm strike feint will totally cover the incoming low Soccer Front Kick to the assailant's shin. Feinting is simple, and basically trivial.

Throwing a small object towards an opponent's eyes will cause him to lift his hands instinctively

High palm Strike, low shin Kick

Feints are tactically extremely important, but this book is about *Feint Kicks*: Kicks that start one way to cause a reaction, and then evolve into different maneuvers taking advantage of the opening created by this original misguided reaction. We shall describe *Kicks* which turn into other *Kicks* in order to surprise the opponent. The Art of feinting is certainly not limited to Kicks. It is much more encompassing than that and will not be treated here. A feint can be a full move, a step, a rhythm break, a head fake, an eye move, and many other things. Feinting is a very important part of any Martial Art, but at a tactical level far beyond the scope of this book which is concentrating on individual moves. An example of a feint turning into a Kick, but *definitely not a Feint Kick*, is presented in the side Figures: a fake "shoot" to lower the opponent's guard and attention). Further in the text, we shall also present a few examples of Near-feint Kicks and Feinting Kicks intended to prepare a punching attack.

A feint but not a Feint Kick: Two fake lunges towards the opponent's legs turn into a high Roundhouse Kick and a kneeing follow-up

Feints can be very subtle and innocuous-looking moves, but which still are traps that can cause an opponent to react in a way that will make him vulnerable. In the example below, simple footwork can become a great set-up for a surprising kick. The example below is certainly not a Feint Kick, but a still an effective surprising kick at the end of a misdirecting set-up. If you look at it in the context of *Stop Kicks*, it would be an ***'Attack on Recovery'***. In the example, you simply move your front foot forward, as if stepping to attack; as your opponent reacts with a classic Reverse Stop Punch or Counter Punch, you pull the foot back. It looks as if you have decided to abandon your attack and retreat. As your opponent abandons his own counter and pulls back, you suddenly hop forward with a rebounding Front-leg Hopping Front Kick. Follow up with an Oblique Jab as you land. As you can see, feinting is ubiquitous, and it is basically a Mind Game.

Feinting Footwork to Front Kick on recovery

Feint Kicks are different from Double Kicks, Multiple Kicks and kicking combinations. What we consider as *Double and Multiple Kicks* (that we will expose fully in a coming book) are **two Kicks in succession**, *both* kicks aiming to score and hit the opponent *powerfully*.
Feint Kicks are generally Near-double Kicks in the sense that they are mostly two Kicks in succession, ***but*** with the first kick aiming *exclusively* at eliciting a reaction from the opponent that will open a target to the second kick. The purpose of the first Kick, whether it is powerful and fully developed or it is half-baked or only hinted, is not to score at all, but just to misdirect. Sometimes, the difference with a Double Kick can be borderline, and more mental than physical, but it is a really different concept and must be approached as such.
For example, I shall present my personal experience with the Front-chambered Roundhouse kick, a very classic Feint Kick, in which you want your opponent to believe you are front-kicking low and therefore cause him to open himself to a high Roundhouse Kick. I used to train endlessly on the heavy bag to deliver a nearly *fully-developed* Front Kick, *touching* the bag at full extension, before turning into a Roundhouse. This particular Front Kick was not powerful but it was fast and convincing. This hard work helped me to make this kick a great success in tournaments where I was fighting experienced "hard-to-convince" opponents. It should be noted that, against less experienced fighters, this would have been totally unnecessary, and a Front Kick *Chamber* would have been more than enough for misdirection (while also allowing for a more powerful Roundhouse Kick). We shall dwell on these nuances when covering said Front-chambered Roundhouse Kick.
It is important to bear in mind that the way the first Kick, -i.e. *the feint-*, is delivered will be highly dependent upon the particulars of the specific encounter. The point to remember here is that a lot of the difference between a *real* first Kick and a *feint* Kick is in the mindset and the specific situation.

Another important point to make about Feint Kicks, is that they generally should be preceded by some brainwashing of your opponent: Just like Pavlov's dogs, you should condition him to expect a certain attack by delivering it fully for a few times. Then deliver the same opening attack as a feint!
It is also extremely important to remember that it is not recommended to use sophisticated feints against an un-experienced opponent. Somebody who is not used to sparring will not easily read the signs you are trying to send. You risk completely missing the misdirecting part by being too subtle and sophisticated, and will so place yourself in danger. This is also one of the reasons why sophisticated and spectacular Feint Kicks are often more "tournament" Kicks than Self-defense Kicks. Keep in mind that, -against a strong but unexperienced opponent-, your feints must be much *cruder*.

Feint kicking must also be used very carefully against forward-rushing stop-fighters! You will have to gauge the leanings and tactics of your opponent before choosing your own strategy. If your opponent lunges forward with a Stop kick or a Stop Punch as soon as you initiate a committed attack, he will not pick up on your misdirection: he will already be upon you! This kind of opponent calls for feinting a starting attack with a head fake or a body move, and then stop-kicking him in his own stop-attack; numerous examples are scattered in our previous book about *Stop Kicks*.

With all this said, it is still clear that, -when wisely used-, Feint Kicks are a great fighting tool. As always in the fighting Arts, everything else being equal, doing the unexpected will always bring you victory.

The layout of this book will follow the same pattern of the previous ones in the series, for consistency purposes. It should be understood, though, that the examples presented in the "Typical application" and "Self-defense" paragraphs will be relatively trivial and limited in numbers. Feint kicks are, by definition, complex kicks leading by stealth towards a successful kick aiming at concluding the confrontation. Basically, most examples presented will be based on a first move aiming at conditioning the opponent to expect one type of attack, followed by the delivery of the Feint Kick itself. And then sometimes, a suitable follow-up. There are not too many variations on that theme, and examples will be straightforward.

Training Feint Kicks

We shall now add just a few words about drilling those Feint Kicks.

Drilling Feint Kicks is based on common sense; we shall give a few pointers in the text, but the general principles are briefly covered here.

- *Drill the underlying basic Kicks*: There is no Feint Kick if you have not fully mastered the basic Kicks. And mastering means: keep drilling the basics. You will not develop a successful Front-chambered Roundhouse Feint Kick if you have not achieved good technique for the basic Essential Front Kicks and Roundhouse Kicks. It is recommended to drill the underlying Kicks just before training the complex Feint Kicks.
- *Drill the Feint Kick in front of the mirror*: You must see what your opponent will see. Make sure to eliminate gradually any tell-tales of your real ultimate intentions. It is recommended to drill the first half part of the kick, the Feint-part, alone. Until it looks convincing. Then work on the transition. Then only, start working on the full Feint Kick.
- *Drill on stationary targets*: Hit the heavy bag with the end-Kick, as power is needed to make the maneuver worthwhile. A technique ending "out-of-breath" with no residual power (because of the convoluted trajectory), is not a Kick; it is a tap or a feint.
- *Drill with a partner*: There is no alternative to having a partner "reading" you, checking the realism of your Feinting start.
- *Use in free-fighting and competition* to assess your progress: There is no alternative to learn good feint-kicking and its use in different situations against different types of opponents. You should learn as much from a failed attempt as from a successful one. Remember that learning is a process, especially when using what you learn must be intuitive. Keep your ego in check and focus on the goal.
- *Train for flexibility*: Feint Kicking often requires convoluted hip movements that will be easier and faster with good flexibility. The reader is invited to consult a previous book about Plyo-Flex training, and, -if possible-, add *Plyo-Flex* training to his schedule.

Specific training drills and pointers will be presented in the text. The reader is invited to pay attention and try them all.

The Kicks

1. The Front-chambered Roundhouse Kick

General

This is probably the most classic of the traditional Feint Kicks: You cause your opponent to try to block an incoming mid-level penetrating Front Kick which will unexpectedly turn into a high Roundhouse Kick, connecting at the now unprotected head. There are two extremes in the possible deliveries; at one end of the spectrum: the Small Roundhouse Kick as presented in our previous book about *Essential* Kicks. At the other end of the spectrum, we have a fast Penetrating Front Kick going nearly all the way to full extension before recoiling back partially into a Full Roundhouse chamber, and then a Full Roundhouse Kick. Both extremes will be presented here. Both are important as opponents react differently to feints: Some less skilled fighters will be easily convinced by the short version, when seasoned opponents will need to see the long version to start believe a Front Kick is coming. And, of course, you will have all other nuances in between. The Front Kick-feint is usually delivered from the rear leg, as the signals thus sent are much clearer than for a front-leg Front Kick. This is the classic execution, but we shall present a front-leg version for the sake of completeness and as an encouragement to striving for excellence. All variations are worth exploring and drilling, in order to prepare the fighter for all possibilities.

The Front-chambered Roundhouse Kick is a must-practice kick, as a Feint Kick first, but also for speed, flexibility and overall kicking proficiency.

The photo series below exemplifies the principles explained before: the conditioning of the opponent to the mid-level Front Kick set up, the development of the Front kick-feint up to the necessary point where it causes an attempted block, and the evolution into a high Roundhouse Kick.

The Front-chambered Roundhouse kick and its preparation

Description

The short version of the kick mentioned above, which is basically the *Essential* Small Roundhouse Kick, is presented below. You basically chamber a fully classic rear-leg Front Kick, but, -from the front chamber-, you smoothly and gradually develop a high Roundhouse Kick by pivoting with the hips and twisting the leg. This is simple, natural and fast, but needs drilling to learn to develop power for.

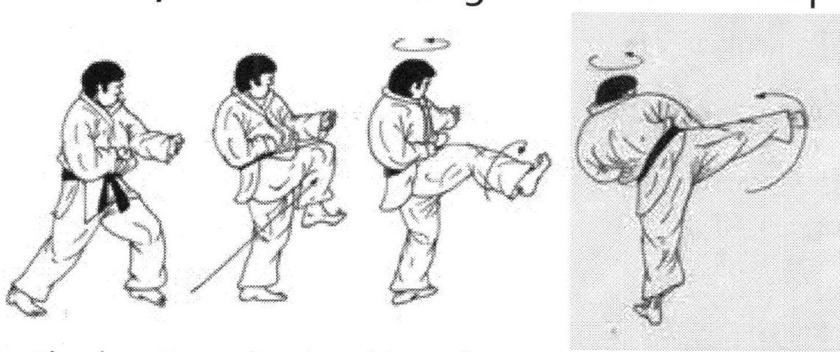

The short Front-chambered Roundhouse Feint Kick, aka basic Small Roundhouse Kick

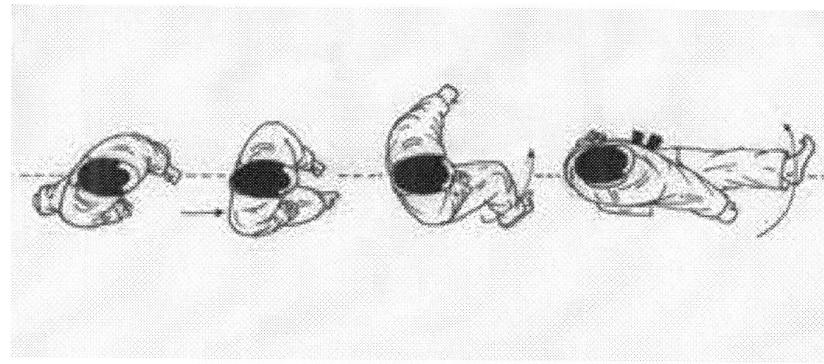

Top view of the Front-chambered Roundhouse Feint Kick

Front view of the Front-chambered Roundhouse Kick

Side view of the Front-chambered Roundhouse Kick

The *long* version of the kick is presented below: you deliver a fast Front Kick <u>until you provoke a reaction</u>; speed is more important than power as you do not need to score. This can be up to the full extension of your Front Kick if necessary: what is important is that it goes fast and causes a reactive blocking move. As soon as the opponent lowers his guard to block or check the kick aiming for his groin or lower torso, you retract the leg partially and pivot into a Roundhouse chambering position. You then deliver the Roundhouse Kick with maximum power to his unprotected head. This version is more powerful because of the dynamic recoil before the final kick. It is also more convincing than the short version, because the Front Kick travels a long way before evolving. It is more difficult though, and requires serious training. With the feint part of the kick being so 'long', the difference between this Feint Kick and a *Double Kick* is speed, focus and mental attitude!

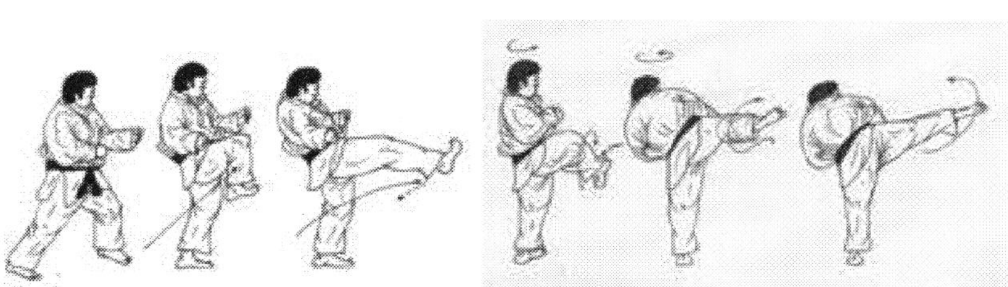

*The **long** Front-chambered Feint Roundhouse Kick*

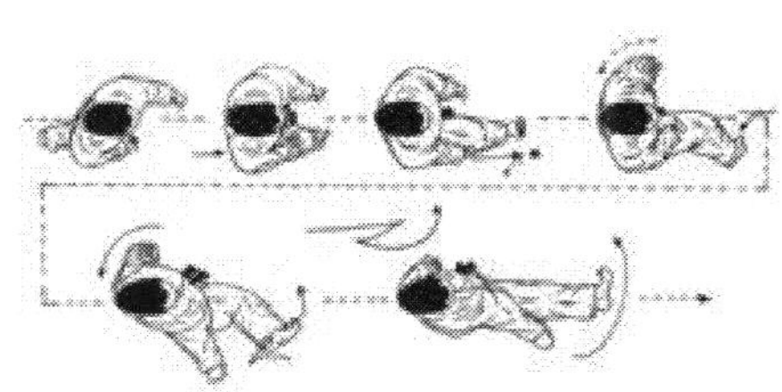

Top view of the long Front-chambered Roundhouse Feint Kick

All variations between both extremes are valid and relevant to specific situations and relative strength of opponents. The photos series below show the difference, in front view, between these two extremes.

The ***short*** *Front-chambered Roundhouse Feint Kick, compare to following series*

*The '**long**' Front-chambered Roundhouse Feint Kick, nearly a full Front Kick start*

Key points

- Master Key: A convincing Front Kick, both mentally and physically. According to the situation, a chamber may suffice; but you must be ready to go further into the Front Kick-feint.
- The Front Kick delivery must be with loose muscles for speed, with no unnecessary contractions. No need for power at the early stage.
- Ideally, the technique should follow one or more full Front Kick attacks on your part. The feint-chamber should be identical to the Front chamber of your Feint Kick. In some cases, it can be *exaggerated* on purpose to better fool the opponent.
- The hip thrust of the starting front chamber is critical to the momentum needed to make the Roundhouse powerful enough to be a relevant Kick.
- Most of the time, a follow-up will be warranted.

The Front Kick-chamber must be as convincing as possible: vintage picture of Marc De Bremaeker in tournament

Typical applications

The Figures below show the traditional application: You deliver a full-powered Front Kick at belt level and *slightly on your opponent's out-side*, and retract the leg back in your original focused stance. In matching stances, this should be an easy kick to block; you have to kick outside just enough to still cause the block, but not more. Make sure your Front Kick is a realistic attack. It is also recommended to keep your guard up, or even fake-punch while retracting the kicking leg, in order to prevent a counter by the opponent. Repeat immediately and make sure the chamber looks identical; but this time, you will switch into a high Roundhouse Kick as soon as your opponent repeats his 'easy' downward block. Backfist his face from his in-side while lowering the leg. Let the foot rebound on the floor into a low Roundhouse to the opponent's front leg or into a sweep as illustrated. Keep pounding.

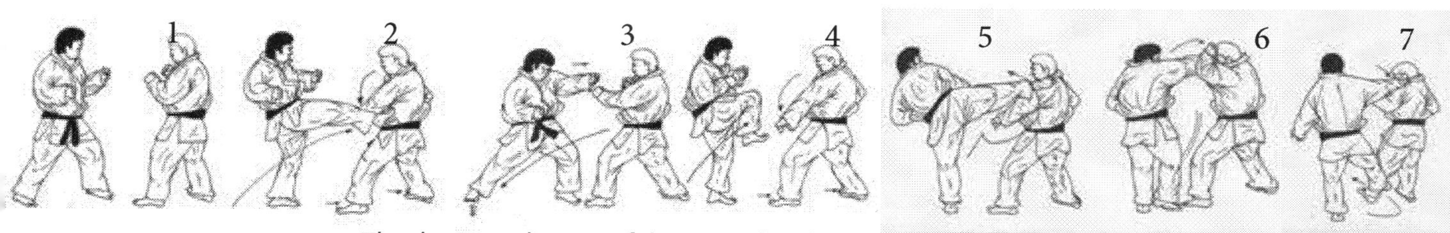

The classic application of the Front-chambered Roundhouse Feint Kick

A very useful variation of the classic Front-chambered Roundhouse Feint Kick, is the one starting with a *Low* Front Kick. The Low Front Kick, as described in our previous book about *Low Kicks*, is a very painful attrition Kick, easy to deliver with no telegraphing and which will always cause a reaction if repeated. The shin is a very sensitive anatomical part of the body, and once kicked there, your opponent will certainly try to avoid being hit again. In this version with a Low Front Kick, the chambering is minimal, but it is enough to make sure that the kick is discernible by the opponent to get his attention down. This is also a version in which the starting kick should be delivered nearly all the way, or even delivered fully before evolving into a high Roundhouse. This is up to you and the specific circumstances. It is a great variation, easy to succeed with and well worth drilling.

The Low Front Kick variation, easy and very efficient

We have mentioned that this Feint kick is *usually* not powerful enough to conclude an engagement, except maybe in a points-type tournament. The Kick should be followed by a finishing blow, or more likely, a combination follow-up. Therefore, of course, the whole Front-chambered Roundhouse Feint Kick could also simply be the confusing start of a longer combination attack. The photos below illustrate this concept, with a starting painful Front-chambered Roundhouse Kick to the kidneys; the follow-up being a Back-fist Strike and a high front-leg Hook Kick.

The Front-chambered Roundhouse Feint Kick as the confusing start of an aggressive combination

Specific training

- Drill the underlying basic kicks before any Feint Kick training (See Illustrative Photos at the end of the section). Remember to drill the Front Kick for *speed*, with relaxed muscles.
- Practice in front of the mirror; concentrate especially on fully identical chambers for the Essential Front Kick and the Front-chambered Roundhouse Feint Kick.
- Use a marked heavy bag especially for training the long version: *touch lightly* the bag with the Front Kick, and then hit forcefully with the Roundhouse Kick. It is best to use a 'belly-bag' or a bag to which you add a lower thick layer of foam for extra distance. In a separate drill, add a chair in front of you to force you to execute a high and clear Front-chamber for higher discernibility.
- Partner training is key. Practice the Feint Kick first, with comments by your helper. Then alternate the technique and regular Front Kicks. Then deliver both Front Kicks and Feint Kicks at random, with your partner trying to block.
- Try the Feint Kick in free-fighting, but remember not to over-use a feint maneuver, lest it loses its surprising facet.

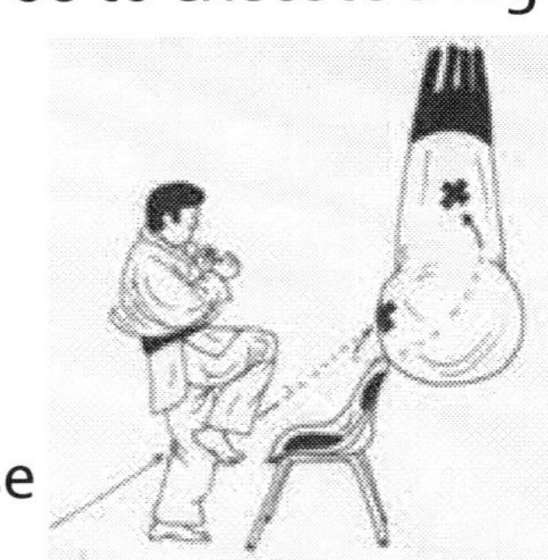

Drill with high chamber over a chair and onto double-marked belly-bottomed hanging bag

Self-defense

The Figures below illustrate the *front-leg* version of the kick, much less in use but still valid, especially if aiming towards the opponent's groin. In order to cause a reaction, the starting front-leg Hopping Front Kick is directed at your assailant's groin; if necessary the kick should be an Inward-tilted version (See our book about *Essential Kicks* for the Inward-tilted Front Kick). Even an untrained fighter will lower his hands in primal protective reaction! If you are in a sport setting, make sure you do not contact, but only feint towards the opponent's groin area. As soon as your opponent lowers his hands reactively, you turn the groin kick into a high Roundhouse. This version of the Front-chambered Roundhouse Kick is usually less powerful than the classic version, because of the lack of hip thrust in front-leg kicks. Make sure you immediately follow up, in this example with a Back-fist Strike, an Outer Reap Throw (*O Soto Gari – Judo*) and a Stomp Kick.

A front-leg Front-chambered Roundhouse Feint Kick and its follow-up

The Figures at the top of the next page show a classic application already presented with the Low Front Kick to the assailant's shin as a start of the Feint Kick. But the sequence below aims at illustrating the principle of Progressive Conditioning: you deliver a series of attacks which purpose is to gradually focus your opponent's attention down, before the decisive high attack. In this example, you will first aim loosely at your opponent's groin with an Essential Outward-tilted Front Kick. This will get his attention, down. The immediately following Low Front Kick to his front shin is a very fast and easily successful technique which also irritates and distracts. Retract the leg backwards. You can now repeat the technique a few times, or proceed according to the specific circumstances. As you have his attention downwards, and probably his guard as well, you can then repeat the Low Front Kick as a Feint Kick turning into a very surprising high Roundhouse to the head. You can touch his shin, or only feint fast towards it according to the situation and relative skills. Follow up by sweeping his front foot when coming down. Punch or catch him as he is off-balance with his back to you, and deliver with a Low Stomping Side Kick into the back of his knee.

Lower the opponent's guard with gradually lower kicks; then deliver a Low Front-chamber Roundhouse Feint Kick

If you are a good user of the high Penetrating Front Kick, the Essential Front Heel Kick version or the Front Pushing Stop Kick version, the following variation could be of interest to you. After a few Front Kicks at sternum or even face level, you can start the Front Chamber to cause a high block, and then pivot to deliver a *Low* Roundhouse Kick to the opponent's side knee. This is a surprising move, quite easy to execute, but generally requiring a follow-up.

The surprising high-Front-chambered Low-Roundhouse Feint Kick

And last, but not least, we shall mention the more sophisticated approach to the traditional Front-chambered Roundhouse Feint Kick. Once you have mastered the kick and some of its variations, and if it is a technique you 'feel' and are comfortable using, then it is worth taking it a bit further. The classic technique is a feint based on a low straight attack turning into a high circular one.

Other Feint Techniques that we shall meet further on are based on opposite side trajectories or on different level attacks. To make the Front-chambered Roundhouse Feint Kick more effective, you can add to it an element of opposite side trajectory by turning the Front Kick Feint into the *Outside-tilted Front Kick* already mentioned in this section. The straight Low Attack then acquires some light circular properties that will increase the misdirection. Remember that it is all going very fast, and that you will emphasize the chamber tilt to make it even more obvious. How much you tilt your Front Kick is up to you and the circumstances, but this is definitely the next level of the technique. It works better than the basic technique, but it requires more training and good hip flexibility. This was the version I did use to execute in tournaments eons ago, with a lot of success. I warmly recommend drilling this version gradually, once you have mastered the basic technique; in parallel, serious *Plyo-Flex* training would help acquiring it.

The next level: the Outside-tilted Front-chambered Roundhouse Feint Kick

Illustrative Photos

It is very difficult to illustrate Feint Kicks with real fights photos. In this very bad picture of a free fight, Roy (back to camera) clearly blocks a mid-level Kick that never comes. Marc's Kick is already in high Roundhouse mode

The classic Penetrating mid-level Front Kick

The classic high-level Roundhouse Kick

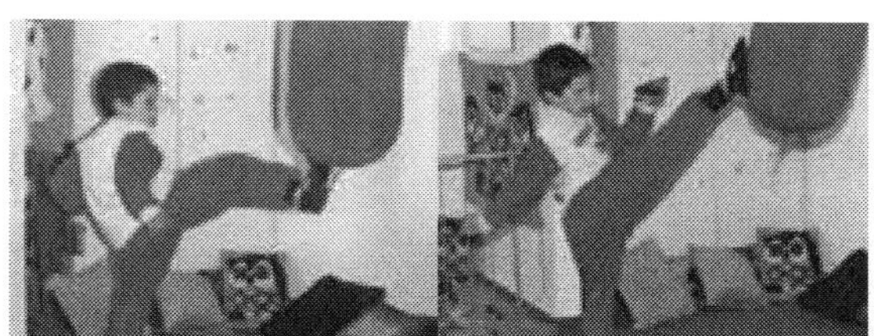

Front to Roundhouse kick work by Nimrod De Bremaeker, 5 years-old

The Essential Inward-tilted Front Kick

The Essential Outward-tilted Front Kick

2. The Roundhouse-chambered Front Kick

General

This kick is the inverse technique of the previous one: you make your opponent believe that a powerful Full Roundhouse is on its circular way towards his side; in the classic version towards the side of his head. When he reacts to protect himself, you slam his open centerline with a straight Front Kick, usually at lower belly level. This awesome kick was popularized in the early eighties by the British National Karate team led by famous *Ticky Donovan.*

This kick is extremely confusing to the adversary, as it is much less common than the previous Front-chambered Roundhouse Kick. It is less in use because it requires much more skill, training and hip flexibility. Once it is mastered, it is very efficient, but should only be used against a skilled martial artist: only an experienced free-fighter will respond to a realistic Roundhouse Chamber. Such a technique would be wasted on an inexperienced fighter.

This kick is nearly exclusively delivered with a starting rear-leg chambering because the chamber must be clearly visible for the feinting technique to work, and because such a convoluted Front Kick needs distance to gather speed and power. One of the salient points of this kick is that, properly executed, it can gather as much power as a regular Penetrating Front Kick.

We shall also show that, in some cases, the sinusoidal trajectory of the kick can be accentuated to become an Outside-tilted Front Kick, as described briefly in the Illustrative Photos of the previous section. Such a Kick will take the feint even further, but it will be even more difficult to execute: an example will be presented at the end of this section.

Description

The Photos below show the traditional execution of the classic Full Roundhouse Kick, although it is rarely executed this way in real fighting. The full chamber, as seen in these photos, is shouting out loud: 'a Roundhouse is coming, a Roundhouse is coming!'. But then, it could turn into a powerful Front Kick ... Like always with feint-kicking, it is all about conditioning your opponent first.

Roundhouse full chamber in tournament – Marc De Bremaeker vs Roy Faige

The traditional Full Roundhouse Kick; check this chamber!

The Figures show the execution of the rear-leg Roundhouse-chambered Front Kick. From the Roundhouse Chamber position, the leg starts to gradually turn into a Front Kick as the body redresses and the hip pivots back into straight position. The change can be as early or as gradual as needed in the circumstances and according to your opponent's reaction. Of course, the technique will work better if you have first got the opponent used to get a Roundhouse Kick after a Roundhouse chamber; the classical version being a few high head Roundhouses, followed by the Feint Kick ending as a lower abdomen Front Kick.

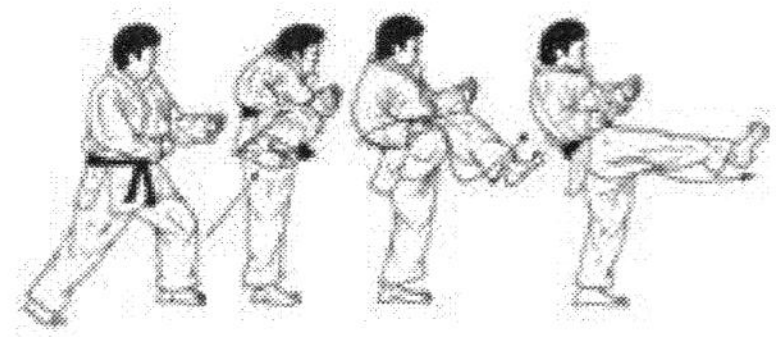

The Roundhouse-chambered Front Kick

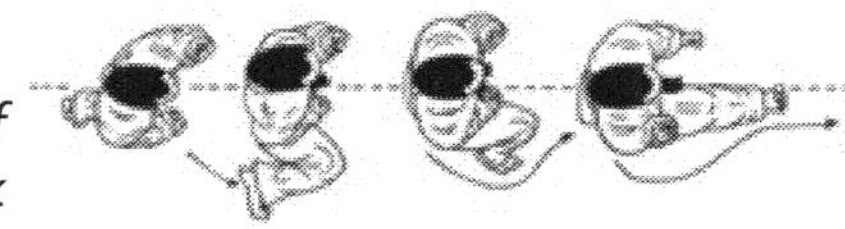

Self-explanatory top view of the Feint Kick

High Roundhouse head Kick followed by the Roundhouse-chambered Front Kick at lower belly level

Key points

- The chamber must be that of a classical Full Roundhouse Kick, and in some cases, even *exaggerated*. The body should lean sideways to shout out: "Roundhouse coming!".
- There is no stopping at the end of the chamber: the kick must be one uninterrupted smooth movement.
- Ideally, the kick should follow at least one Full Roundhouse Kick attempt.
- This is a sophisticated feint, not to be used against unskilled fighters.

Always start after a Full Roundhouse conditioning attack, always emphasize the full chamber

Typical applications

The Illustrations belowshow the classical application: you deliver a rear-leg high Full Roundhouse Kick. You then retract the leg back rearwards while jabbing to keep the opponent in check. You can repeat several times if the situation warrants it, until you are sure that such an attack will cause a high outside block. You then repeat the identical start of the same Roundhouse attack; but, this time, as soon as he reacts to the typical chamber, you turn it into a Penetrating Front Kick to his undefended lower abdomen. You follow up as you land forward, for example with a Hook Punch that you can blend into a Body Drop Throw (*Tai Otoshi - Judo*) after a full pivot.

The classic use of the Roundhouse-chambered Front Kick and a follow-up

Specific training

- Always start your training sessions with the drilling of the basic underlying kicks.
- This Feint Kick definitely requires training in front of a mirror.
- You should also train with a protected partner: work on the feint Kick first; have him check you for realism. Then alternate Roundhouse Kick and Roundhouse-chambered Front Kick. Then throw the two Kicks at random as your partner tries to identify and block.
- Drill the Kick with a hanging tennis ball on your side: you must aim at kicking the ball from under with your Roundhouse chamber, before you can start to develop the Front Kick (illustrated). You can also have a partner place his open hand at the right level instead of the hanging ball.

Use a hanging ball to force a high and full Roundhouse Chamber when drilling the Feint Kick

- Work the Feint Kick on the marked heavy bag (with the mark in front of you), with a chair on your side to force a high and full Roundhouse chamber (illustrated).
- Work on the heavy bag, alternating Full Roundhouse Kick and Roundhouse-chambered Front Feint Kick.
- This specific Feint Kick requires serious training for good hip flexibility. Good exercises (illustrated in order) would

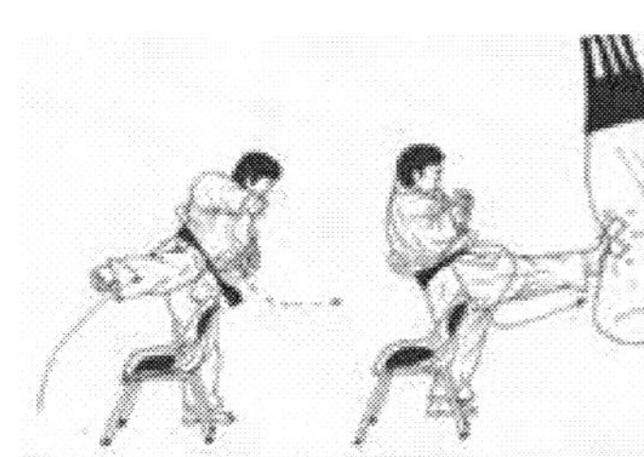

Front-kick the marked heavy bag with a chair on your side to force the high Roundhouse Chamber

be: Roundhouse Chamber Lifts with partner, Cobbler Stretches, Bent Cobbler Stretches, Wide-angle Forward Bends, Wide-angle Side Bends and Sitting Roundhouse Kick Drill. There are many more possible exercises and additional assiduous Plyo-Flex training will certainly boost your progress together with your overall kicking proficiency.

Various helpful and recommended stretching exercises

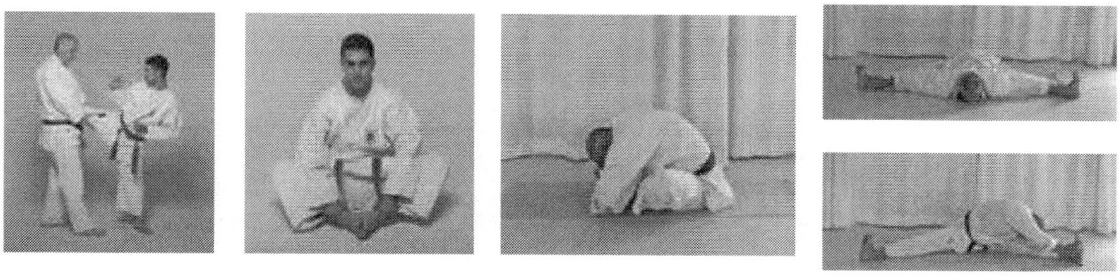

Self defense

The Photos below illustrate the *Low* Roundhouse Chamber-variation of the Feint Kick. Instead of a high Roundhouse Kick, you feint the chamber of a 'Low Kick', a low Roundhouse Kick to the side of the opponent's thigh or knee. Of course, it should be executed, as illustrated, after a few 'conditioning' real 'Low Kicks'. When appropriate, you then start the Low Roundhouse feint and evolve into a straight Penetrating Front Kick as the opponent starts to react, usually by lifting his knee outwards.

The Low Roundhouse-chambered mid-level Front Feint Kick, after a few conditioning kicks

In the same spirit, the Figures below show the use of the kick against a serial "leg-blocker" of Low Kicks, who lifts his shin turned up and very much outwards as often done in *Muay Thai* boxing and *Kyokushinkai Karate*. In this case we shall illustrate the use of the *Upward* Front Kick variation towards the opponent's groin; it is fast, easy and more appropriate to Self Defense. Note that the Outside Leg Block tends to have the negative side effect of opening the groin to possible strikes. After a few of your 'Low Kicks' (Straight-leg Roundhouse Kicks to the thigh) have been shin-blocked by your opponent, you will repeat with an exaggerated preparation: open your stance and chamber high and clear. As soon as he lifts his front leg to block, switch smoothly to the Upward Front Kick to his groin area. The kick can also be slightly outward-tilted, as will be detailed further in the text. In any case, follow up! For example as illustrated...

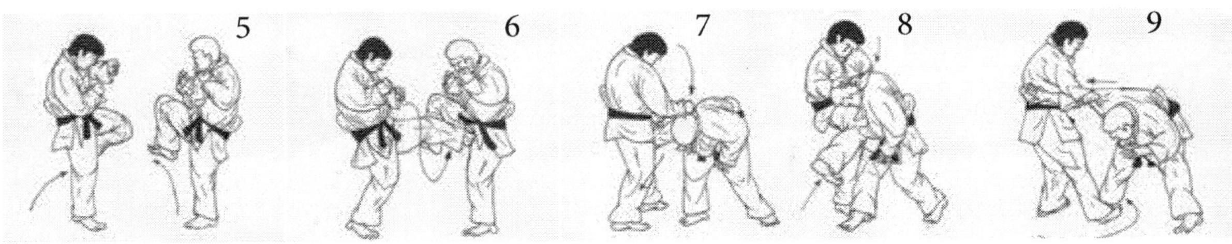

The Low Roundhouse-chambered Upward Groin Front Feint Kick and its vicious follow-up

As mentioned in the introduction of this section, the Roundhouse-chambered Front Kick does not lend itself well to the front-leg Roundhouse opening, mainly because the body is already twisted and leaves no room for the hip thrust of the Front Kick. The best way to use this Feint Kick with a Hopping Front-leg Roundhouse Kick is illustrated at the top of next page. You deliver your typical Front-leg high Roundhouse Kick, and then chamber the leg back powerfully to land it rearwards *where it will rebound into a rear-leg high Roundhouse*. It is recommended to lift the 'reverse' hand while pulling the leg back, in order to keep the opponent at bay and to maintain his attention *high*. This is basically a Double Roundhouse Kick: Front-leg and (same) rear-leg in series. It would be wise to execute this full Double Kick at least once before going for the Feint Kick. When executing the feinting version, you execute the basic Roundhouse-chambered Front Feint Kick from the 'rebounding' phase. Follow-up, for example as illustrated on the next page, with a Low Soccer Front Kick and Hook Punch. →

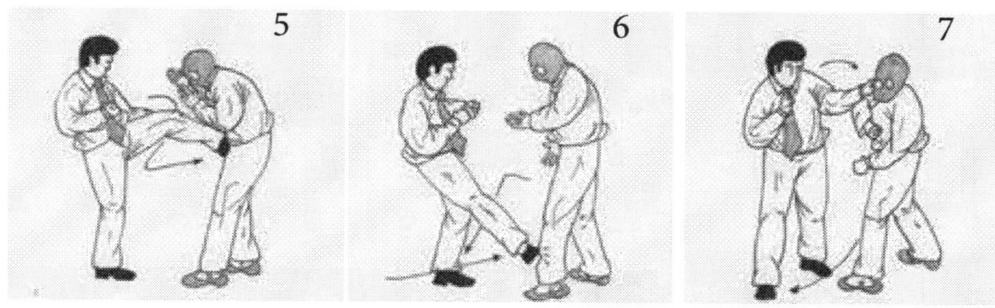

Front-leg Roundhouse Kick rebounding into Roundhouse-chambered Front Feint Kick; and follow-up

Exactly like with the previous Feint Kick (Front-chambered Roundhouse), this Roundhouse-chambered Front Kick reaches a higher level of sophistication if the Front Kick part is traded for an *Outside-tilted Front Kick*. This is certainly more confusing to a trained opponent, but it is much more difficult to execute: it takes even more hip flexibility, more training and it requires more speed because of the huge 'uncovering' during the fake Roundhouse chambering. It is not a Feint Kick to try on an untrained opponent, who will certainly miss the hint, but it is a better Feint technique if you have mastered it. It is a great Feint Kick against opponents in very deep Side Postures, as they feel protected from straight attacks by the narrow side stance they present. The Figure illustrates the delivery of the kick. It is an important variation to train for, even if you will never use it.

Front and Top view of the Roundhouse-chambered Outside-tilted Front Feint Kick

As a last example, will shall illustrate the kick at lower levels, for the fighters who prefer not to kick high. The principles stay the same, and the technique is very efficient if you take the time to drill it at these specific levels. It needs thorough training to become a good Feint Kick, and the fact that it is delivered lower does not mean that it requires less hip flexibility. To sum it up, if it is a technique you feel is more appropriate to your morphology or psychology, do not expect it to be easier than the higher versions! Au contraire; it takes more work to make it convincing.

In the illustrations below, you deliver a first Roundhouse at kidney level to get your opponent familiar with your use of the technique. As you repeat the same chamber, you let him react, and then deliver a somewhat stomping version of the Low Front Kick; an Outward-tilted Low Front stomp Kick would even be better. The follow-up illustrated is a rebounding Hand-on-floor Side Kick to the throat of the bent-over opponent, but it could be many other things.

The Mid-level Roundhouse-chambered Low Stomping Front Feint Kick

Illustrative photos

Kin Geri: the Upward Groin Front Kick

An Essential Front-leg Hopping high Roundhouse Kick

The Low Stomping Front Kick, slightly outward-tilted

3. The Roundhouse-chambered Side Kick

General

What we call the *Roundhouse-chambered Side Kick* is in fact the "short" version of this important Feint Kick; the longer version is different in its mindset and execution and will be presented in the next section as 'the Long Roundhouse feint to Side kick'.
The (short) Roundhouse-chambered Side Kick starts as a rear-leg Full Roundhouse chamber that turns into a Side Kick chamber while you pivot onto your standing foot; the Side Kick releases naturally from the chamber. In fact, another way to present this Feint Kick is as a regular rear-leg Side Kick, but with the chambering going *through* a Roundhouse-type chamber instead of going *through* the usual Front-type chamber. This Feint Kick is a basic circular feint turning into a straight attack; the 'straight' attack is slightly slanted and comes a little from the *other side* than the original circular attack. On top of that, the misdirection from the Feint Kick can be compounded by an added effect of feinting at one level while completing the kick at another (hi/lo or vice-versa). The short version presented in this section is a very *natural* Feint Kick as the development of the kicking trajectory feels like a normal and smooth movement that does not require special flexibility. It is also quite easy to deliver and very versatile, as the application presented will demonstrate. Its additional advantage is that, should you miss or be stopped-punched, the complex chamber will act as a Block Kick and protect you; examples will be provided. This Feint Kick is very important, not only because very natural, but also because it ends with one of the most powerful Kicks of the arsenal: the Side Kick. An added bonus is that the Feint Kick is *not* less powerful than the regular Side Kick.
Again, just like with the previous kick, this Feint Kick is usually delivered as a rear-leg kick because it starts with a Roundhouse Chamber that needs to be seen and reacted to. The Front View of the execution is presented in the photos below.

Front View of the classic Roundhouse-chambered Side Kick

Description

The Figure on the side shows the top and side view of the classic delivery of the kick, starting with a clear rear-leg Full Roundhouse Chamber. The pivot of the standing leg and the body continues uninterrupted, *but without extending the leg to deliver the kick*. During this "empty" pivot, the chambered leg gradually metamorphoses into a Side Kick-chamber. Once you are in Side Kick Chamber with your side towards the opponent, you stop the pivot and deliver the Side Kick with full hip thrust. Chamber back, of course, and follow up.

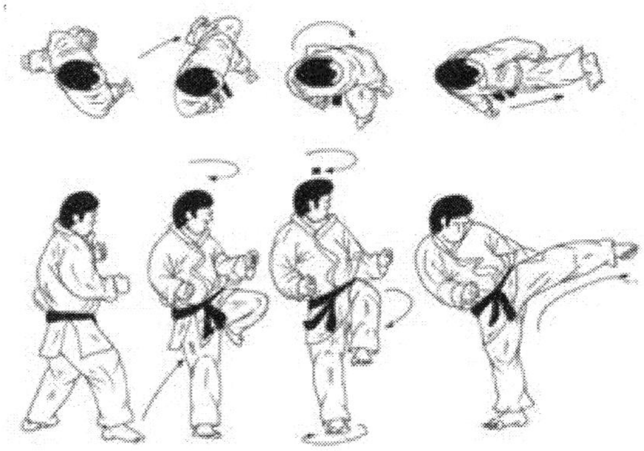

Top and Side Views of the classic Roundhouse-chambered Side Feint Kick

Key points

- Exaggerate the Roundhouse chamber. Not by doing it slowly, but by executing it fully and obviously, with the knee lifted high.
- Do not interrupt the move: this is one smooth circular pivot all the way to the classic Side kick-chamber.
- The pivot comes to a Full Stop when Side chamber position is reached, but the leg extension starts immediately and seamlessly.
- Push the hips into the Side Kick; this is the classic Essential Penetrating Side Kick.
- Ideally deliver after one or more 'conditioning' Full Roundhouse Kicks.

The Feint Kick is best executed after nudging the opponent with a real Full Roundhouse Kick that will get him used to expect more of the same

Typical Applications

The Illustrations below show the kick delivered to a *blocking-type* opponent: the Roundhouse Chamber-feint must be kept short and compact, as much as possible up to the point it still causes a reaction. In this example, from opposite stances, you will first deliver a Full Roundhouse Kick, at least at sternum level, before retracting the leg back into original position (not illustrated). Repeat the same-looking clear Roundhouse Chamber to cause the same blocking reaction. As he lifts his hands against the expected same Roundhouse Kick, you have reached the position to side-kick his exposed ribs. Follow up, for example with a high Back-fist Strike and an Outer Reap Takedown.

Roundhouse-chambered Side Kick against a blocking opponent: kick the ribs exposed by the misguided block

The Figures below show a variation of the kick delivered against a *fleeing-type* opponent: The Roundhouse feint can now be wider, and the Side Kick will be delivered with a hop. The illustrations below show, purposely, an exaggerated hop to make the point clearer; the reader is invited to consult our previous book about *Essential Kicks* for more background on the Hopping Kicks. The *Hopping Side Kick* is a smooth technique with a conceited, very low but long hop to be executed as late as possible while the kick is already under way; it is, in some way, a Feint Kick in itself that fools the opponent about range and distance. In our matching stances-example, you deliver a Full Roundhouse Kick to your opponent's head and retract the leg back as he steps back to control it. As soon as he comes back to regular range, repeat with the same high Roundhouse chamber, this time turning into a Hopping Side Kick to his open ribs. Follow up, for example by landing the kicking foot forward and out, for a rear-leg Straight-leg Roundhouse Kick to the opponent's groin or lower belly.

The Roundhouse-chambered Hopping Side Feint Kick against a retreating opponent

The Illustrations below show the delivery of the kick against a *stop-countering-type* opponent: The Roundhouse feint is very short and the Side Kick leans towards the Back Side Kick-delivery (See *Book of Essential Kicks*). Note that the switch from Roundhouse Chamber to Side Chamber is very much a classic Leg Block. We shall, in this instance, also illustrate the fact that the opponent can also be conditioned to a simple combination attack instead of to a single kick only; it is even more realistic and convincing. We shall show a jab opening, followed by a high rear-leg Roundhouse Kick. In this same stance-example, you carefully deliver the jab, then the rear-leg Roundhouse Kick to the opponent's shoulder; you retract the leg immediately back into original stance while keeping a very closed guard. As you have noticed that the opponent tends to try to stop-punch your attack, you repeat the jab/kick opening, but with a very short Roundhouse *Chamber* and you let the pivot become a shin block of his incoming Reverse Punch counter. Keep your guard up. In this instance, it is best to let the pivot take you a little bit further, and to deliver a Back Side Kick to his exposed abdomen. The advantage of the Back Side Kick is that it can still develop much power at close range and can be as short or as long as necessary. Follow up after landing, for example, with a Spin-back Short Back Kick of the other leg.

Roundhouse-chambered Back Side Feint Kick against a countering opponent

The Feint Kick works also very well with the Low Kick version of the feint, but, in that case, the chambering feint is significantly different. The Straight-leg Low Roundhouse Kick is not a whipping Kick like the regular Roundhouse, but a kick-through Kick pulled by the upper and the hips. The delivery of the Straight-leg Roundhouse Kick ('Low Kick') starts with a twist of the shoulders, then the hips; only then does the leg starts its forward attack. The 'chambering' of the kick is therefore different, and must be replicated realistically for the Feint Kick to be a success. Once the technique is mastered, it is a very easy technique to execute with great odds of success; but serious drilling, especially in front of the mirror, is required. The photographs on the next page do illustrate the case in point.

Front view of the Low Straight-leg Roundhouse-chambered Side Feint Kick

Application: Kick, Kick, Feint Kick!

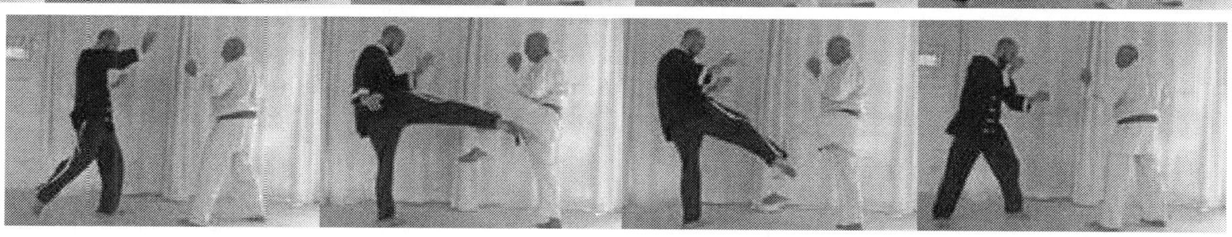

Specific training

- Drill the basic underlying Kicks first, especially the Essential Full Rear-leg Penetrating Side Kick, which general movement is similar (See Illustrative Photos). Then train the Feint Kick.
- Practice in front of the mirror; this is key to a successful Feint Kick. Make especially sure that the start of your Feint Kick looks exactly like the start of the basic underlying Kick.

- Practice on the heavy bag with a chair or an obstacle on your side to force a high and clear Roundhouse Chamber. Drill the Full Roundhouse first, then the Roundhouse-chambered Side Kick, from the same position. As Illustrated here.
- Practice shin-blocking (Shin Block = Side Kick-chamber!) an incoming staff stab by a partner while clearing a chair on your side with a Roundhouse Chamber (See Illustration below on the side).
- A common general Triple Kick drill, presented below, can be tweaked into a more relevant exercise for this Feint Kick. The 'Roundhouse Kick, to pivot Front Kick to Side Kick' becomes a 'Roundhouse Chamber to pivot Front Kick to Side Kick'. Both drills are great for hip flexibility, pivot speed and general kicking proficiency.
- Of course, drill with a spotting partner and try in light free fighting.

Chair and bag drill for the Roundhouse-chambered Side Feint Kick; drill the Full Roundhouse Kick first, with the same obstacle for high chambering

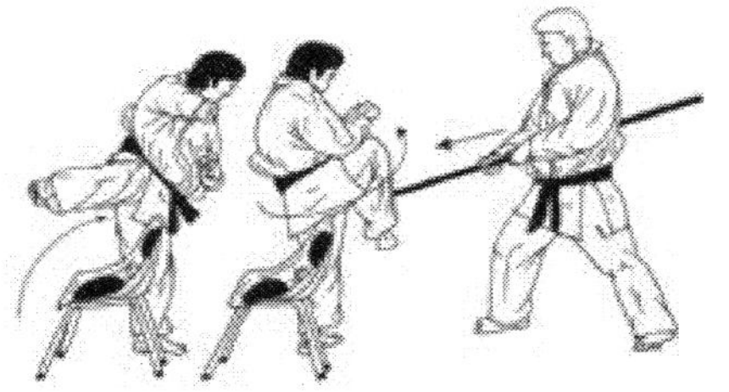

After clearing the chair, block a Staff stab to drill the Feint Kick pivot

Classic Triple Kick Drill: Roundhouse, Front and Side Kicks

Feint Kick Drill: Roundhouse Knee Strike, Front Kick, Side Kick

Self defense

Feint Kicks are certainly no sure things, even when executed flawlessly. They need to be used in the right context and in a way fine-tuned to the specific opponent, who may or may not 'cooperate'. Feint Kicks are particularly tricky against stop-countering opponents. In this case, your opponent may think that he is stop-punching or stop-punching a Roundhouse Kick; if his timing is right and he catches you in chambering development, he will not care much that you originally intended to Side-kick him. Neither will you. This does not mean that Feint Kicks are necessarily useless against stop-countering adversaries, but it certainly must be taken into account: the feint will have to be much shorter and relevant to the counter. If you have mastered the art of Feint-kicking and are comfortable, then a Feint Kick can be a great trap against a stop-countering opponent. We shall illustrate the point here with three examples, as the Roundhouse-chambered Side Feint Kick lends itself well to luring and trapping the countering types. The examples given are also possible 'ways out' in case you do not succeed in your execution or if you did not expect a stop-counter. For all three examples presented below, remember that they come after a few full Roundhouse Kicks that should both test the waters and get your opponent 'used' to expect the full Kick.
In the first example, your opponent will try to stop-punch your rear-leg Roundhouse Kick with a classic *Shotokan Karate-type* sliding-forward Reverse Punch (*Gyacku Tsuki*). Purposely or thankfully, your chambering switch to Side Kick chamber has blocked his punch, but you need to take back the initiative quickly. What simpler than an immediate fast Backfist Strike, started as you are still standing on one leg. Lower your airborne foot simultaneously onto his forward foot in a classic Stomping Side Low Kick. You can then follow-up with a Spin-back Hook Kick for example, or anything else that catches your fancy.

You cannot complete the Feint Kick against a Stop Punch, but you can block, strike and Stomp

If you expect the Counter Punch, or if you detect it in time, you can execute the following variation of the Feint Kick: the Side Kick part of the maneuver becomes a *Hand-on-floor* leaning Side Kick. This classic Essential Kick, presented in detail in our previous book, has the advantage of removing all of your upper body from danger; in this case, the Reverse counter Punch.

It also allows you a very high kick, in this case a Stop Kick, even if you are not flexible. In the example illustrated below, you expect the counter, and therefore shorten your Feint, to immediately plunge into the bent-over Kick. Catching him at the throat or chin would certainly finish the engagement.

The dangerous Roundhouse-chambered Hand-on-floor Side Feint Kick against a counter-punch

The next example illustrates the easier dealing with a *Stop Kick*. In this case, your opponent has learned your (conceited) tendency to attack with a rear-leg Roundhouse Kick, and he plans to stop-kick you in the groin with his own 'timing' Front-leg Hopping Roundhouse Kick. Your Side Kick chamber becomes a Block Kick from which you can easily follow up. A fast Backfist is always possible to start with, but we have chosen to show a devastating Low Side Kick to his standing leg. This kind of 'cutting' kick is extremely efficient, and the reader is invited to consult our previous books about Low Kicks and Stop Kicks on the subject.

The Roundhouse-chambered Cutting Low Side Kick against a stop-kicker

The Photos below illustrate the classic high Roundhouse Feint to Low Side Kick to the knee, after a bit of high Roundhouse conditioning. This is a great basic combination and the Feint is even more efficient at that height level difference: it will be both a high to low feint, and an outside circular to inside straight feint. The Low Side Kick to the knee joint (*Kansetsu Geri* in *Karatedo*) is an easy and efficient crippling attack.

The High Roundhouse-chambered Low knee Side Feint Kick

The illustrations below show the same technique, but based on a *Low* Roundhouse Feint; this is a simple circular outside to straight inside Feint, without the additional confusing height level effect. It is a very fast and strong technique though and its success can be reinforced by the use of the *hand* in-between the kicks to draw the opponent's attention high anyway; this is an easy way to give some 'level' effect as well. The combination presented will be especially efficient against an assailant who tends to try to block a Low Kick with his hands instead of evading or lifting his leg. The combination illustrated gives also a more sophisticated compounded conditioning preparation to the Feint Kick. Start by delivering a full powered 'Low Kick' (Straight-leg Roundhouse to his outside thigh), and retract the leg back <u>*while jabbing high*</u> to keep him away and keep his attention up. Repeat this immediately as your leg rebounds on the floor to attack again. This is the conditioning to a compounded *double* attack. According to the specifics of the encounter you can proceed immediately with a rebounding Kick, or you can break the rhythm in-guard as illustrated. You then repeat with a full Low Kick, a jab while retracting, and the rebounding into the exaggerated Roundhouse *Chamber* of the Feint kick. The opponent expects another Low Kick to his outside knee, followed by a jab, but it turns into a Side Kick to his inside knee. You can follow up immediately with a same-leg high Side Kick, preferably without lowering the kicking foot. Keep him off-balance with more kicks. Should you follow up with a full Low Kick, as originally expected, and not a Feint Kick, it would be both ironic and confusing to the opponent.

Complex preparation to score with the Low Roundhouse-chambered Low knee Side Feint Kick

Illustrative Photos

Applied Leg Block to Side Kick

The classic rear-leg full Side Kick

The low version of the Essential rear-leg Penetrating Side Kick

Essential Side Kick variations: respectively Bent-body and Hand-on-floor

4. The Long Roundhouse Feint to Side Kick

General

This is in principle the same kick than the previous one, but we present it separately to underscore once more the different ways to deliver a Feint Kick. This is the ***long*** version, as opposed to the previous *short* regular version. This is not a "chamber" feint, but *nearly* a Double Kick, the other extreme of the scale. Of course, there are plenty of possibilities in between those extremes, but the delivery is quite different at both ends of the range of possibilities. This Feint Kick starts with a high Roundhouse *Kick*, which is in fact a *long* feint that can even lightly touch the target before it chambers back into a classic Side Kick-chamber. The 'feint' part of the kick can be delivered as a Hopping rear-leg Kick or even as a front-leg Kick. This should convince even the most seasoned fighter that your purpose is a Full Roundhouse. Remember though that it is not a Double Kick as the Roundhouse part is not fully powered, but just very fast into trying to cause a reaction. This version of the Feint Kick has the advantage of *not* requiring a clear or exaggerated full chamber to work: The kick in itself is certainly more convincing than a chamber. This is why, as mentioned, it is also effective with a *front-leg* Roundhouse Feint.
This kick and the previous one, as two extremes of the same basic combination, should both be practiced for a deeper understanding of the complexity and sophistication of Feint Kicks and all their possibilities.

Description

The Illustrations show the classic way to deliver this version of the Feint Kick: A fast, fully developed high Roundhouse that will be folding, - as soon as barely connecting -, into a Side Kick Chamber. Unlike for the previous kick, the leg extends as long as needed and then flexes back into the Side chamber. The whole dynamic of the kick is different from that of the Roundhouse-chambered Side Kick of the previous section; both kicks should be practiced for a better mastery of all the intermediate possibilities. This comparison should remind the reader of the two extremes of the possible deliveries of the Front-chambered Roundhouse Kick presented in section 1: Front chamber only or nearly fully extended Front Kick Feint.

The Long Roundhouse Feint to Side Kick

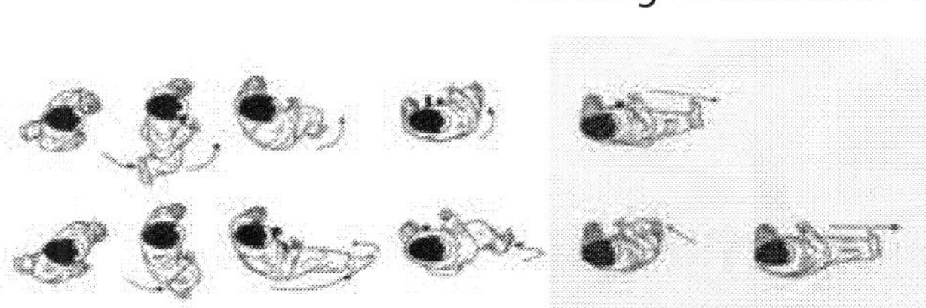

Comparative top view of the Feint Kicks: above is the shorter Roundhouse-chambered Side Feint Kick, below is the Long Roundhouse Feint to Side Kick

Key points

- The Roundhouse Feint must be delivered fast with relaxed muscles. Speed is of the essence. No need for a full chamber either. Of course, previous 'conditioning Roundhouse Kicks should look identical.
- There is no interruption between the kicks: One smooth movement with every part flowing into the other.
- The kick should ideally be executed after one or more high Roundhouses; the high Roundhouse are preferred because directed towards the opponent's eyes to cause a reaction.
- The chambering-back from the Roundhouse Feint is directly into the Side Kick chamber; it is not going unnecessarily through a Roundhouse chamber-back.

Typical applications

Front view of the long Roundhouse Feint to Side Kick

The Photos show the front view of the Feint Kick, The reader is invited to compare to the previous shorter Roundhouse-*chambered* Side Kick. The opponent's reaction to the Roundhouse Feint can be one of three types: getting out of range, blocking in place or stop-countering forward. In the first case, it will often be necessary for you to lengthen the reach of the Side kick by hopping during delivery. In the second and third case, this Feint Kick can be a great 'trap' luring the opponent in, but the kick must then be delivered accordingly. Another important point, already made, is that the Roundhouse Feint can be executed as a front-leg Kick, because it travels most of the way and does not need to be powerful.
The first application example will illustrate two of the comments made above: the Roundhouse Feint will be a front-leg Kick, and the capping Side Kick will be a hopping version. The Illustrations at the top of the next page show a front-leg version start of the Feint Kick against a retreating opponent. Deliver one or more front-leg high Roundhouse Kicks, after a Back-fist Strike to close the distance; the back-fist should be directed to the opponent's *outside*, in order to make the following *inside* Roundhouse Kick all the more threatening. Repeat in an identical set-up, but, this time, fold the nearly completed Roundhouse Kick into a Side Kick-chamber. Hop *while* side-kicking his ribs. Follow up!

Hopping front-leg Long Roundhouse Feint to Hopping Side Kick

Against a counter-attacker, the previous Kick is certainly better, but it will not work with every opponent. Sometimes, you will have to *convince* him that the Roundhouse is real and go all the way to the long Feint. You'll have to be careful when executing the technique against a counter-attacker, especially at the 'conditioning' stage. You will have also to make sure that you start your kick switch as soon as the opponent gets convinced by your Roundhouse Feint and starts reacting. The illustrations below show how you trick an opponent that is fond of retreat/check and reverse punch-counter.

The Long Roundhouse Feint to Side Kick against an evading-back counterpunching opponent

Against a stop-countering opponent going forward at the hint of a Roundhouse, this version of the Kick is *not very practical*. It is better to use the previous version described in section three and executed at the chambering level (Roundhouse-chambered Side Feint Kick); in any case, it would need to be used very carefully.

Specific training

- Work the heavy bag by *lightly* touching its side with the high roundhouse and *powerfully* side-kicking its front. For a more sophisticated drill, hang a ball in a net on the front of the heavy bag at head height; 1 make sure your Roundhouse barely touches it as it starts folding (See Illustration).
- Drill with a partner wearing body protection (for the Side Kick) and holding a focus pad for the Roundhouse Feint. Make sure to feint fast and to only touch the focus pad lightly. 2
- Work with a partner in light free-fighting, alternating real Roundhouse Kicks and the long Roundhouse Feint to Side Kick.

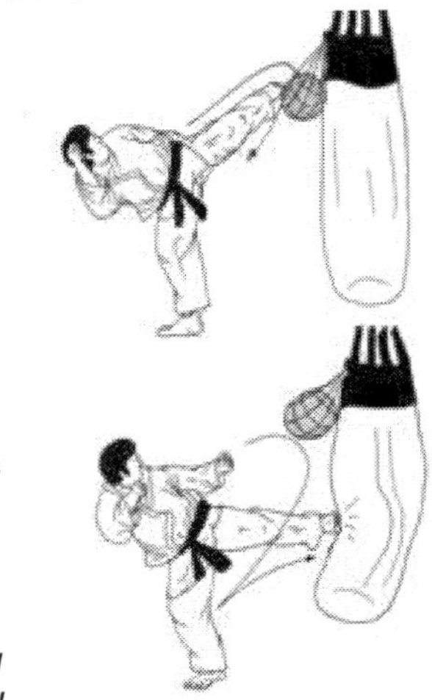

Drill with target ball hanging on a heavy bag: caress the ball with the folding Roundhouse Feint, side-kick the heavy bag hard

Self defense

Remember to always adjust distance with this kick according to your opponent's reactions. If he tends to retreat, hop into the Side Kick; if he tends to come back to counter, shorten the kick.

Adjust distance when executing the long Roundhouse Feint to Side Kick

The illustrations **on the next page** show the version of the kick turning into a Side Kick *to the knee*; the feeling of the kick is even more natural and round when flowing from a *high* Roundhouse into a *low* Side Kick. This example shows the introduction of the Feint Kick into a *Rebounding* Kick combination, in which a front-leg Kick is repeated fast by letting the lowering foot 'rebounding' on the floor for the next iteration of the kick. This kind of Kick lends itself very well to Feint kicks, because the repetition of the same Kick is a great conditioning technique that does not let time for the opponent to think. In our example, you attack with a front-leg high outside Roundhouse and let the lowering foot rebound on the floor, as if on a spring, for another identical Roundhouse Kick. As the opponent usually retreats to block the kick, you will often have to hop between/during the Kicks.

The second 'rebound' will look like another *outside* high Roundhouse, but will turn into a crushing low Side Kick to the *inside* knee of the clueless opponent. Follow up, for example, with a Capoeira-style Hand-on-floor Spin-back Hook Kick to the opponent's head (high Feint/low Kick/high Kick).

Rebounding long and high Roundhouse Feint to low Side Kick, and follow-up

As a general rule, feinting towards the groin is probably one of the most efficient ways to elicit a reaction. No red-blooded male can stay unreactive if a blow is convincingly coming towards his groin, and if only for atavistic reasons. A deep-ingrained reflex will have any man take all precautions necessary to avoid damage to his reproductive organs.

When I was a Karate points-fighter, a long time ago, I used to direct all my feinting moves exclusively towards the opponent's eyes or groin, in a direct and convincing way. Needless to point out that those were not legitimate targets in Sport Karate, but it was never my intention to touch them. Those moves did always provoke the expected reaction, in spite of the fact that my opponents knew consciously that I did not aim for the eyes or the groin; they simply could not resist the unconscious atavistic instinct of self-protection.

Aiming for the opponent's groin, especially with a long Feint is therefore clearly a winning move. The Roundhouse long Feint to Side Kick is a great move for self-defense; the Side Kick is preferably a low Side Kick to the knee, but can also conceivably be a high head Kick, or a mid-level rib Kick. In a self-defense situation, the long Feint can even be a fast light Kick barely touching the groin, but retracting into a powerful fully-hipped Side Kick; 'barely' touching the groin is already scary and painful. The example illustrated on the next page also includes a bit of 'conditioning'.

As you are assailed with a stick attack, you time-stop-kick the open groin of your aggressor with a fast slightly-hopping front-leg Roundhouse Kick. As it is partially checked by your assailant (or even if not), you let your kicking foot rebound on the floor for an identically-looking Feint Kick.
Your once-hit opponent will react to protect his groin, while you fold into a Side Kick chamber. Low-kick his knee powerfully, eventually with a Hand-on-floor bending version as illustrated, and follow up. In this example, we have shown an exotic but very efficient Ground Kick that naturally blends with a Hand-on-floor Side Kick; if it catches your fancy...

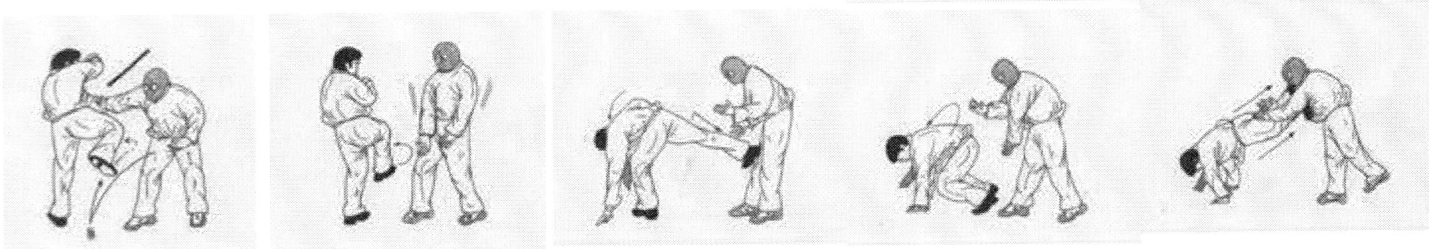

Front-leg Groin Roundhouse, Rebounding groin Long Roundhouse Feint to low knee Side Kick, follow-up

The Illustrations below show this Feint Kick applied to the 'Low Kick',-Straight-leg Roundhouse Kick to the thigh or knee-, of hard Martial arts like *Muay Thai* or *Kyokushinkai* Karate. You condition your opponent with a first fast 'in & out' *Low* Kick that he will block with his front shin. As you repeat, you will develop the kick just enough to have him execute the same block, but you will avoid the block by smoothly switching to a Side Kick chamber. In the example, you deliver an unexpected *high* Side Kick while hopping if necessary. It could be a low Side Kick as well.

Low Kick Feint to high Side Kick

To cap up this section we shall present a photographic comparison between the classic same-level Feint Kick, and the low knee Long Feint to mid-level Side Kick.

The classic mid-level Roundhouse Long Feint to Side Kick

The low and long knee Roundhouse Feint to ribs Side Kick; touch the knee for best results

Illustrative Photos

The Essential Groin Roundhouse Kick

The classic Hopping Roundhouse Kick; check the reference on the floor

Classic Side Kick finishes: respectively high and low

5. The Front-chambered Wide Step

General

The coming technique comes somewhat in contradiction to what I wrote in the introduction of this book and of the general introduction to the 'Kicks' series. To add insult to injury, this technique comes early in the book because of its importance. The first part of the technique is to be believed by the opponent to be a Front Kick. The second part is a range-shortening long Step that will *generally* allow for a Punch or other Hand technique. The second technique can sometimes be a Kick, generally rear-leg and powerful, but the preferred embodiment will be the much faster and more natural punching follow-up. The reason is simple: the Front chamber-misdirection will be much less effective for a second Kick after the long and wide stepping. It will be easy to understand from the examples presented below.

You Kickers out there, make no mistake: this is a very important technique and a relatively safe way to close the distance to your opponent. You basically fake a Front Kick and use the feint to execute a large step while your opponent is busy trying to block a kick which is never coming; it will be easy and natural to strike him in the head while he is busy dealing with the 'Front Kick'. To console yourself, you kicking enthusiast, you can complete the hand technique with a subsequent appropriate kick!

The basic principle behind this technique is akin to the schoolyard bullying game: look at my foot; ouch, I just slapped you...It is the simplest of misdirection's! But although technically easy to perform, this Feint Kick needs drilling: the feint-chamber needs the right mindset to be convincing, and its use can be humbling a bit at the beginning of training when not yet mastered.

This is a must-drill technique that allows to close surprisingly long ranges, and even lends itself to further hopping if required. The Front Chamber Feint can be as long as necessary, and all the way to a nearly full long Penetrating Front Kick.

The long and hopping Front-chambered wide Step, with jabbing lunge Punch

Description

The Figures below show a classic way to drill this important Feint Kick, which principle is easy to understand and to execute. You deliver a first full-fledged Penetrating Front Kick at the opponent's lower abdomen level. Let the kicking foot land back rearwards and then rebound in a real and high similar Front chamber *to start developing the kick towards his lower abdomen, again*. Your opponent will lower his guard to counter the Feint Kick. You do not extend the leg fully though, but push with the hips while doing the longest step possible. In this example, you even hop slightly forwards. Classically, you jab to his face while landing, and follow up with a Reverse Punch and a further incremental step. Of course, this is only one possible example between many, and the experienced fighter will develop his own combinations and techniques on the same basic principles.

A classic drill: Front Kick, rebounding Front-chambered wide Step, Jab/Cross punching combination

Key points

- Always keep your guard up, remember that you are basically rushing the opponent and could be stop-countered.
- The chamber must be fast and powerful, exactly like for a 'real' Front Kick. The hips start to push forward as well, just as if... Remember that the length of the Feint Kick will depend upon the circumstances and the reactions of your opponent.
- Always execute the technique after a real and convincing Front Kick; and make sure the Feint Kick looks exactly like the beginning of your previous Kick.
- In a sport setting, aim the Front Feint Kick towards the belt knot of the opponent; in a self-defense situation, aim the Feint Kick clearly at the opponent's groin.

Typical applications

One of the most typical variations of the basic technique is the finishing up on the outside of the opponent, with the lunge punch becoming an evading twisting jab very typical of the *Wadoryu* school of Karate. In this technique, the long step also inches gradually out from the chamber position, in order to finally land well out of the center-line.

The front-hand Punch is delivered from the opponent's outside while twisting the hips forcefully while pulling in the rear leg; this fantastic little maneuver, -called **Nagashi Tsuki** in *Wadoryu Karatedo*-,allows punching while evading out and forward. In this case, the stepping out and the evading punch place you out of the trajectory of a possible countering punch.

The long and evading-out version of the Front-chambered Step, followed by Nagashi Tsuki

The basic technique lends itself to a fast punching follow-up, as presented. This version should be thoroughly drilled, as it is easy and important to master for many possible situations; its importance includes learning *not* to fall in this trivial trap yourself. But, of course, having closed the distance with the long step, you will often find yourself in a position lending itself to follow up with a kick as well. The Illustrations below show an example of a Front-chambered Wide Step followed by a kick, very useful against a 'blocking-type' opponent. See how you deliver a short but full-powered rear-leg Front Kick towards your opponent's belt knot and retract your leg back in original position while jabbing to keep him away. You then repeat the Front Chamber as a feint and, as he starts to block again, you hop-step widely forward *and on his out-side*, all the while catching/controlling his front "blocking" hand. From this position you can deliver a powerful rear-leg Roundhouse to his head and follow up with a low stomping Side Kick to his knee.

Front-chambered wide Step followed by a Kick

Specific training

- Drill in front of a mirror
- Drill with a partner acting as a target and as a spotter for the "veracity" of your Front chamber.
- Work on long stepping by marking the floor, but keep checking the convincing chamber in the mirror. Once the technique is familiar: Make your step gradually longer; add some hopping; and drill evading out while stepping.
- Drill the step over a belt at knee level, hold by a partner.
- Develop your distance-closing by stepping and hopping by seriously drilling Plyometric exercises; some of the most relevant drills are illustrated in the Photos below. Refer to our previous book for more information (Plyo-Flex – Plyometrics and Flexibility Training for Explosive Martial Arts kicks and Performance Sports)

Drill distance-covering for the Feint Kick by marking the floor and increasing range gradually

Drill long-stepping after clearing a belt at knee-height by front-chambering

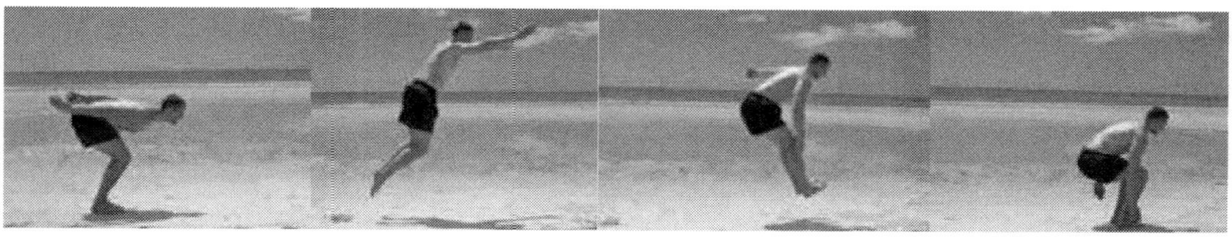

Plyometric Long Jumps in series

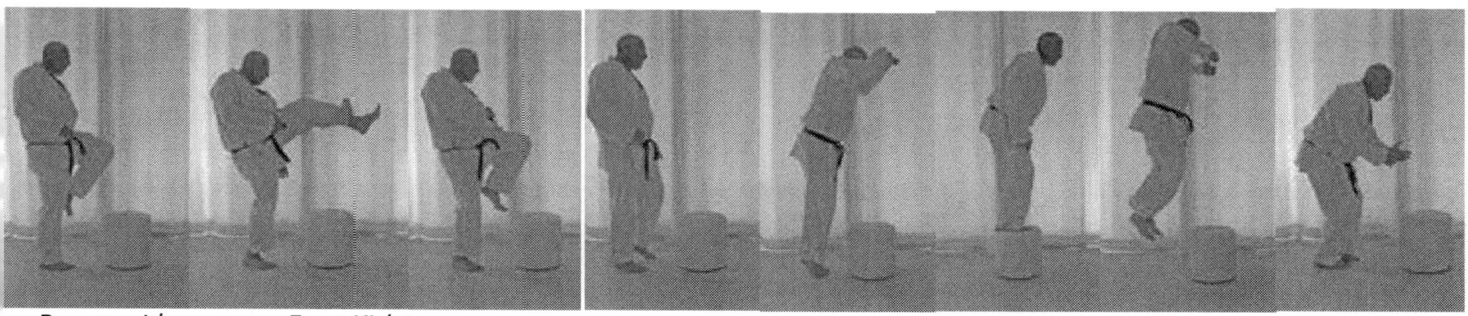

Repeat with no pause: Front Kick to on-box Jumps

Plyo-Upward Stairs Jumps in series

Self defense

The Front-chambered Wide Step is a great tool to handle 'serial retreaters', opponents who flee rearwards at the first sign of an attack. This type of fighter is used to retreat enough to keep away from your attack or attack combination, counting on the fact that an attack will always be shorter and take more time than a step. What they forget, though, is that stepping forward is usually faster and gets further than stepping rearwards! In the example below, you condition the opponent with a real but too short Front Kick; you then execute the Front-chambered Wide Step to catch up with him. In this example, we cap up the step with a rear-leg powerful groin...real Front Kick.

A very close punching relative (or a significant variation) of the classic Front-chambered Wide Step, is what is commonly called the 'Superman Punch'. Superman Punch is the popular generic name for a type of pendulum punching maneuver starting from a Front Chamber-like position and using the pulling back of the leg to give additional power to a punch. The Punch in itself has been popularized by MMA events where it often appears as a Flying Punch, in which you jump-rush your opponent to strike him from above (It is to be noted that a Flying Punch does not necessarily includes a leg scissoring movement). The Superman Punches and the Flying Punches can be either of the jab- or of the cross-type; and they both can smoothly evolve from the Front Chamber Feint. These versions starting from what is akin to a Front Chamber Feint, are close relatives of the Front-chambered Wide Step

and are worth mentioning and illustrating here.
All variations can be executed 'flying' or rooted on the ground. As this is not a treatise about punching, the reader is invited to experiment and choose the execution most suited to his temperament and experience.

Static 'Superman Punch in place; definitely a Front Kick Feint!

Flying 'Superman' Jab from Front Chamber

Hopping 'Superman' Reverse Punch from Front Chamber

One of the great variations of the technique, is the one where the wide step lands on the opponent's front foot in a crushing <u>Stomp</u>; the self-defense aspect will be clear to all. The Feint Kick Step can land as a Side Stomp Kick or an outward-tilted Front Stomp Kick according to the circumstances. When doing this variation, it is always good to keep the opponent's attention up, at mid (Front Kick Feint) and high (Punch) level; this will make the Stomp easier to successfully execute. In the example below, a high reverse punch is used to keep the higher level busy, and the Stomp Kick is a Side version. Follow up with a Roundhouse Elbow Strike while switching to a fast *second* Stomp Kick, this time outward-tilted for more hip power.

Front-chambered Stomping long Step and follow-up

The Figures below illustrate an applied *front-leg* version of the Feint Kick. The front-leg Front Kick being less powerful, it is better to execute both parts of the maneuver, -the 'conditioning' real kick and the feint-, as aiming at the groin; it will give a more stressing and convincing effect. The advantage of the front-leg version of the Kick and of the Feint Kick is its speed, leaving less time for the opponent to think. In this example, you attack your flee-prone assailant with a Hopping Front-leg Front Kick towards the groin. As he retreats, you lower your kicking leg forward and you repeat the attack immediately by half-stepping with the rear leg into a new Hopping front-leg Front Kick. That one, though, is a Feint and will turn into a step that will help catch your retreating opponent with a jab to the face. As he keeps fleeing, you overwhelm him with a powerful rear-leg Soccer Front Kick to the shin and, as you lower the leg deep on his out-side, with an Oblique Roundhouse Kick to the head. The reader has probably noticed: Hi, Lo, Hi... The follow-up illustrated is an interesting sweep of the front leg to force him to give you his back, followed by a hard version of *Jiu-Jitsu's Sukui Nage* Throw, in which you grab his groin from behind (the belt in training!) to lift him up. Caution is warranted when drilling this dangerous technique.

An applied Front-leg Front-chambered wide Step

As a last example we shall illustrate, at the top of next page, the feint part of the kick as a Feint *High* Front Kick, keeping the opponent's attention up all the time until the real attack comes lower. If you are a high kicker and the high Front Kick is part of your arsenal, you can unsettle a menacing assailant with a series of high Front Kicks that will get him retreating. Once he is conditioned to expect more high Front Kicks, you turn a high Front Chamber-feint into a Wide Step. The Step will be followed by a groin mid-level Front Kick. You can then finish him off with a low Straight-leg Roundhouse.

High *Front-chambered wide Step, followed by rear-leg groin Kick*

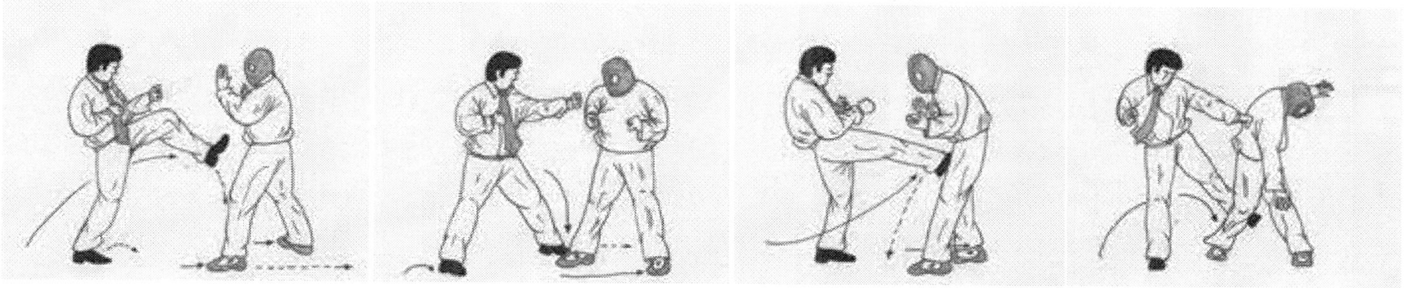

Illustrative Photos

Front-leg Front Kick, upward version

A classic Karatedo training series with high punches and mid-level Front Kick

A variation of Wado-ryu's Nagashi Tsuki

6. The Hook-chambered Roundhouse Kick

General

As its names indicate, this Feint Kick starts like a Hook Kick coming towards one side, and finishes as a Roundhouse Kick connecting with the opposite side. This is a very natural Feint Kick for the flexible fighter, but much more suitable for the tournament scene than the street: It takes an experienced sport fighter to get sucked in into a Hook Kick feint. The Hook Kick is a relatively sophisticated kick, not very much used out of the sport arena; it is, moreover, difficult to spot which is not the best of qualities for a misdirecting Feint Kick. This Kick is a perfect example of something not to use on a novice, but to use only on an experienced fighter.

Because of its delivery and trajectory, it will generally be the front-leg technique that lends itself better to the feint bit. It is relatively easy to perform, -in both the short and the longer feint versions-, because the 'switch-kick' hip movement is very natural. The final scoring kick comes from the opposite direction of the expected one; it is a side to side feint maneuver.

Here is probably the place to mention one of the best kicking Artists ever, *Bill 'Superfoot' Wallace*, who popularized the Universal Chamber position from which all three Side-, Hook- and Roundhouse-Kick could develop to surprise the opponent. Wallace proved his kicking mastery in the Golden Age of both points and full-contact sport Karate. The Universal chamber is mentioned in our previous book about *Essential Kicks* and represent the essence of the mastery of feint kicking.

Front-leg Hook Kick followed by a front-leg Hook-chambered Roundhouse Kick; front view

Description

The Illustrations below do show the delivery of a medium length kick: It could be shorter (simply pivoting with the cocked chamber leg), or longer (delivering a nearly full kick and folding back to Roundhouse chamber). In this case, you lift the front leg into a very clear high Hook Kick chamber and with your back slightly towards the opponent to reinforce the feint. You pivot with the hips back while extending the leg halfway into a (fake) Hook Kick; you start flexing the leg back into a chamber after passing through the centerline. You now are in perfect Roundhouse Chamber position from which you kick.

Side and top view of the classic mid-extension Hook-chambered Roundhouse Kick

Key points

- Make sure the chamber is convincing and credible.
- Do not interrupt the movement: transitions are smooth and natural.
- Do not use on an inexperienced opponent, who will not understand the feint.
- Always deliver after one or more conditioning Hook Kicks, chambered in exactly the same way.

Typical applications

The Photos show the classic execution of the kick in same-stances situation. The Feint Kick is preceded by a conditioning Hook Kick.

The applied high Hook-chambered Roundhouse Kick

The Figures show the classic application in *opposite* stances, and illustrate how suitable this Feint kick is in the Side Stance position beloved by kickers. Deliver a front-leg Hopping high Hook Kick. Lower the leg and repeat immediately with an additional hop, lifting the same leg in a convincing Hook Kick Feint. As the opponent lifts his hands in-side to block the incoming Hook, smoothly switch to an *out-side* high Roundhouse to the back of his neck.

The high Hook-chambered Hook Kick in opposite stances

As mentioned, this Feint Kick usually executed in its front-leg form, as it is the most common form of the Hook Kick in fighting sports. The rear-leg version is a great Feint Kick as well, but it is more difficult to execute and also more rarely applicable.

The rear-leg Hook-chambered Roundhouse Kick

The extreme version of this Feint Kick, very suitable to sport practice, is presented below. It is rather a *Missed-kick Trap* than a Feint Kick, as explained later in the book: Your kick will miss **on purpose**, and you will stop-kick or stop-punch your opponent as he takes advantage of this seemingly golden opportunity to counter. The Hook Kick is an easy kick for "missing": if you kick too high, you also kick shorter but it still looks like a real Kick. It is best, of course, to execute after a few 'blank' missing kicks. In the example below, you deliver a very high front-leg Hopping Hook Kick that your opponent evades easily by leaning back. The missing kick folds into a Roundhouse chamber. When the opponent comes back naturally forward to counter, you catch him with a high Roundhouse, hopping if necessary.

A close relative: Missing Hook Kick Trap into Roundhouse Kick

Specific training

Hopping Roundhouse Kick in series

Hooking the Hook Kick into Roundhouse Chamber

- Drill the basic Roundhouse and basic Hook Kicks first.
- Drill hopping forward on one leg in Roundhouse Chamber position, delivering Roundhouse Kicks with each hop. The kicking leg does not lower, for a minimum of ten repetitions (As illustrated).
- Drill the Hooking Hook Kick, 'hooking' right into perfect Roundhouse Chamber position (Second Illustration).
- Drill the Ground Roundhouse and the Ground Hook Kicks to strengthen the hip muscles (See Photos on the next page; refer to our previous book about *Ground Kicks*).
- Work the heavy bag, barely grazing it with the passing Hook Kick feint, but hitting hard with the subsequent Roundhouse Kick. For a shorter feint drill, you can hang a ball from the front of the bag at Hook Kick height and make sure you barely graze it on your way in (See drawings on the next page).

The Ground Roundhouse Kick and The Ground Hook Kick

- A Medicine-ball or a Basketball on top of a standing bag can be of great drilling help for the high Roundhouse version: your Hook Kick feint barely grazes the ball without moving it, but your Roundhouse Kick will try to kick the ball as far as possible! (As illustrated by the drawing).
- Drilling with a moving partner is supremely important: Practice both Hook Kicks and Hook Feints while he helps by 'spotting' you.

Barely graze the ball with the Hook Kick, kick it out powerfully with the Roundhouse!

Self defense

The Photos below present the even more confusing *high-low* version of the kick, more appropriate for real world fighting as the kick targets the groin. High Hook Kick Feint to groin Roundhouse...

The ***high****-Hook chamber feint to (****low****) groin Roundhouse Kick*

The figures below show the same basic technique, but with a more complex, and therefore realistic, conditioning phase. Take the initiative with a cross-step and high Back-fist Strike turning into a front hand catch. While trying to keep control of the opponent's hand, deliver immediately a high Hook Kick; your fiddling with his hand will keep him misdirected. Lower the kicking leg and repeat at once the whole maneuver: high Back-fist followed by the high Hook chamber. This time, he will probably concentrate on keeping his front hand free, while preparing to smother the coming Hook Kick into his lifted hands to his *high out-side*. But you pivot with the leg still cocked and deliver an unexpected Low Roundhouse Kick to his open groin (*low in-side*). Follow up as you land the kicking foot, starting with a Side Elbow Strike for example.

Offensive application of the high Hook Chamber to low groin Roundhouse Kick, and follow-up

The principles of the *Tap Kick* will be detailed further in the text, but we shall give a suitable example here. A 'Tap Kick' is an important Feint Kick-type in which the Feint goes all the way to touch the opponent at the intended 'feint target'. From this touching, the kick continues to develop to powerfully hit the final *real* target. It is, in some way, the ultimate long feint; and there is nothing more convincing than actually touching the target. Of course, what the opponent does not know yet, is that you concentrate on speed and misdirection at this stage, not on power. As the opponent reacts to the harmless 'tap', your Feint Kick evolves into a real kick directed at another target. Tap Kicks need to be fast and to provoke some reaction; they are usually directed at the legs or groin where they are most effective. Of course, high Taps are conceivable, but less common. In the example presented below the Tap Kick is a front-leg Hook Kick to the assailant groin (*low in-side*) as soon as he initiates a forward move. A fast and light kick touching the groin area will always provoke a reaction, even if partially blocked. You immediately and smoothly fold the kicking leg into Roundhouse chamber to follow up with a *high out-side* head kick. From there, you could lower the leg into a naturally-following *Low* Spin-back Hook Kick.

Groin Hook Tap Feint Kick to high Roundhouse Kick

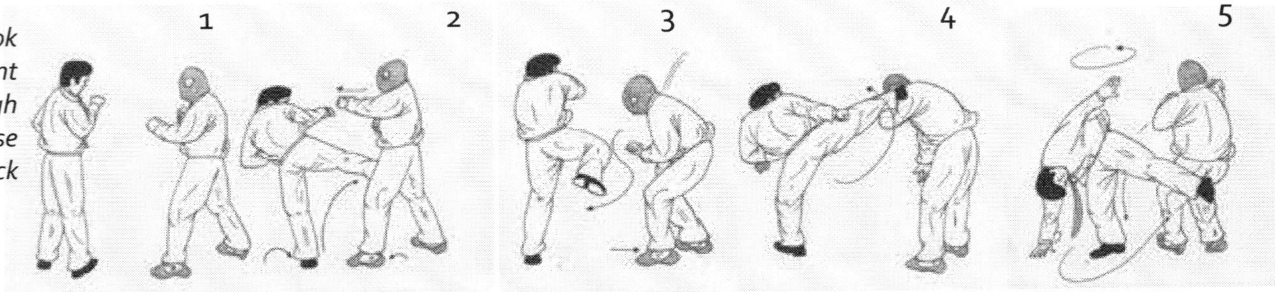

We shall cap this section about the Hook-chambered Roundhouse Kick by briefly reminding the reader of the Essential Spin-back Roundhouse Kick, which is, in fact, a Spin-back Hook-chambered Roundhouse Kick. The kick is mentioned in this book, and is presented in detail in our previous work about *Essential Kicks*. The variant presented here is the actual delivery of a short Spin-back Hook Kick into the opponent's guard; this disruptive Feint will turn into a full Roundhouse Kick coming from the other direction.

A feinting-applied Spin-back Roundhouse Kick

Illustrative photos

The basic Essential front-leg Hooking Hook Kick

Another example of Hook-chambered high Roundhouse Feint Kick

Hook Tap Feint Kick to the knee provoking the necessary reaction for a successful high Roundhouse Kick and follow-up

Another example of high Hook-chambered groin Roundhouse Feint Kick

7. The Front-chambered Hook Kick

General

This kick, starting with a Front Kick-feint, will generally be a rear-leg start. Somewhere during delivery, the Front Kick turns into a Hook Kick. Technically, it is a very easy kick to perform and, - if well executed- , it is usually very successful. This is basically a straight-to-circular Feint Kick, but it generally adds a dual level-feint aspect: the Front Kick will usually aim at mid-level, while the Hook Kick will generally conclude at high level. Therefore the Front-chambered Hook Kick will more than often be a low/high straight-to-circular Feint Kick. It is in some way a poor man's Roundhouse-chambered Hook Kick because it is easier to perform, especially for the less flexible Artists. But one should also remember that the Hook Kick is not that powerful a Kick and that it needs to be accurate to be decisive, especially in a real-life situation. There will very often be need for a follow-up, and we shall offer a few examples.

The Front Kick-feint can be as "long" as needed, and it is therefore usually very effective as a lure, especially when in the general direction of the groin. Relatively easy, often successful, confusing, what is not to like?

The Front-chambered Hook Kick; simple but effective

Description

The Illustrations on this page and the Photos at the top of next page show the classical "short" version of the Feint Kick: You deliver a convincing rear-leg Front Kick Chamber as if targeting the opponent's groin. You seamlessly start pivoting in this chamber position until you have your side towards the opponent. From this *Side Kick-like* chamber, you start to deliver the high Hook Kick to the head (The only worthwhile target for the Hook Kick, together with the groin).

The short Front-chambered Hook Kick

Front view of the Front-chambered Hook Kick

Key points

- This is one uninterrupted movement: the transitions between the chambering phases are smooth and rounded.
- The classical "short" version is usually too short for use against an experienced fighter, and the Front Kick must be partially developed to count as a Feint. The Front Kick-feint does then have to chamber back somewhat during the pivot towards the Hook chamber.
- Never deliver this Feint Kick if you have not delivered at least one full Front Kick (with identical chamber) just before.

Typical applications

The illustrations below show the more realistic application with a "long" Front Kick-feint. In fact, the Front Kick-feint could go all the way to a touching *Tap Kick* if the conditions are suitable. In this sporting example, you deliver a powerful rear-leg Front Kick towards the opponent's belt knot, then chamber back to replace the foot rearwards where it came from. Repeat if you feel it is needed to get him accustomed to this teasing delivery. You can then repeat the kick, but faster this time and with more hip thrust (or even with a hop). You are in fact extending the Front Kick nearly all the way, not far from touching him, in order to force a reaction and to have him lower his guard to check the longer-than-expected kick. As soon as he reacts to the Front Kick, you chamber partly back while pivoting on your standing leg. You are now in position to deliver the smoothly following Hook Kick to his unprotected head. You can finish up, for example, with a Spin-back Back Kick to his now open mid-section (low feint/high kick/low kick).

Applied 'long' Front-chambered Hook Feint Kick

Specific training

- Work the heavy bag, touching it lightly with the Front Kick before getting into Hook Kick-mode. Drill for speed and smooth transitions.
- For coordination and speed, practice the kick in its front-leg version (See Illustration).
- Work with a partner, spotting you and moving around. Alternate real Front Kicks and Front-chambered Hook Feint Kicks.
- Drill hopping during the pivot from Front Chamber to Hook Chamber. Drill slowly at first, then increase speed gradually without harming the technique: It must stay a realistic feint. Use the mirror.
- It is important to learn to deliver power with this type of kick, as it is not trivial. For scoring in sport contexts, speed is enough; but for real-life kicking, drilling for power is imperative. The best drill is kicking the medicine ball off a standing bag: lightly touch the bag with a fast Front Kick, then hook-kick powerfully through the ball standing on top. The difference in range from the standing bag to the center of the ball makes for a realistic Feint Kick drill (See Second set of drawings).

The front-leg Front-chambered Hook Feint Kick

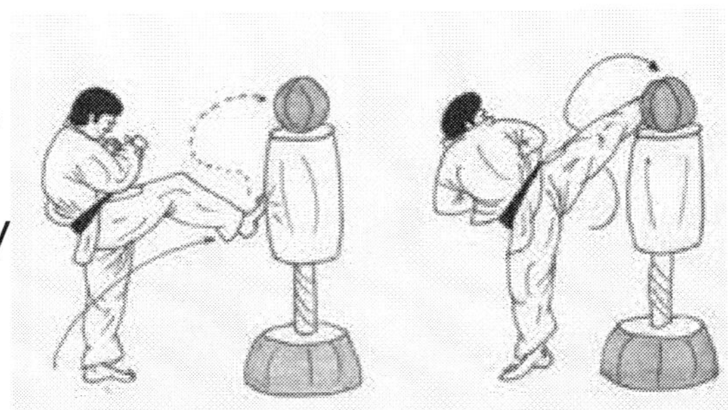

Drilling the Front-chambered Hook Kick for power: kick the ball as far as possible

Self defense

The illustrations at the top of the next page show an example of the ultimate "short" version of this Feint Kick: Front feint-kicking the shin and/or knee of the opponent. After a few Low Front Kick attacks to his shin, -especially when he shows inklings to attack or move forward-, you repeat with a Low Front Kick feint, that will turn into a high Hook Kick as his attention is definitely down. This is a surprisingly easy and successful maneuver, and many will fall into this trap. A good follow-up is the following: while you land the hook-kicking foot forward, punch towards his eyes to keep his attention up and deliver a full-powered rear-leg Penetrating Front Kick to his groin or lower abdomen (as the circumstances dictate).

The Low Front Kick Chambering Feint to high Hook Kick

The Illustrations below will remind the reader about the importance **1**. of *feinting* towards the groin for its atavistic reactivity, and **2.** of the usual necessity of *following up* after a Hook Kick. Start by conditioning him to mid-level Front Kicks. Then, kick clearly towards the groin, with a long Front Kick-feint. As soon as he reacts (as he has no choice), let the Feint turn into a high Hook Kick to the face. And now the featured follow-up: chamber the leg after the Hook Kick and, from this Universal chamber, roundhouse-kick the other side of his head. If difficult for you to double-kick without lowering the leg, you can lower the leg between the kicks and let it *rebound* forcefully on the floor for a fast follow-up. Do jab or back-fist while lowering the leg after the Roundhouse Kick, but make sure you lower the foot *behind his lead foot*. Deliver a downward knee strike to the back of his knee to get him down on one knee, and switch legs for a following debilitating Downward Knee Strike to his exposed Achilles' tendon.

Front Kick Feint towards the groin, high Hook Kick; sophisticated follow-up

As mentioned more than once, the Hook Kick is not a powerful kick and is usually reserved for targeting the head, preferably in a surprising way for more effect. Versions aiming at lower targets, like the Low Hook Kick described in our previous book (*Low Kicks*), are more anecdotic kicks used to divert attention and allow for further attacks, or are part of takedown moves. The only exception to this rule is, understandably, the groin. This area is the most sensitive of the male body, and is always a prime target. Feinting a mid-level, or even a high level Front Kick, and turning into a groin Hook Kick will therefore work exactly as all the preceding moves described; there is no need for further illustration. The reader can practice all the preceding applications and direct the Hook Kick part towards the opponent's groin. Executing the Hook Kick at groin level is easier for less flexible Artists, is faster, and it can be executed from closer, if necessary, with a slightly bent leg 'hooking' into the groin.
The example we shall nevertheless present is a near-miss of the Feint Kick against a 'timing' counter-punching opponent (Illustrated below). The following maneuver is relevant whether or not you have conditioned the opponent with preparatory Front Kicks. As you chamber the Front Feint Kick, the opponent does not retreat or does not prepare to block, but he initiates a counterpunch at mid-level. This is the most classic *Shotokan Karate* stop-punching maneuver. By pivoting immediately to the Hook Kick chamber, you will simultaneously block his incoming attack; this is reminiscent of many Stop Kicks described in our previous book (*Stop Kicks*) to which the reader is invited to refer. From this position, the short groin Hook Kick will be fast and easy. The follow-up illustrated is a full-powered rear-leg Crescent kick to the head, and a classic *Kibisu Gaeshi* Ju-Jitsu Takedown (One-leg Lift).

Application of the Front-chambered **groin** *Hook Kick*

Illustrative Photos

Another example of Front-chambered high Hook Kick

8. The Roundhouse-chambered Hook Kick

General

This is in some way the next level of the previous kick: instead of a Front Kick Feint in the centerline, you go a bit further with a Roundhouse Kick-feint coming from the (opposite) side. The Roundhouse-chambered Hook Kick is more difficult to execute, as it requires more hip flexibility. This said, this is a classic and must-drill Feint Kick, in the vein of the principles behind the *Universal Chamber*, presented in our *Essential Book of Martial Arts Kicks*.

Universal chambering, side and near-front views

The 'Universal Chamber' is a position from which the cocked leg can develop equally easily a Side Kick, a Hook Kick or a Roundhouse kick, generally at high levels. The position is not static, of course, and is relatively safe: the chambered foot blocks access to the groin, the chambered lower leg protects the trunk which is also half-bent rearwards, and the hands are in guard near the head. This way of kicking was popularized by one of the most famous kicking champions of recent times, *Bill 'Superfoot' Wallace*, who used to reign supreme in both points and full contact Karate. From this Universal Chamber, one can easily misdirect a trained opponent by moving the hip slightly in a way suggesting one of the options, while in fact executing another. Of course, this kind of subtle feinting is difficult to explain, and it will work only on experienced fighters attuned to body changes. Do not try subtlety on novice or unsophisticated opponents (Variations of the Universal Chamber are presented below).

Examples of applied Universal chambering

In actual use, the kick will usually be a front-leg version, as a rear-leg Roundhouse Feint would take longer and be slightly too obvious. A rear-leg version is probably better used with unexperienced fighters, who are slower and who need more obvious moves to be convinced. We shall again remind the reader that the Hook Kick is fast and deceptive, but not the most powerful of kicks: it is more often a sport kick than a self-defense one. That is also why the reader needs to remember to aim for the head or the groin, and to always follow up.
In any case, this is one of those kicks to be drilled for general hip flexibility and for overall kicking proficiency, even if it is not your cup of tea.

Description

The first set of Figures and Photos shows the classic ***rear-leg*** delivery for a more thorough and difficult training that will make your front-leg version easier and faster. Start with it. Chamber a regular rear-leg Roundhouse and pivot on the standing foot *without extending the kicking leg*. Only when your side faces the opponent, do start to extend the leg partially (as needed), *while* pivoting a little bit more. Stop pivoting, and extend the leg back in the other direction to deliver the intended Hook Kick.

The classic rear-leg Roundhouse-chambered Hook Feint Kick

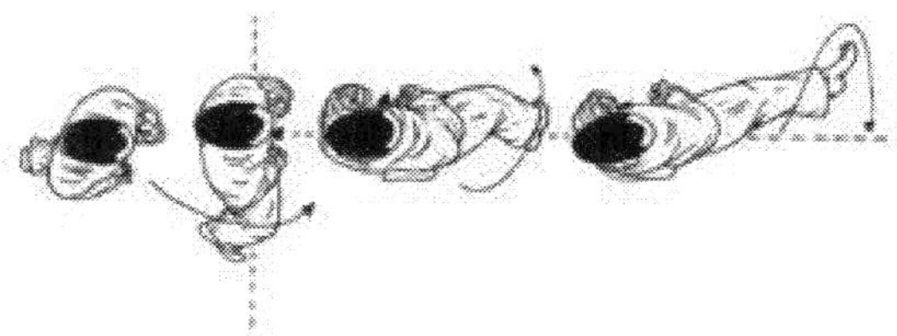

Top view of the rear-leg Roundhouse-chambered Hook Feint Kick

Front View of the rear-leg Roundhouse-chambered Hook Feint Kick

The second set of Figures and Photos shows the delivery of the more sporty and practical ***front-leg*** version: You hop directly into front-leg Roundhouse chamber or into Universal chamber; you then pivot slightly in *with the leg chambered*, for a better Hook Kick starting position. Kick through.

The sporty front-leg Roundhouse-chambered Hook Feint Kick

Front View of the front-leg Roundhouse-chambered Hook Feint Kick

Key points

- The nuance between a Hook chamber and a Roundhouse chamber is very subtle: Make sure to exaggerate the 'Roundhouse impression' of your chamber.
- Try to always execute this Feint Kick after a previous real Roundhouse attack opening with the same original chamber.
- The leg trajectory is rounded, smooth and uninterrupted. Use the Roundhouse 'overshoot' of the hips like an elastic band to maximize the power of the Hook Kick.
- Always follow up after a Hook Kick.

The Roundhouse Chamber must be convincing – **Grace Wong**

Typical applications

The Figures below illustrate the classic front-leg sport application of the Kick, and this time from a slightly rear-view for completeness of the picture. This will also be a hi/lo feint. Deliver a first front-leg Roundhouse to your opponent's midsection, preferably aiming for the belt knot. Repeat, -either after a break, a step or a 'rebounding foot'- , and develop the kick towards the same target, but while evolving into the high Hook Kick to the back of his neck. As a follow up, you could let the kicking leg rebound on the floor for a real body Roundhouse this time.

Mid-level Roundhouse Chamber to high Hook Kick, after a conditioning mid-level Roundhouse

Specific training

- Work the heavy bag, rear- and front-leg, grazing it while passing with the chamber, and then connecting with the Hook Kick. You can also add a hanging ball to the front of the bag to touch through on your way in, as we have done before.

Graze the bag on your way in, Kick the bag on your way back

Specific Training (Continued)

- Repeat with a chair between you and the bag, and/or a chair on the side for a "full" chamber. Drill with various length of the feinting leg, i.e. a more or less "extended" chamber.
- Train with a moving partner, who should be helping you by trying to spot the feint. Alternate randomly real Roundhouse Kicks and feinting Roundhouse Kicks.
- Work systematically on your hip flexibility.

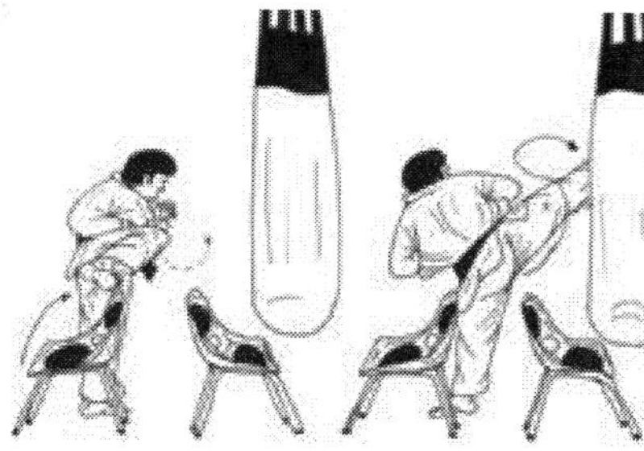

Use chairs to force you to exaggerate the chamber and the chambered pivot

Self defense

For Self-defense, lower Kicks are often more practical. The Photos below show the Roundhouse Feint delivered low, as a 'Low Kick' to the knee or thigh, and turning into a high head Hook Kick. The principles are identical as for the previous applications; you have to make sure that the Feint looks real and shifts to the Hook Kick as late and as smoothly as possible.

Low Roundhouse Chamber to high Hook Kick

The Illustrations below show an application of the rear-leg version of this Low Kick Feint. This is a very effective combination because the Low Kick (Straight-leg Roundhouse) is very disturbing to an assailant's concentration. Deliver a first Low Kick to the side of his thigh/knee. Repeat with a slightly exaggerated chamber. As he gears up to move the leg or smother the hit, you pivot and glide into the high Hook Kick to his face. Lower the leg in front and follow up, for example with a Spin-back Hook Sweep Kick of both his legs.

Low Kick-chambered high Hook Feint Kick and follow-up

Illustrative Photos

Vintage photo: Experienced Champion Mishka Daglietski still falls for the feint and tries to block Marc's Roundhouse that has become a Hook Kick

High Roundhouse, followed by high Roundhouse-chambered Hook Kick

9. The high Spin-back Hook Feint to Downward Heel Kick

General

This is basically the Spin-back Downward Hook Kick, as described in our previous book about *Essential Kicks*; it is simply delivered in a more 'feinting' frame of mind. This basic Kick is the natural evolving follow-up of a Spin-back Hook Kick, in case your opponent ducks under it or crouches to minimize its impact. Refer to sections 'The Downward Hook Kick' and 'The Spin-back Hook Kick' in our previous book for a full understanding of the underlying Kick. We shall limit ourselves here to a simple presentation and application.
In the case of the Feint Kick, you purposely will execute a recognizable *Spin-back Hook Kick*, and do so as high as possible. You should strive to lift the foot higher than your opponent's head, so as to have enough accelerating range for the *Downward Heel Kick*. The reader is also invited to note that, the movements being uninterrupted, the Downward Hook Kick will in fact be on an oblique trajectory.

The Spin-back Hook Kick

The Spin-back Hook Feint to Downward Heel Kick

Description

The Drawings describe the kick as the high full Spin-back Hook Kick it is until the centerline is reached. The Kick is delivered in such a way that it reaches its apex at the centerline. But the body pivot then stops and the hips turn to face the opponent while the kick evolves into a slightly diagonal *Axe Kick* (Downward Heel Kick); the diagonal vector is due to the overall momentum of the kick that is not stopped, but progressively diverted.

The high Spin-back Hook Feint to Downward Heel Kick

Impact of the diagonal Spin-back Axe Kick

Key points

- This is a kick that must be delivered with full commitment from the start; there is no way back. The power comes both from the spin-back and from the downward trajectories.
- Always deliver after at least one *high* Spin-back Hook Kick; it is best if the opponent finds it easy to duck under the kick.
- The Hook Kick must be executed as high as physically possible, both for the Feint effect and for acquiring range for downward acceleration.
- Keep your guard up at all times; you are relatively close to the opponent.
- Always follow up.

Typical applications

Most applications presented are against an opponent crouching or ducking to evade or smother an incoming Spin-back Hook Kick. It is important to remember that, for fast and flexible Artists, the Kick is certainly valid by itself and can be used with surprising effect against opponents that do not bend down or cringe to smother it.

But the Photos below will illustrate the classic working combination for the use of the kick. Drill the Spin-back Hook Kick and Spin-back Hook to Downward Heel Kick in uninterrupted series; as the partner ducks under the second Hook Kick, he gets slammed with the Axe Kick.

High Spin-back Hook for conditioning, then Feint Kick; drill one after the other in series

The Figures below illustrate the same combination starting with an opening jab for a more convincing effect. The opening jab will reinforce the conditioning effect (Jab = will be followed by Spin-back Hook Kick) and will further overwhelm the opponent (second jab follows closely the first Spin-back Hook Kick) and therefore nudge his urge to crouch. Jab and use the hip movement to start delivering a full classic Spin-back Hook kick to your opponent's face. Lower the leg back after a full turn and repeat immediately. The second jab should crowd him. This time aim the following Hook Kick even *above* his head, if possible; but turn the kick into a Downward Heel Kick, whether he crouches or not. Follow up, starting with a Low Kick from the other leg, for example. The combination, without its conditioning preface, is also illustrated by the Photos that follow on the next page.

A great combo: Jab, Spin-back Hook kick, Jab, Spin-back Hook Feint to Axe Kick, Low Kick

Jab preceding Spin-back Hook Feint to Downward Heel Kick

Specific training

Hold the focus pad for a downward diagonal trajectory

- Drill the basic kicks thoroughly: the Spin-back Hook Kick, the Downward Heel Kick, the Downward Hook Kick and the Spin-back Downward Hook Kick. Refer to our previous work about *Essential Kicks*.
- Work seriously on your hip flexibility. Refer to our previous work about *Plyo-Flex* training.
- Training with a partner is essential. It is best to have him protected or to use focus pads. Be always careful when drilling this Kick.

Self defense

Once you have conditioned your opponent that, when you spin back, a Hook Kick is coming, you can then vary kick heights. This could contribute to the 'overwhelming' effect and therefore cause him more convincingly to duck and crouch. The Figures below show the same combination as before, but starting with a first Spin-back Hook Kick at *groin level*. This should get his hands down first, but then befuddle him as you next spin-back high. As he hopefully ducks, turn the move into a diagonal Downward Heel Kick. Follow up, for example with a Downward Hammer-fist Strike and an Outward Ghost Kick.

Groin Spin-back Hook Kick followed by high Spin-back Hook Feint to Downward Heel Kick; interesting Ghost Kick follow-up

The following Photos illustrate the use of the kick after the Leg Block of an incoming 'Low Kick'. The circular vector of the Leg Block will take you naturally into a fast spin-back, close to the assailant. This maneuver is threatening enough to cause the expected crouching that invites the evolution of the Spin-back Hook Kick into a hard-core Axe Kick. [Leg Blocks are briefly presented in our previous book about Stop Kicks]

The perfect opportunity for a high Spin-back Hook to Downward Heel Kick: follow-up of a circular Inside Leg Block

Illustrative Photos

Diagonal impact of the Spin-back Hook to Downward Heel Kick

Technical execution of the Spin-back Hook Feint to Axe Kick

10. The Roundhouse Feint to same-leg Spin-back Hook Kick

General

This Feint Kick is a very close relation of one of my favorite same-leg Double Kicks (to be presented in a coming book about Multiple Kicks): the Roundhouse to Spin-back Hook Kick. The only difference is that the starting Roundhouse is fully executed in the Double Kick, but only partially in the Feint Kick. How sketchy and incomplete the feint-part of Kick will be is highly dependent upon the specific situation and the relative level of the protagonists. In some cases, the starting Roundhouse Feint can be reduced to a little bit more than a chamber. In others, the Roundhouse will have to go all the way and even touch the opponent; in this case, it will be delivered with speed and flexibility instead of power.

This Feint Kick is a very effective and surprising kick if you are fast and flexible, if you have drilled it seriously and if you have well-conditioned your opponent to expect a powerful Full Roundhouse. It may seem far-fetched, convoluted and of a too-long trajectory to some, but I would implore them to give it a serious try. I have been using it and its Double Kick counterpart for years, with surprising success. It is a Kick of choice against a counter-attacker or an opponent that tends to block powerfully while staying in place.

In any case, the Artist is encouraged to practice this Kick seriously, if only for speed, conditioning, versatility and overall kicking proficiency.

Description

Remember that the Roundhouse Feint must be convincing and well-perceived. The classic execution is the high Feint/ high Hook Kick version, but all permutations are possible, as we shall see. The Illustrations show how you lift the knee in a clear Roundhouse chamber. If needed, as per the situation and your opponent's reaction, you may have to start the developing the Kick. Stop the pivot as soon as you have elicited a reaction, and lower the leg while starting pivoting in the *opposite* direction. If you are proficient, the kicking leg stays airborne, but it straightens low and gets close to the standing leg (in order to accelerate the pivot of the body). If you are less proficient, the foot touches the floor to rebound as you proceed with the Spin-back. Once you have your back to the opponent, you keep accelerating but start to lift the leg up for the Hook Kick.

The high Roundhouse Feint to same-leg high Spin-back Hook Kick

Description (Continued)

Top view of the Roundhouse Feint to same-leg Spin-back Hook Kick

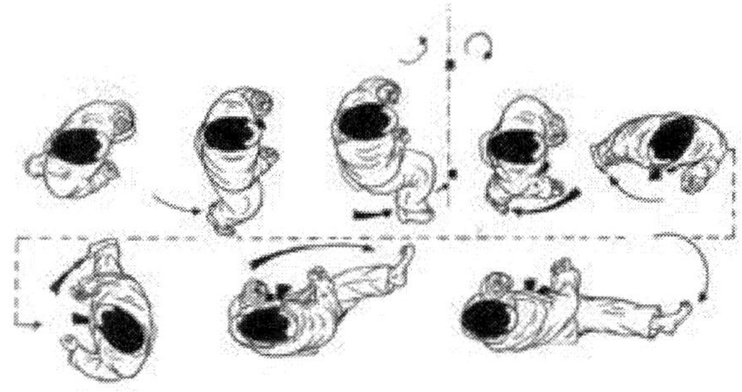

Key points

- The forward move is interrupted as soon as the opponent reacts.
- From the point the forward move has been stopped, this is one uninterrupted and fully committed movement; in the opposite direction.
- Use the swinging leg and the arms to accelerate the Spin-back; this requires training but gives a lot of accelerating power.
- Always execute after a previous real Roundhouse Kick that is chambered in the exact same way.
- Deliver with relaxed muscles: this is exclusively a fast kick, no power needed. Muscle tension will only slow both the Feint and the ultimate Kick.
- The Hook Kick is, of course, a kick-through maneuver. Do not slow the acceleration before impact!

Typical applications

The Photos below and those at the top of next page show the slight difference in execution of the two basic variants of the 'high Feint/high Kick' permutation: with or without letting the kicking leg touch the ground between the Feint and the Kick.

Foot landing during the high long Roundhouse Feint to same-leg high Spin-back Hook Kick

Typical Application (Continued)

Fully airborne high long Roundhouse Feint to same-leg high Spin-back Hook Kick; no foot landing during execution

This kick is not to be used against a "runner" (a fleeing opponent): Use it against a 'blocker' or a counter-attack fan. The Illustrations show a typical application of the Feint-version of this kick. Attack your opponent's lower back with a rear-leg Roundhouse Kick; this is a relatively easy but very painful maneuver at kidneys level. Retract the leg rearwards, but let it 'rebound' on the floor. Repeat a clear Roundhouse chamber, but stop and spin-back into a high Hook Kick as he braces for your Roundhouse and initiates his counter-punch. In this example, your Spin-back Hook Kick will catch him near completion of his reverse punch. This is the *'mid-level Feint/ high Kick' permutation*. Follow up, for instance with a Spin-back Short Back Kick of the other foot (opposite Spin); this in turn would be the perfect set-up for a sacrifice *Sumi Gaeshi* throw to bring him to the floor for ground control. The *Sumi Gaeshi* takedown (Corner Reversal Throw) can either be **Judo**-type with a seat-lift, or an old **Jiu-Jitsu**-type where the 'lift' is a full Kick to the groin.

Applied mid-level Roundhouse Feint to same-leg high Spin-back Hook Kick; and suggested follow–up

Specific training

- Drill the full Double Kick (The Roundhouse to same-leg Spin-back Hook Kick), but drill for SPEED and not for power.
- Drill the Feint Kick on the heavy bag.
- Drill the Feint Kick by *kneeing* the heavy bag with the Roundhouse Chamber. Better, knee a hanging medicine ball hanging in front of the bag.
- Repeat with a chair forcing a high and exaggerated Chamber (Illustrated).
- Drill *Plyo-Flex* exercises to improve Hip Flexibility.

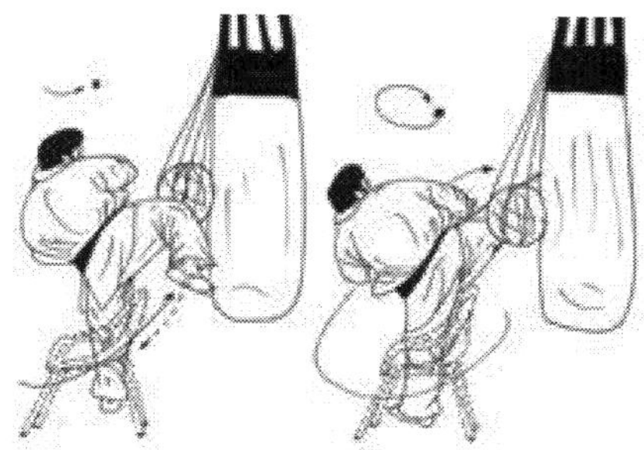

Use a ball-hanging heavy bag to drill the Kick; when proficient, add a chair for exaggerated chamber

Self defense

The Figures below show a variation of the 'low Feint/high Kick' permutation, with the *Hand-on-floor* version of the Spin-back Hook Kick. In this example, in opposite guards, you attrite your opponent's inside front leg with 'Low Kicks'. When he starts to react to your prodding with leg blocks, repeat with a clear chamber. As he starts blocking, you stop and spin back, while bending the body away from a possible counter. If the opponent is close, you should "hook" in at impact (**Hooked** Hook Kick – See *The Essential Book of Martial Arts Kicks*). Follow up; we have illustrated a Hip Wheel throw follow-up (*Koshi Guruma - Judo*), but anything goes...

Applied **low** *Roundhouse Feint to same-leg* **high** *Hand-on-floor Spin-back Hook Kick; and follow–up*

Last but not least, we should remind the reader that the Hook Kick can also be delivered with great success to the opponent's groin, where some additional 'hooking' can do even more damage. The illustrations below show the *high Feint/low Kick* permutation, in which a groin Spin-back Hook Kick follows a same-leg high Roundhouse Kick. Not only is the groin Kick redoubtable, but the change of plane (hi/lo) will give the Feint Kick an additional advantage. This example also shows a *front-leg* Roundhouse Feint, that is additionally a 'timing' Stop Kick (For more about 'timing' Stop Kicks, the reader is invited to refer to our previous book *Stop Kicks)*. As the assailant initiates forward momentum with a punch, you hop forward in a classic 'timing' Stop Roundhouse Kick to the head; keep it fast and loose. As soon as you have connected and jammed his intended attack, you can start your Spin-back pivot. Let your 'hooking' Hook Kick catch him in the groin as his hands are still lifted. A natural follow-up, would be the use of the pivot for a fully-powered Crescent Kick to his now unprotected head. As the assailant is now seriously mellowed, a punishing Large Outer Wheel Throw (*O Soto Guruma – Judo*) would be easy to execute.

*Applied front-leg **high** Roundhouse Feint to same-leg **low** groin Spin-back Hook Kick; and follow–up*

Illustrative Photos

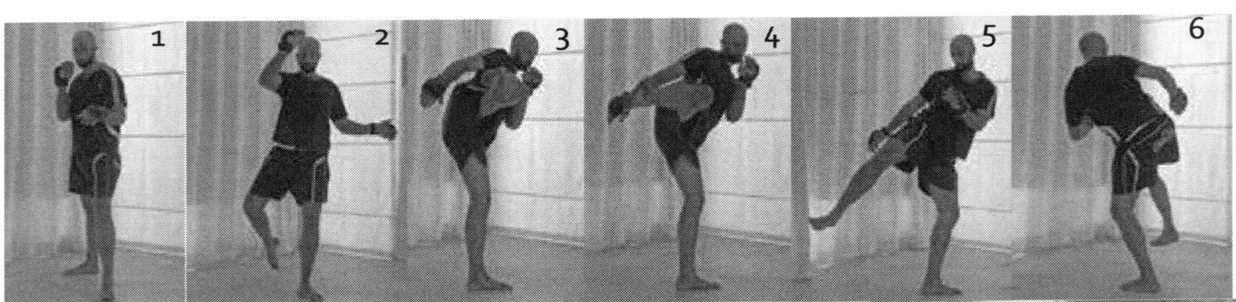

The corresponding full Double Kick: Roundhouse Kick to same-leg Spin-back Hook Kick

11. The Side-chambered Roundhouse Kick

General

This is a relatively easy Feint Kick to perform, as it glides smoothly and naturally. It should be mentioned, though, that it requires some training to make the Feint look clear. Some training will make you learn the 'feeling' of a discernable feint into the smooth development of the kick. But it is a very efficient maneuver, as the expected straight Kick and the actual circular Kick come from totally different angles, and can moreover be delivered in lo/hi permutations. The Feint Side Kick can also be extended easily for as long as needed to exact a reaction, and so without hampering much the switch to the Roundhouse.This is a must-practice Kick, front-leg and rear-leg, although the front-leg version is more common and natural.
This is again the place to refer the reader to the theory of kick-delivery from the Universal Chamber position. The Universal Chamber is common to all three of the Hook, Roundhouse and Side Kicks, and its purpose is to confuse the opponent as of which will be ultimately delivered (See previous books). These principles are important to understand for our purpose here, as it is the opposite effect that is required. In the case of Feint Kicks, you *want* your opponent to identify the kick that is supposedly coming, and you must exaggerate the Chamber position accordingly. The difference can sometimes be very subtle, and it is important not to overdo it: the slightest the hint necessary, the better.

Description

The front-leg delivery (of the Feint Side Kick) is the most common practical use of this kick, but the classic learning drill is, as usual, the rear-leg version. The practice of the rear-leg version is the best way to learn to emphasize the Side Kick chamber, and to execute the Feint Kick in a complete and exaggerated way. Later, the principles ingrained will allow for a much more subtle and effective feint. The Figures at the top of next page describe the classic ***rear-leg*** delivery of the Kick: Go directly into classic Side Kick Chamber. Start extending the leg and lift the foot in a regular Side Kick-move, but simultaneously pivot on your hip outwards, thus giving the foot a slightly curved trajectory. The emphasis on the 'curving' move will be as deemed by the circumstances and by your opponent's reactions: you could go from Side Chamber directly to Roundhouse Chamber, or you could have to extend the leg in a nearly-full Side Kick before retracting it into Roundhouse Chamber. But, as soon as your opponent obviously expects a Side Kick, you complete the hip pivot and flex the leg into the Roundhouse Chamber. Kick. The classic delivery is that of the high kick.

Description (Continued)

The classic rear-leg Side-chambered Roundhouse Kick

Top View of the rear-leg Side-chambered Roundhouse Kick

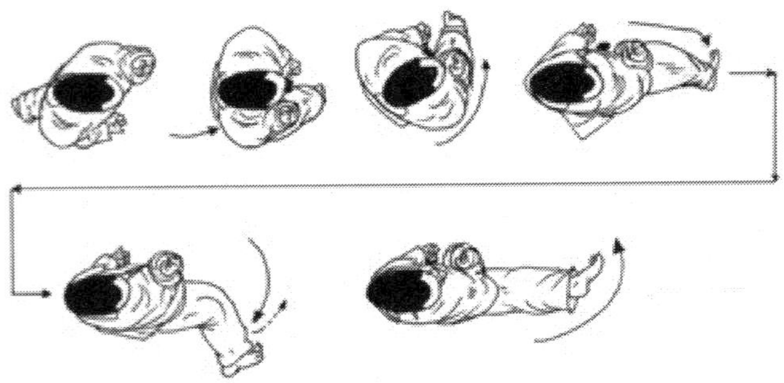

Front View of the rear-leg execution

The Photos <u>below</u> and the Illustrations at the top of next page show the more practical ***front-leg*** delivery. In this case, it is preferable to hop into a slightly exaggerated side kick chamber, giving your opponent a little more of your back; something like the preparation for a Back Side kick. This will give you some more range for the curved extension of the leg. It is of course best delivered after a previous 'real' Side Kick.

The front-leg execution of the Side-chambered Roundhouse Kick; after a 'conditioning' Side Kick

Description (Continued)

The common front-leg Side-chambered Roundhouse Kick

Key points

- The chamber must be clear, and with your side towards the opponent.
- Lift the knee as high as possible.
- The move from the Side Chamber to the Roundhouse Chamber is smooth, curved and uninterrupted.
- The Roundhouse Chamber must not be an "all the way" classic execution with the heel close to your buttocks; you start kicking as soon as you have enough range to do so effectively, as per your proficiency and the specific situation.
- Always execute the Kick after a previous mid-level or low-level Side Kick to condition your opponent to react to the chamber.

Typical applications

The Illustrations below show the typical *front-leg* application in **opposite** stances, with mid-level Feint and high actual Kick. Preferably after at least one 'real' mid-level front-leg Hopping Side Kick, you deliver another 'feinting' one aiming again at your opponent's belt level. You execute the Feint for as long as necessary to elicit a reaction, even crashing into his guard if necessary. Turn the successful Feint into a high Roundhouse Kick to the back of his neck, with a hop if necessary. Follow up; a very effective an ironic subsequent technique would be a rebounding same-leg Side Kick to his now-opened middle.

Applied classic front-leg Side-chambered Roundhouse Feint Kick in opposite stances

The Photos below will show the same classic application, *but* in **same stances** and after two conditioning mid-level Side Kicks.

The same-stance applied Feint Kick after two preparatory Side Kicks

Specific training

- Work the heavy bag from different distances, grazing the bag with your curving Feint Side Kick, and then hitting *as hard as possible* with your Roundhouse (to force you to chamber enough). A 'bean-shaped' bag is even better for drilling this Kick!
- Repeat with a chair between you and the bag (Illustrated)
- Drill with a partner, alternating 'real' Side Kicks and Feint Kicks. Lightly touch his guard with the Side Kick, before launching the high Roundhouse. Your partner should help you to make the Feint real-looking.
- A great way to drill for a better intuitive understanding of the maneuver and for a more flexible hip joint is the following: Execute a full mid-level Side Kick, but *obliquely* to avoid touching your partner or the heavy bag; from this position, bend the leg into Roundhouse Chamber to execute the Kick *fully* on the other side. This is a great drill, highly recommended, and also very good for general kicking proficiency.

Drill on the bean-shaped bag, eventually with a chair for more complete Chambers

Full Oblique Side Kick to other-side Roundhouse: a good drill

Self defense

The following application is a more 'keep-the-pressure'-version of the classic applied Feint Kick, with the added twist of linking a high Back-fist strike with the mid-level Side kick. The high Back-fist is a classic maneuver used to cause the opponent to lift his guard in order to create an opening for the naturally-following Side Kick. In this case, it will add a realistic layer of complexity and help overwhelming the opponent's senses. As described in the Drawings below, you will 'condition' your opponent to a well-known high Back-fist/mid-level front-leg Hopping Side Kick. You will repeat immediately but, this time, you will execute a Feint Side Chamber after the Back-fist strike; he will expect the Side Kick even more, after previous combination. But you will, instead, deliver the high Roundhouse Kick to the unprotected head. You can follow up with the easy transition to a high Spin-back Hook Kick, and an *Essential* Upward Hook Back Kick.

Cross-step high Back-fist Strike preceding the mid-level Side-chambered high Roundhouse Kick; and follow-up

In theory, this Feint Kick lends itself to all permutations of low/mid/high levels for both part of the Kick. Although some exotic permutations can work for some Artists and add an element of surprise, the basic application presented above in several versions, is by far the most common. The only other permutation encountered from time to time is the low Side Kick Chamber Feint to high Roundhouse, and mostly as a Stop Side Kick, an Obstruction Side Kick or an Attrition Side Kick (More about those in our previous books about *Low Kicks* and *Stop Kicks*).

In the coming example, you stop-kick any attempt of your opponent to move forward with Low Side Stop Kicks to his moving front leg. This will frustrate all possible attacking moves. Illustrated are a hopping step for a front-leg kick, a lunge step for a jab and a full step for a lunge punch. When your opponent is well conditioned to this attrition by obstruction-kicking devoid of follow-up, you can use the Stop Kick as a Feint. Lightly touch is front knee as a Stop Kick, but meld smoothly into the high Roundhouse; it is best to execute the *Body-bent* version of the Roundhouse as you are close and in Stop Kick-mode. A good follow-up would be to land the kicking foot deep behind the opponent and Stomp-kick the back of his front knee.

Front-leg Low Side Stop Kick to high Roundhouse Feint Kick; follow-up

Illustrative Photos

Technical Roundhouse Kick from Side Kick Chamber

Illustrative Photos (Continued)

A hooking Upward Back Kick

Another hooking Upward Back Kick

Stomp Kick to the back knee joint

Back knee Stomp Kick

12. The low to high Roundhouse Feint Kick

General

This is our first example of a pure 'level' Feint Kick: same kick, same direction, but two different height levels. The name says it all: you make your opponent believe that a low Roundhouse Kick is coming, and you then kick over his lowering guard for a *high* Roundhouse. This Feint Kick requires flexibility and some practice, but it is thereafter very effective, especially if you direct the feint towards your opponent's groin: It is very difficult to stay impassible when you have something flying towards this area.
It is a very fast kick, as you are already more or less in chambering position for the second 'real' kick. In fact it is basically a near-Double Kick, with emphasis on speed and on a feinting mind-frame for the first kick.
Whatever your personal feelings about its use, it is an important Kick to drill for speed, hip flexibility and overall kicking proficiency.

The low to high Roundhouse Feint Kick after a 'conditioning' Low Kick

Description

The following Illustrations and Photos describe the delivery of the front-leg version of the kick, which is the most common, -especially in sport fighting-, because of the high speed of the feint. This 'feint' part of the Kick is always a partially-developed Roundhouse Kick, as it needs to be convincing. It should also always be "aimed" below the belt, to allow for a meaningful height differentiation. In the author's opinion, you should in fact aim to deliver a fast no-power "touch" Roundhouse from where to proceed. Touching is always the best possible Feint because it adds a stimulus to another of the five senses, on top of just sight.
You can also simply lift the nearly-straight leg towards the target, aiming to touch.

The classic low to high Roundhouse Feint Kick

Description (Continued)

All variations are valid, so long as you convince your opponent that you are attacking his legs or groin. As soon as your opponent reacts, the leg is retracted into a Roundhouse Chamber while the knee is lifted, the knee doing thus a kind of "bobbing" move, as shown clearly in the front view. Kick high and chamber back. When delivering the 'real' kick, one should lift the knee as little as needed, in order to refrain from an early warning; the best approach is to lift the chambered knee *while already extending the leg for the high Kick*. The reader will have to work out his own most comfortable and efficient version, to be checked and proofed in free-fighting against an array of different opponents.

Front View of the Feint Kick

This Feint Kick is best delivered after a 'real' full low Roundhouse Kick

Description (Continued)

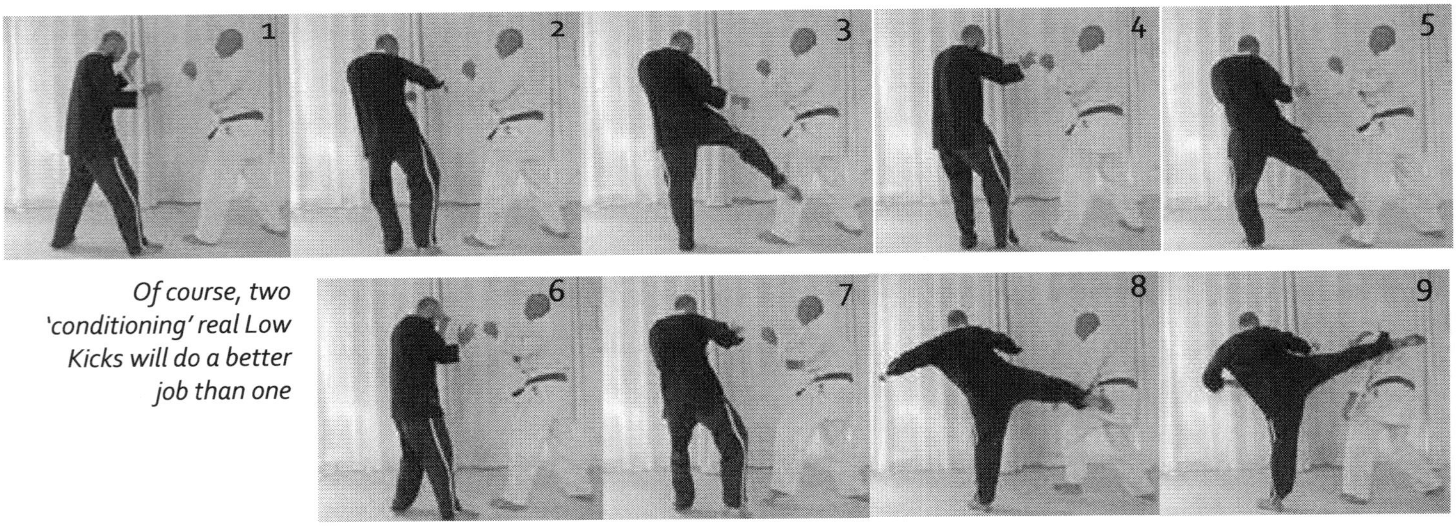

Of course, two 'conditioning' real Low Kicks will do a better job than one

Key points

- Keep developing the fast Feint Kick until you cause a reaction; if not it is a meaningless maneuver.
- From the retraction of the feinting move to the completion of the Kick itself, you must move in a smooth rounded movement; no abrupt 'stop and go'.
- Keep your guard up.
- It is preferable to deliver the Feint Kick after one or more real low Roundhouses.
- The kick is surprising but not very powerful: kick a few inches *through* the head, chamber back with a whipping effect and *always* follow up.

Typical applications

The applications will basically be all very similar: there is not much besides the Feint Kick itself, its preparatory conditioning and its follow-ups. The Figures at the top of next page show the typical application of the Kick, front-leg style. In sporting mode, you will feint to the belt knot; in real-life mode, you will aim for the groin. Hop and lift the front foot in a nearly straight line towards the target, as a fast low Roundhouse. In this example, the opponent blocks the kick. Repeat immediately and obviously, but start cocking the leg back as soon as you have the opponent react. Deliver the high Roundhouse as he is lowering his guard. Follow up with a *high* Back-fist Strike (coming from *opposite* direction to previous high Roundhouse) as you land the kicking foot. You can then finish him up with a real *Low* Kick from the other leg.

Typical Application (Continued)

Applied low groin Feint to high Roundhouse Kick, with conditioning and follow-up

Opposite view of conditioning Kick followed by the Feint Kick

Specific training

- Drill the full Double Kick, full-powered both low and high.
- Train in front of a mirror: the start of the *conditioning* kick and the Feint Kick must be identical.
- Train with a partner holding focus pads: Touch low pad lightly to rebound into the high Kick. Kick through the high focus pad before chambering back.
- Drill on the *marked* heavy bag: lightly touch the bag with the low Straight-leg lift, cock and kick high. You can also practice the fast "touching" roundhouse alone for speed. Working on a pear-shaped heavy bag is recommended.

Self defense

The 'Low Kick', -Straight-leg Roundhouse Kick to the thigh or knee-, is of course a suitable low Roundhouse for this Feint Kick. Whether front-leg or rear-leg, it will work miracles if the opponent has been previously painfully hit.

Low Kick for conditioning followed by Low Kick Feint to high Roundhouse; both front-leg and rear-leg are illustrated

The Illustrations below show a practical rear-leg version of the 'Low Kick' directed at the opponent's knee, in a classic *hi jab/hi cross/lo kick* combination. Repeat the combination but cap it with an exaggerated chamber instead of the kick. Turn the low Feint into a high Roundhouse Kick as he reacts. Follow up, for example with a palm jab to the face as you lower the leg. You can then sweep of his front leg to get his back, catch his shoulders and throw him brutally to the floor with a traditional Jiu-Jitsu takedown. Just pull the shoulders down while pivoting down and out around him, as illustrated.

Practical combo with 'Low Kick' turning into high Roundhouse

We shall cap this section with an example in which the Feint Kick itself is not delivered but only hinted at. This example will remind the reader of what was already said in the introduction: feinting is much more subtle than simply techniques. Feinting is a thing of the mind, just like misdirection in magic. Often only body moves will be enough to make the opponent believe that a certain technique is coming. This is an important skill that can be developed by focused free-fighting. In the example below, you will use a hip movement to hint at a possible Low kick. As it does not come and you retract into regular guard, the relieved opponent will also come back forward into regular guard.... to be kicked in the ribs in a typical "**Attack on Recovery**" (See our book about *Stop Kicks*).

Fake the start of a Low Kick, retract back as the opponent reacts rearwards, and then kick the relieved opponent as he recovers forward

Illustrative Photos

Roundhouse Kick, respectively: Low to knee, low to groin and high to head

The mid-level (solar plexus) version of the Kick: the middle to high Roundhouse Feint Kick

13. The Side Kick to Reap Throw

General

This is an old favorite move of mine, sneaky and usually quite easy to succeed with. It is especially great if you like to get your opponents to the ground for grappling. The principle is simple: You deliver a Side Kick to your opponent in order to close the distance, and you lower the leg close to him, basically between his legs. You can then proceed to reap his front leg in a classic Reaping Throw, whether from his out-side (*O Soto Gari*, Large Outer Reap – *Judo*), or his in-side (*Uchi Mata*, Inner Thigh Throw – *Judo*). This move is similar to the **saving** technique after an unsuccessful Side Kick has been brushed aside by your opponent. It is slightly different though: in the present case, you deliver the Feint Side Kick expressly from the start in a way which will allow for the longest step possible, and landing where you really want it. In many ways, this is the same principle as the Front-chambered Wide Step, already encountered above: the Feint Kick intends to disguise your making a wide **positioning step**. In this case, you position yourself for a subsequent takedown.

Classic Judo *O Soto Gari*

It should be noted that, -if possible-, you should reap both his legs and not only his front one in a classic *O Soto Guruma* Judo Throw. Should you be an adept grappler and ground-fighter, you could also finish your *Uchi Mata* by going to the ground, *MakiKomi*-style. All variations are relevant, once you have mastered the principle. The Takedowns are illustrated below for completeness.

A picture being worth a thousand words, we shall describe this Feint Kick directly in typical applications.

Classic Judo O Soto Guruma; sweep both *legs*

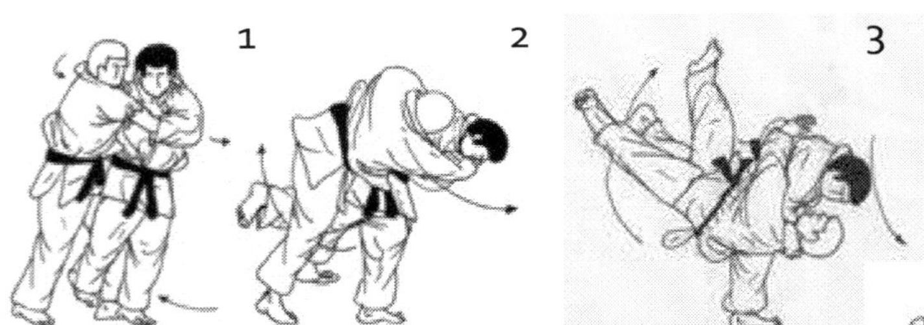

Classic Judo *Uchi Mata; sweep the inside thigh*

Uchi Mata to Makikomi Sacrifice Throw

Descriptive applications

The classic and didactic application would be an immediately repeated Side Kick turning into the Takedown set-up; it could even be a rebounding Kick. The Photos below show how, after a front-leg Side Kick, you let the landing foot go back up immediately into a *Side Kick Feint to Outer Reap Throw.*

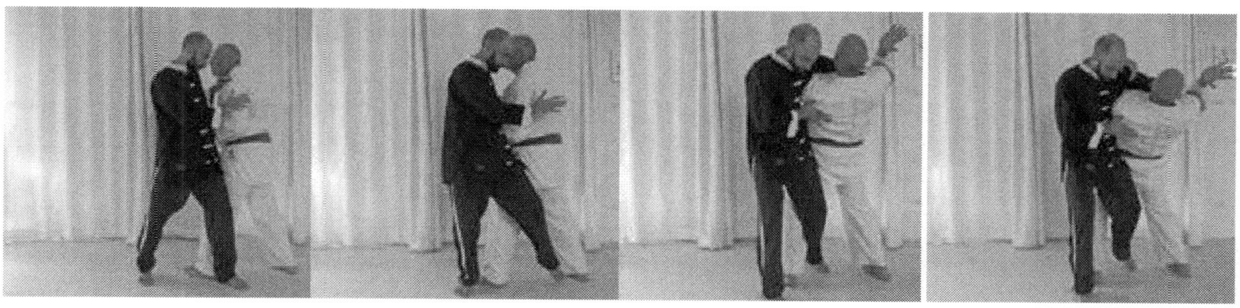

Typical Side Kick Feint to Reap Throw after a conditioning 'real' Side kick

The Illustrations at the top of next page show a rear-leg Feint Kick leading to an Outer Reap Throw, after evading back. In opposite stances, you retreat in the face of a classic jab/cross attack (*Kizami/Gyacku Tsuki combo – Karatedo)*. As your opponent chambers back his futile Reverse Punch, you close back the distance with a long-range rear-leg Side Feint Kick; Side Kick that you purposely direct to his out-side whether he succeed in diverting it or not. You do not need to fully chamber the Side Kick before extending the leg, but you must fully commit and thrust your hips forward for a long 'step'. Deliver a Ridge-hand Strike to his face while landing behind his front leg. Sweep his leg in a classic *O Soto Gari*, and start punching him already while he is falling down. Follow up.

Retreat purposely to set up the Side Kick to Reap Throw

The next Figures show a **front-leg** version in **opposite stances**. In this example, the Side Kick Feint is a low Side Stop Kick or at least its beginning (if it is enough to interrupt the opponent's attack). As the opponent starts a Reverse Punching move, you hop forward into Side Stop Kick chamber. You can fully kick the incoming knee, just touch it or even bypass it if it is adequate. But, in all cases, your Side Kick will develop in front of him in a wide step leading to an Inside Thigh Reap Throw (*Uchi Mata*). Keep your guard up while kicking and be ready to check the incoming Reverse Punch if it does not stop as expected. Land with a Side Elbow Strike, then get hold of his neck from behind to help the forward Takedown. Follow up.

Front-leg hopping Side Stop Kick to Inside Thigh Reaping Throw

It nearly goes without saying that the Side Feint Kick can touch the opponent, or even be delivered fully, without harming the principle of this technique. The Kick can also hit and then 'slide'. It is all about intent during execution; this is also why this Feint Kick deserves a lot of drilling: it can become an effective intuitive follow-up maneuver. The Illustrations at the top of next page illustrate such a 'follow-up' version of the technique. In this example, you hit & lift your opponent's guard, or the start of his jab, with an Upward Side Kick; and you then hop into a same-leg Penetrating Side Kick to the ribs without lowering the kicking foot (If this is difficult, you can let the kicking foot touch and 'rebound' on the floor). You deliver the Kick fully, but with the intent to lower the leg behind his, in order to reap them out. In the example it is a double-leg Reaping Throw (*O Soto Guruma*), but it could be a simple *O Soto Gari* as well.

→

The Feint Kick can be a 'real' Kick that subsequently slides into position

Key points

- The Kick is delivered slightly off, but as close as possible to the opponent's body; unless you choose to touch and slide
- Keep your guard up; this technique brings you very close to your opponent.
- Always follow up: a Takedown is an opportunity to strike or to bring the fight to the ground for submission techniques. A takedown is usually not a finishing technique by itself.

Specific training

- Judo and Ju-Jitsu Throws are sophisticated techniques that build upon placing the opponent into specific off-balance positions. This is not simply about reaping the leg; you will need to invest in good form and serious drilling. Practice the Takedowns in their basic Judo form for a good understanding.
- Only a partner can make you "feel" the technique.
- Work on the heavy bag by kicking powerfully as close as possible to the bag but not touching it, and then catching the bag in a "neck" embrace as you land.

Use the long heavy bag to drill the Feint Kick all the way through the leg reap

Self defense

The Illustrations below show an aggressive pre-emptive combination ending with our Feint Kick. As your menacing assailant initiates his attack, you stop him in his tracks with a surprising all-out rear-leg penetrating Front Kick. Stop any further advance or attack with a front-leg Stop Side Kick to the knee of his front leg; lean back all the way to a Hands-on-floor version to keep away from danger, if necessary (Refer to our previous book about *Stop Kicks* for more information). You can then proceed with an additional front-leg Body-bent Side Kick but more obliquely towards his *rear knee*. Whether you hit and slip on the knee or just past in front, is up to you and the specific situation. This last Side Kick is delivered as a Feint Kick to Inside Thigh Reap Throw. For added safety, it is recommended to deliver a Back-fist Strike as you land, as you have your back to the assailant. Follow up.

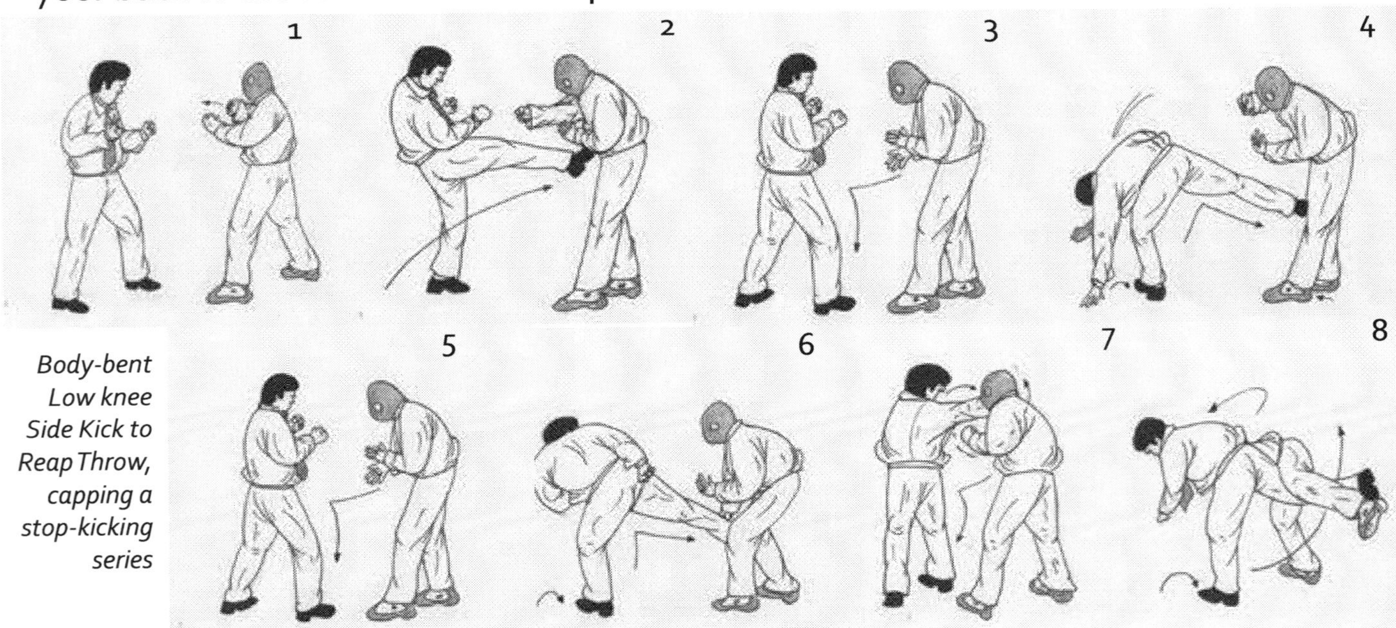

Body-bent Low knee Side Kick to Reap Throw, capping a stop-kicking series

This Feint Kick can be adapted to other kicks and Side Kick variations. The conversant Artist will discover his own personal variations. In the previous example, we have already illustrated the *Body-bent-* and the *Hand-on-floor-* versions of the Side Kick in context. The example at the top of next page illustrates the Feint Kick with a *Roundhouse Feint*, or, more precisely, a **Roundhouse-chambered Side Feint Kick**. In opposite guards, you condition your opponent with a close rear-leg Roundhouse Kick that you let rebound into his guard. You then repeat a clear Roundhouse chamber close to him, but, instead of delivering the kick he expects, you basically knee-strike through his guard. You can then extend and lower the leg on his outside, Side Kick-like, for the Takedown. The mind must be set for a real full <u>Roundhouse Knee Strike into his guard</u>!

A Roundhouse-chambered Side Kick Feint to Outer Reap Throw

And this technique is also very natural after a *Hook Kick*, whether a Hook Feint Kick, a Tap Kick (just 'touching') or a Full rebounding Hook Kick (not kicking through, but only a few inches into the target). Hook Kicks turning into Reaping Throws are presented in the figures below.

Front-leg Hopping 'timing' Hook Stop Kick turns into **Uchi Mata**

Spin-back 'timing' Hook Stop Kick turns into **O Soto Gari** *followed by Stomping Kick*

Illustrative Photos

Applied Outer Reap Throw after a full Side Kick

Illustrative Photos (Continued)

Outer Reap Throw after full rear-leg Hook Kick

Conditioning Kick, then Straight-leg Roundhouse Feint to the body into **O Soto Gari**

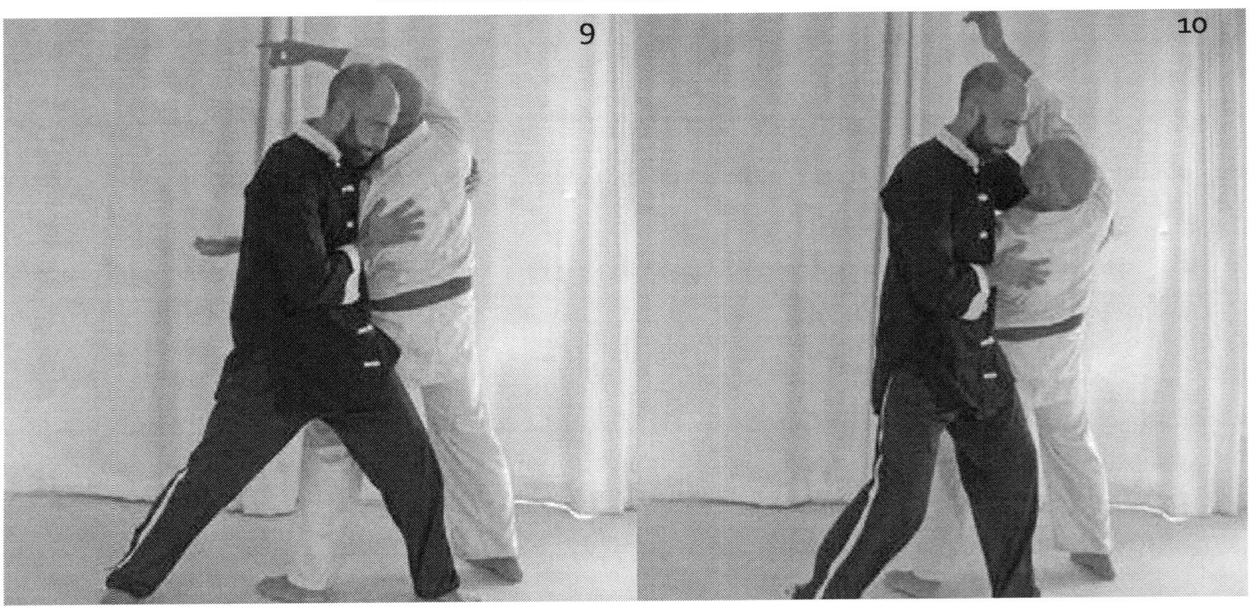

14. The Spin-back Outward Over-tilted Front Kick

General

This is an exotic close-combat Kick from the Korean Arts that we have included mostly for the sake of completeness. The rationale behind the Kick is to turn an expected Outside Crescent Kick into an exaggerated Outward-tilted Front Kick, and by doing so, to extend its range and overtake the block. This Kick is quite difficult to execute as the foot tilt is extreme, and its success is based on a real belief by the opponent that it is an easy-to-block Outside Crescent Kick that is coming. The kick has also the disadvantage of being delivered from extremely close, which is always a dangerous proposition. Moreover, the most-used version is the Spin-back variation in which you additionally present your back and lose some eye contact.
It is an interesting Kick though, very surprising in very close combat, and it could be a useful additional tool for a *flexible* fighter fond of Outside Crescent Kicks.
We shall present it relatively briefly.

Description

The Illustration shows the basic training Spin-back version in front view. The kick starts just as a classic Spin-back Outside Crescent Kick. But, at the end of the Spin-back, you do not start to lift the leg straight as for the regular Crescent, but you keep it half-flexed, as if chambered. You keep pivoting as in an Outside Crescent Kick, but, at the last moment, you let the leg fully pivot outwards,- ankle, knee and hip -. The kick becomes so an exaggerated Outward-tilted Front Kick, very high and slightly towards your rear; you connect with the ball of the foot like a Front Kick, and not with the blade of the foot like for the Outside Crescent.

Front View of the Spin-back Outward Over-tilted Front Kick

Key points

- Only for use in close combat and after fully mastering the technique.
- Preferably to be executed as a surprising Feint Kick after a few regular Spin-back Outside Crescent Kicks.
- Lean your head and body away from the opponent for added safety.
- Keep your guard up and always follow up.
- The leg pivot outwards comes at the last possible moment, for surprise sake.

Typical application

The Illustrations below show how to use the kick after a real Spin-back Outside Crescent Kick. The opponent counters as he feels you are too close for a repeat performance, but you block his punch while spinning again. Not only will your over-tilted foot catch him from close-up, but it will also easily overtake his guarding (or blocking) arm. This is also a great partner drill for this kick, to be executed smoothly with no interruption between the kicks.

Spin-back Outside Crescent Kick followed by Spin-back Outward Over-tilted Front Kick

Specific training

- The feeling can only be understood from training with a partner, preferably holding a focus pad.
- Drill on the heavy bag, alternating the Feint Kick with regular Spin-back Outside Crescent Kicks. In the Feint Kick, make sure you connect with the ball of the lifted toes, just like for a Front Kick.
- Also train the regular (non-Spin-back) version.

Self Defense

All rules needing exceptions, we shall illustrate in the Self-defense section the regular no-Spin-back version. The Feint Kick without Spin-back is less of a feint and is also less powerful, but it is great to overtake the opponent's block of an expected Outside Crescent Kick. It is a great diversification option for the frequent user of the Outside Crescent Kick.

The Figures below illustrate a tactical trap against an assailant you have found fond of rear-leg Roundhouse Counter Kicks. After you have familiarized him with your rear-leg Outside Crescent Kick, you deliver an additional one which purpose is to be too short and inviting his Roundhouse Kick counterattack. As he kicks, you evade forward and out to deliver your Outward Over-tilted Front Kick to his face, crashing through his ineffective guard. Follow up as he crumbles back, for example with a high Front Heel Kick from your other leg.

Lure opponent into a regular no-spin Outward Over-tilted Front Kick

The following no-spin example will be an *offensive* combination this time. Ideally, it should also follow some conditioning of the opponent to expect easily-checked regular Outside Crescent Kicks. Once you have hopefully conditioned your opponent, you open your attack series with a classic Indirect Progressive Low to High Jab. So simple, but effective! This simple maneuver will help you to achieve many things: you close the distance, overwhelm him, put him on the defensive and block his field of vision. You can then get hold of his blocking hand while hopping forward into a front-leg Outside Crescent Kick that will turn into a close Outward Over-tilted Front Kick to overtake his checking guard. As you are now very close to him, you need to follow up as most suitable to your fighting style. A long-range fighter would push the opponent away and keep kicking him. A good ground-fighter would take the opportunity to take him to the floor. In the example, we have illustrated grabbing him as the kicking leg is lowered to take him down with a classic Side Drop sacrifice throw (*Yoko Otoshi – Judo*).

Offensive **no-spin** *front-leg Hopping Outward Over-tilted Front Kick, and follow-up*

Illustrative Photos

The Essential mid-level Outward-tiled Front Kick

Drilling the classic Outward-tilted Front Kick

Opposite view of the Drill

Apex of the Spin-back Outward Over-tilted Front Kick, side and front views

15. The Curved Side Kick

General

The **Curved** Side Kick has been briefly presented our Book about *Essential Kicks* in the context of a comparison to the classic Oblique Side Kick. It has also been mentioned in our Book about *Low Kicks* in the context of the Low Side Stomp Kick. This unorthodox Kick is a very important technique in the author's opinion, and the reader is encouraged to dwell on it and check our previous treatises.
The Kick will be presented again here, with some emphasis on its "Feint" aspects.
Basically, the Curved Side Kick is a Penetrating Side Kick delivered from an orthodox Side Kick Chamber but <u>developed on a slightly curved trajectory</u> in order to avoid an obstacle on the centerline, like a guarding limb. This is obviously a great kick against fighters with a closed Side Stance, but it is also an ideal Feint Kick after an orthodox Essential Penetrating Side Kick. The kick is very efficient, still powerful, but a little bit shorter than the regular Side Kick. It is nearly exclusively used in its front-leg version; and generally at mid-level. It could be construed as a bit of an hybrid between a Side Kick and a Hook Kick, but it is in fact much closer to the Side Kick.
I consider it an important advanced Kick which practice will also develop your general kicking proficiency and adaptability to changing circumstances. A must-drill Kick!

Description

The preceding paragraph, the references quoted, and the Drawings tell the whole story. Because the difference between the Curved and the Regular Kick is subtle, it is difficult to illustrate it through photos; we have tried anyway in the Front View pictures below.

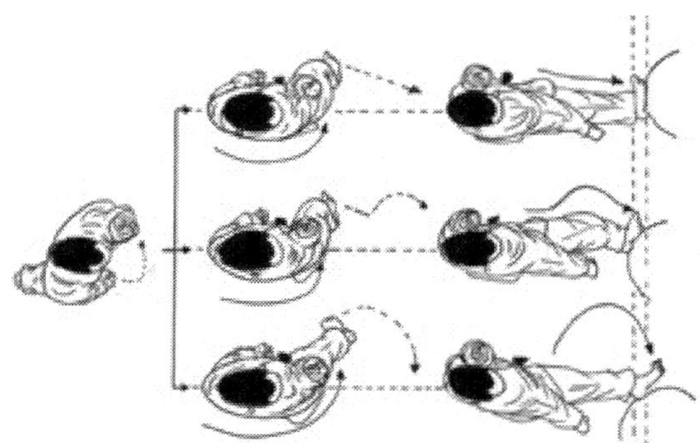

Orthodox Side Kick, Curved Side Kick and Hook Kick, respectively

The Regular straight Side Kick

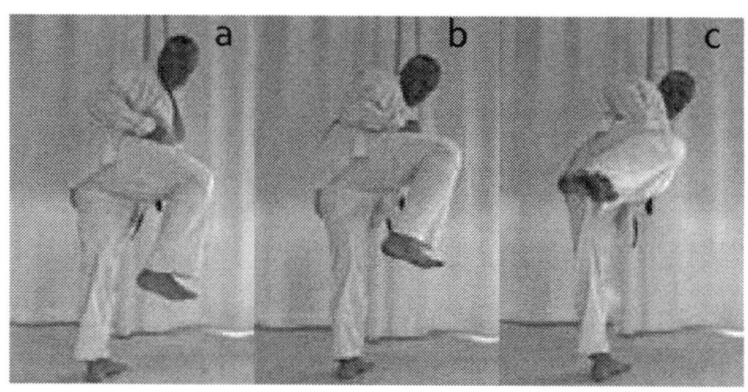

The Curved Side Kick

Key points

- "Curve" the kick just enough to avoid the obstacle and minimize the wideness of the circular move. Though somewhat bastardized, it is mostly a *straight* Kick.
- Chamber fully as you would a regular Side Kick.
- It is always better used after an orthodox Side Kick into your opponent's guard. Remember that the Side Kick is one of the most powerful kicks; kicking hard into someone's guard will always cause pain.
- Make sure you do not telegraph the move; especially do not side-step and do not turn it into an Oblique Side Kick.

Typical application

There is not much to delve about the use of the Curved Side Kick as a Feint kick: deliver conditioning regular straight Side Kicks, then surprise your opponent with a Curved one. As illustrated by the photos below, you will execute a conditioning front-leg straight Penetrating Side Kick **1. short of-**, **2. below-** or **3. into-**your opponent's guard. You can even execute all three options in series before the real show. You then repeat with a long-hopping Curved Side Kick this time (4), aiming for the solar plexus. Follow up.

Kick straight but short of the opponent's guard, then kick straight below his guard; then kick straight into his guard; then curve-kick into his solar plexus

Specific training

- Drill on a standing, then moving partner, in side guard. Make sure you curve the kick just enough to go around his guard.
- Drill on the heavy bag, hitting a mark on the side-front, and avoiding an obstacle on the centerline, like the back of a chair.

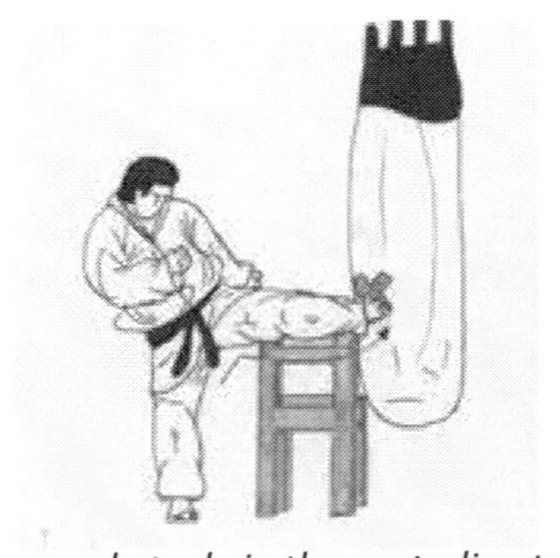
Use an obstacle in the centerline to learn to curve the kick just enough

Self defense

Here comes a great 'Rebounding Kicks'-drill; it is a good exercise and a very efficient combination. The illustrations below show how good the Curved Side Kick is against fighters in the Side Stance. The Side Stance is typical of front-leg kickers, and gives them the false sense of imperviousness to straight Kicks like the Side Kick. And therefore, you will be able to surprise them with a Curved Side Kick after two straight blank ones. In the example, you stop-kick the front knee of the assailant as soon as he starts moving to attack. The low Side Stop Kick then gets back to the ground to <u>rebound</u> into a Penetrating Side Kick to his guarding arm (If you are nimble and experienced, you can execute an airborne 'no-back-to-the-floor' Double Kick). This kick will both hurt his arm and reinforce his sense of security from straight Side Kicks. You then let the leg rebound again on the floor and hop forward into an unexpected Curved Side Kick; in a self-defense situation, you should aim for the general groin area. If you have scored, the opponent will crouch forward, right into a new Rebounding Kick: this time a hybrid between a shorter Curved Side Kick and a *Small Heel Back Hook Kick* to the solar plexus or head, as per the circumstances. (The Small Heel Back Hook Kick is a basic Kick presented in our previous work about *Essential Kicks*). You could finish him up with yet another <u>Rebounding Kick:</u> an *Upward Hooking Back Kick* into his exposed groin.

Low Side Stop Kick, rebounding orthodox Side kick; rebounding Hopping Curved Side Kick; follow-up

Illustrative Photos

Front-leg Hopping orthodox Side Kick into opponent's guard

Front-leg Hopping Curved Side Kick around the opponent's guard

The related Essential Small Heel Back Hook Kick

Various versions of the mentioned Essential Upward Hooking Back Kick

An applied Low Curved Side Stomping Kick

16. The Spin-back Front Kick

General

The Spin-back Front Kick is a fantastic kick, extremely surprising when well-mastered and especially useful in Sport bouts with experienced opponents. We have categorized it into this *Feint Kicks* book on purpose, rather than in the 'Front Kicks' chapter of our *Essential Kicks* book. The Spin-back being very much associated with Circular Kicks, it makes this kick a very effective Feint Kick rather than a Front Kick variation.
There are two ways to deliver the kick, and both versions are equally confusing to the opponent: you either **Spin & Kick**, or you **Spin to Step & Kick**. It will become clearer in the Illustrations below. But note that it is imperative to practice both for versatility: These kicks are easy to execute once you have invested in some training and have mastered the unnatural switch from the *circular* Spin-back to the *straight* Kick.
I used to score a lot with this technique and strongly recommend it to the avid kicker. The important thing to remember is that a Feint Kick is as much a thing of the mind as a thing of the body. You have to meaningfully intend the feinting, and make sure the opponent sees it as a *circular* Spin-back Kick (Outside Crescent or Hook) for as long as possible. The way to do this will be different from opponent to opponent, and it will only be fully understood with intuition derived from focused practice.

The 'Spin & Kick' Spin-back Front Feint Kick; it is the rear leg that kicks

The 'Spin, Step & Kick' Spin-back Front Feint Kick; it is the rear leg that steps, it is the original front leg that kicks

Description

The Figures and photos below describe the *basic* 'Spin & Kick' version of the kick from all other angles: A regular Spin-back, a stop of the pivot and a lift of the spin-back-leg directly into a regular straight Front Kick-chamber. You kick with the original rear leg. You have fooled him with the Spin-back into believing a high circular Kick is coming; the kick ultimately comes in straight and at mid-level. As an interesting comparison to Roundhouse Kicks variations, this version of the Feint Kick would be in the vein of the (fantastic) Essential *Spin-back Roundhouse Kick*.

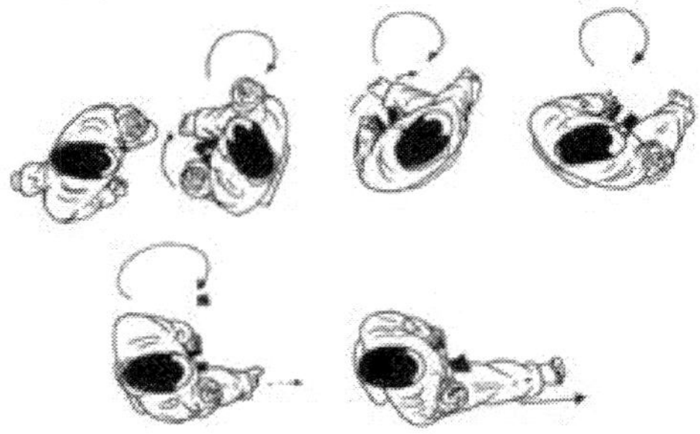

Top view of the basic Spin-back Front kick

Front view of the basic Spin-back Front Kick

Back view of the basic Spin-back Front Kick

Another Front view of the **basic** *Feint Kick,* **Spin&Kick**.

The next Figures will then describe in turn the "Spin-back, Step & Kick" variation of the Spin-back Front Feint Kick, which is probably easier to master *and allows for a longer range*. The Spin-back leads the original rear leg into a step that stops the pivot and allows for a stance from which the other leg can deliver a Penetrating Front Kick. The opponent expects the same high circular Spin-back Kick and finds himself at the receiving end of a straight mid-level Front Kick, but with a step in between. It is a great Kick against retreating opponents. To go back to our analogy to Essential Roundhouse Kick variations, this one is reminiscent of the *360 Spin-back Roundhouse Kick* (The reader is invited to refer to 'The Essential Book of Martial Arts Kicks')

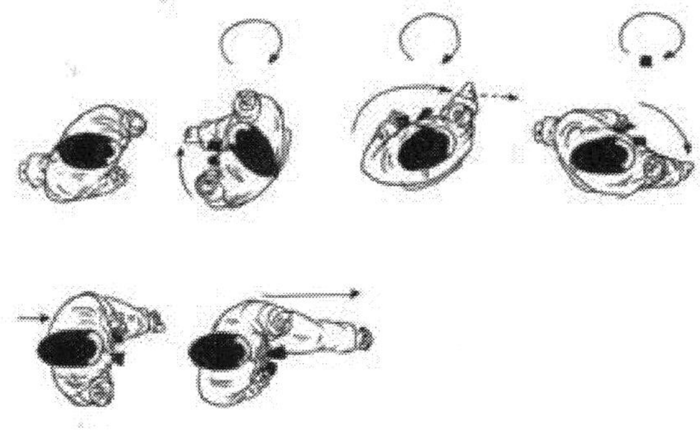

Top view of the Stepping version of the Spin-back Front Kick

Front view of the Step & Kick version of the Spin-back Front Kick

Back view of the longer range version of this Feint Kick

Applied stepping Spin-back Front Feint Kick after a conditioning Spin-back Outside Crescent Kick

Key points

- Always use after conditioning the opponent with at least one circular Spin-back Kick.
- The key to success is in the "Stop Pivot", at the last possible moment, for instantaneous transition from spin-back to straight kick. This must be done at the right time and right place to avoid an oblique kicking trajectory. This must be seriously drilled as explained below.
- The First part of the Feint Kick must look and feel like a Spin-back Circular Kick.

Typical applications

The Illustrations below show a classic application of the basic version of the Feint Kick. Deliver a Spin-back Outside Crescent Kick into your opponent's guard. This is by definition, a relatively short kick. Repeat immediately the Spin-back, but turn the kick into a longer Front Kick at his belt knot level, while he'll be still trying to avoid or check the Crescent Kick which is not coming. As a follow-up, you could lower the leg deep to his out-side while palm-striking his face, and then deliver a rear-leg high Roundhouse Kick.

Classic *Spin-back Front Feint Kick after conditioning Spin-back Outside Crescent*

Of course, there are many possible variations on this theme. The Photos below illustrate a reinforced conditioning of two Spin-back Outside Crescent Kicks in series: the first one into the opponent's guard, and the second towards his head to get him to retreat. As you so cause the opponent to retreat, the use of the stepping variation of the Feint Kick is more adequate.

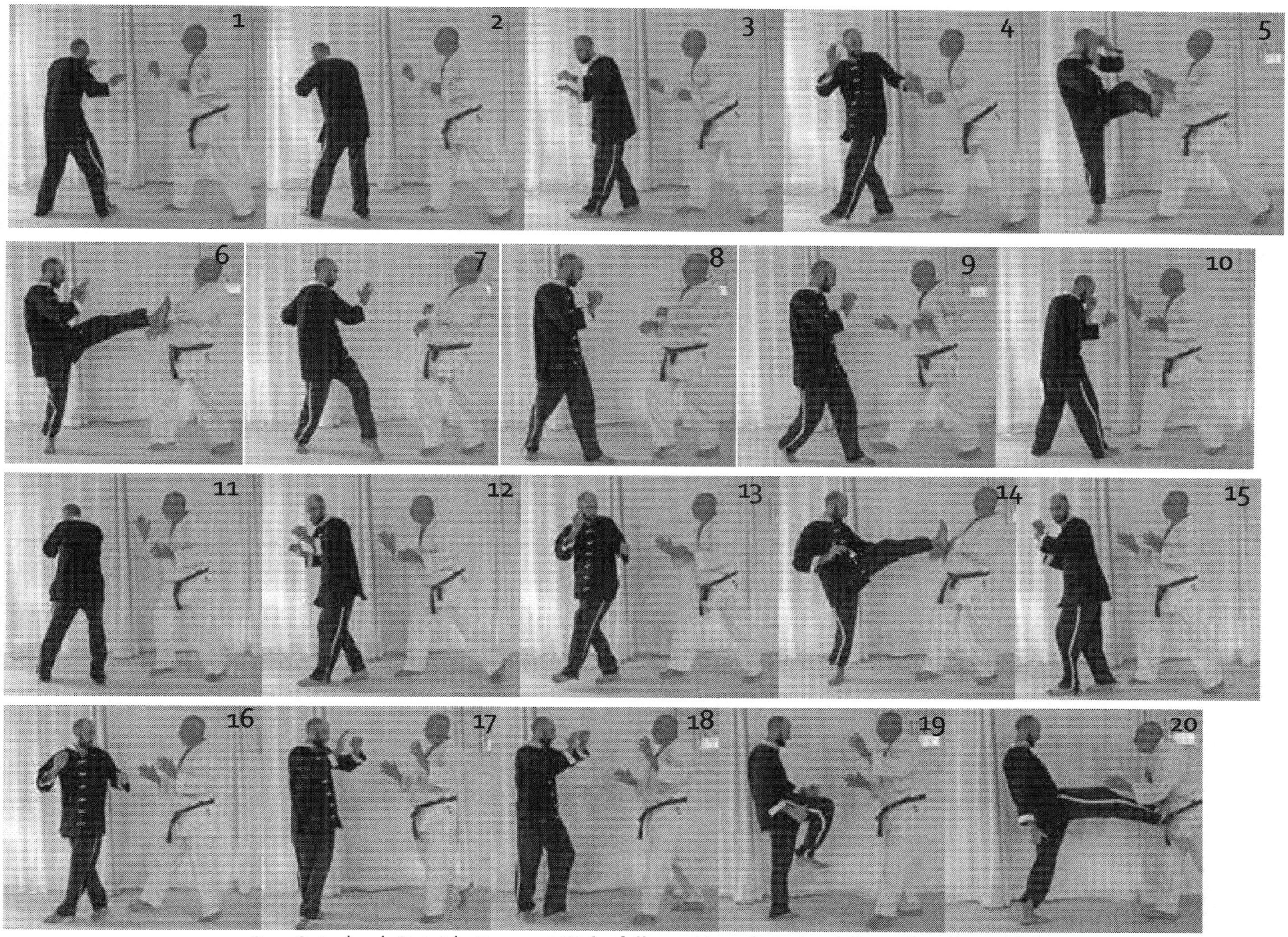

Two Spin-back Outside Crescent Kicks followed by a Spin-back ***Stepping*** *Front Kick*

Specific training

- The key quality to master is the full transition from Circular to Straight at the right place. Any gradual transition will result in an oblique Kick which will graze or miss the opponent. There are plenty of drills to train for this, and they must be practice often and seriously. Use something like a chair or a heavy bag to limit the circular move, and use a *narrow* target (Makiwara, old tire, marked bag, etc) to ensure you stop at the right place and kick straight. The non-exhaustive Illustrations give a few examples.
- Train on the marked heavy bag. Drill for a fast Spin-back and an instantaneous '<u>Stop Pivot</u>'. Make sure you kick fast and straight.
- Work on both variations (basic and stepping) and hit the bag at body and at head level.
- Drill while alternating with *Circular* Spin-back Kicks: this is, at the beginning, a humbling experience! Mark my words, then try it.
- When the heavy bag training is mastered, drill with a partner who should be trying to spot the Front Kick.

Use an obstacle to limit the circular drift and kick a narrow Makiwara target

Use the heavy bag to limit the circular drift

Use a chair to limit the circular drift, of the stepping version in this example

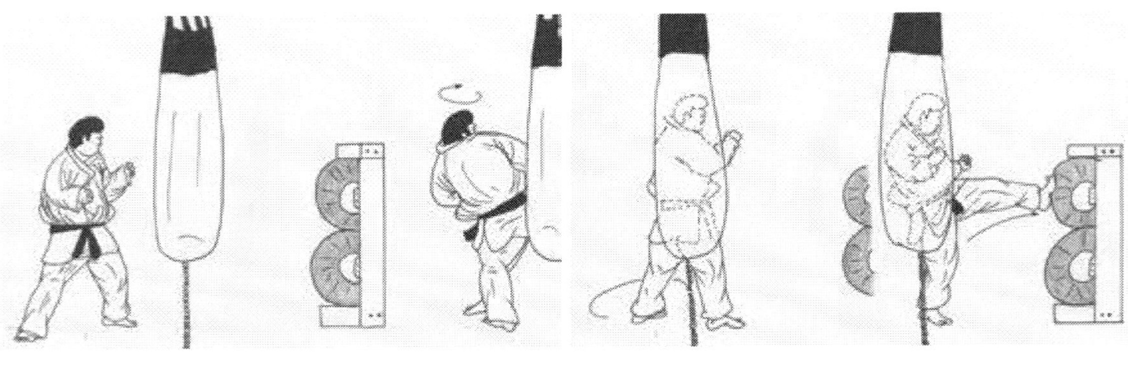

Use the heavy bag to limit the circular drift (of the step in this example) and kick a narrow tire for straight precision; the tire could be hold by a partner

Self defense

The Illustrations below show a stepping version of the Feint Kick ending in an Upward Front Kick to the opponent's groin. This is an interesting technique for use against a compulsive counterpuncher. You first jab to cause your opponent to start his Reverse Stop Punch. But you are already spinning back for a Hook Stop Kick that your opponent will (or will not) evade by stopping his punch and leaning back rearwards. Now that he is conditioned to await a Spin-back Hook Kick, you can proceed by

repeating the Jab and Spin-back. This time, he will probably keep his distance (with his hands held high) to let the Hook Kick fly by and then step-in for a Counter Punch. But your Spin-back becomes a step and is followed by a Groin Upward Front Kick. Follow up, with a Knee Strike for example.

Fake Spin-back Hook Stop Kick turns into stepping Upward Front Kick to the groin

The illustrations at the top of next page do show this Feint Kick applied to a ducking/ bobbing/weaving opponent. After you have ascertained that he will probably evade down your high Spin-back Hook Kicks, he will suddenly find himself crouched in front of a Front Kick Chamber. Execute an Upward Front Kick to his face or groin, according to the range and the circumstances. A great follow-up after a groin Kick would be a Guillotine Choke all the way to the ground.

Spin-back Front Feint Kick against a ducking opponent, and Guillotine follow-up

The Spin-back of this Feint Kick can be a Spin-back **Punch** Feint as well! The Spin-back Fist Strike, whether back-fist or hammer-fist is an extremely powerful technique, one that knocked me out for good once. Bad memories. Therefore, the Spin-back of the Spin-back Front Kick can be *accompanied* with a Fist Strike, or it can be executed with the Strike as a conditioning *feint*. In other words, you can do a back-fist strike while spinning-back into Front Chamber if you simply do the kick; or, you can use the Spin-back Strike as a high Feint while kicking mid- or low-level.

We shall present here both versions of the Kick, classic and stepping, in a Spin-back Feint Punch context. You'll execute the stepping version if the opponent retreats a lot from your attack, and the classic version if he stays around or comes back to counter. The important point to note is that the Spin-back Back-fist Strike is so powerful that the opponent will either be badly hit, or he will place himself in range for one of the versions of the Spin-back Front Kick; there are no real other alternatives.

In the classic version presented first, you condition your opponent with a classic Back-fist attack turning into a Spin-back Back-fist on the other side: an Out/In overwhelming assault. When you will repeat the same opening, your opponent will most probably retreat to get out of range while lifting his guard; only to be kicked in the groin by a classic Spin-back Front Kick. Follow up.

In the stepping version presented next, based on the same opening and conditioning combination, your opponent retreats more. You will step at the end of the same Spin-back Backfist to deliver a Front Kick with the other foot. In this example we have presented a knee-to-groin Double Front Kick, but it could be any Front Kick with follow-up. The point made in the example is that you kick **low** after the high feints and the fact that *you keep your punching arms high and extended on purpose to draw attention up and limit his vision range*!

Compounded Spin-back high Back-fist into classic Front Feint Kick

Back-fist, Spin-back Back-fist into Stepping Low Front Kick to the knee, no-floor-touch groin Kick

Illustrative Photos

*The Essential Spin-back Roundhouse Kick. Another potential Feint Kick and the 'Roundhouse' equivalent to the **classic** Spin-back Front Kick*

*The Essential 360 Spin-back Roundhouse Kick. Another potential Feint Kick and the 'Roundhouse' equivalent to the **Stepping** Spin-back Front Kick*

17. The Spin-back Flying Front Kick

General

This is, obviously, the jumping version of the previous Feint Kick; more precisely, of the *stepping* version of the Spin-back Front Kick. You do a Spin-back flying jump ending with **scissoring** into an airborne Front Kick. This kick is very efficient because the jump allows for a fast transition to the Front Kick. This is not a technique suitable for everybody, but it is an interesting kick, especially if you remember that a 'Flying' Kick does not necessarily need to be high, but can also be *long and low*.
The Feint is again based on the expectation of a Circular Kick (Hook or Outside Crescent) after a normal Spin-back, and this is what must be emphasized for the eyes of the opponent. Remember always that successful Feinting is a matter of the mind.

Description

The Illustrations show clearly the rationale behind the kick: You spin back and lift the flexing leg as if preparing a Spin-back Outside Crescent Kick. Up to there, it is just identical to the stepping version of the previous kick. But this time, instead of a doing a regular step, you will jump up and step *on an invisible high stepping stone*. You obviously jump off the standing leg while keeping the spin-back movement. The leg you just jumped with will be the front-kicking leg, as you scissor in the air. The illustrations are self-explanatory.

The Spin-back Flying Front Kick, flying version of the previous stepping kick

Key points

- The various stages described are executed smoothly and in a continuous fashion.
- The Spin & Jump must be coordinated in order to allow for the Front Kick to develop as you come back to face the opponent.
- The Spin-back must look identical to a Spin-back Outside Crescent Kick, grounded or airborne. The opponent expects a circular Kick and must get an overpowering *Straight* one.

Typical application

As the jump is starting just before the Front Kick itself, you need not to get him conditioned to a *Flying* Spin-back Circular Kick. Causing him to expect a regular grounded Spin-back Kick is enough to get him to lift his hands to block a close high kick coming from the side. The illustrations below shows such an application with a grounded conditioning kick and a jumping Feint Kick. You jab and spin-back into a regular high Outside Crescent Kick through his guard. You then immediately repeat the Spin-back, but to execute a long (and relatively low) Spin-back Flying Front Feint Kick to his abdomen. Following up should be quite easy.

Preparatory high Spin-back Outside Crescent Kick followed by Spin-back Flying Front Feint Kick to mid-level

Specific training

- The most difficult thing in this kick is the switch from the circular Spin-back to the straight Front Kick: You'll need to train on the heavy bag for that and make sure you do not slip obliquely.
- Once you have mastered the straight trajectory on the heavy bag, you can start drilling with a moving partner.
- A great way to understand and practice the jumping part of the Kick is to use a chair or a stool as a real stepping stone upwards; see illustration below. Later, you will try to 'imagine' a stepping stool when executing the kick.

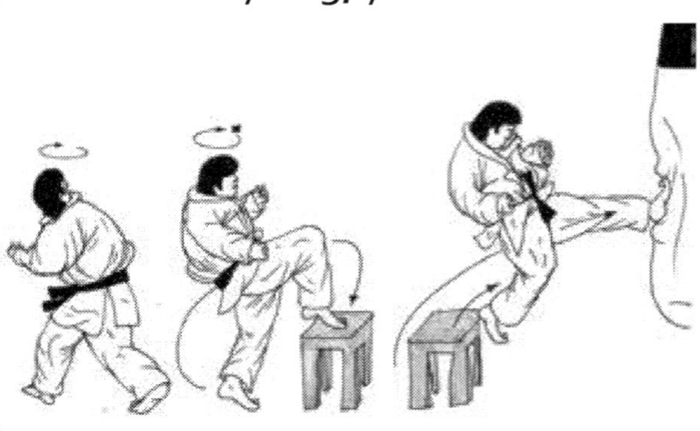

Using a stool to develop the jumping part of the Spin-back Flying Front Kick

Self defense

The Illustrations below show the conditioning phase being a Hand-on-floor Spin-back Hook Stop Kick. In this example, the contrast between the bent-over Kick and the Flying Kick will add to the opponent's confusion. The immediate execution of the Feint Kick after a painful Stop Kick will also keep the pressure on the opponent and have him retreat with his hands up. The Stop Kick is also on an attack that you have *caused* with a Punching Feint, as you have identified the assailant as fond of counterpunches. So, let us put it all together. You feint half-a-punch until your opponent reacts, as much explained in our previous work about *Stop Kicks*. As your opponent starts his counter, you spin-back and down into a classic Hand-on-floor Spin-back Hook Kick, keeping your upper body away from him. If your kick catches his head, good! If not, it will at least hurt his joint by flying through his extending arm. You complete your pivot by landing in guard after a full circle. Keep your opponent off-balance by starting an identical technique: Punching Feint and Spin-back. But this time, you do not expect a reaction to your Punching Feint (although it may come). As soon as you start your Spin-back, the opponent will probably retreat out of range and cover himself. Your Spin-back takes you into a scissoring *long* Flying Front Kick that will help you cover the distance to your unsuspecting opponent. Kick mid-level or groin according to the circumstances. You can follow-up, as illustrated, with a landing Reverse 'superman' Punch and a Low Straight-leg Roundhouse Sweep Kick (Refer to our book about *Low Kicks*).

The Figures below show the Feint Kick delivered after conditioning the assailant to a preparatory *Flying* Spin-back Kick. You deliver a (too) short Flying Spin-back Outside Crescent Kick towards your assailant's head. When you'll repeat the Spin-back attack, your opponent will feel safe with a short retreat. But your kick will turn it into a long scissoring Flying Front Kick to his groin. As he bends over in pain, you can follow up, for example with a *Tawara Nage* Choking Takedown.

Get the opponent used to a short and high Flying Spin-back Outside Crescent Kick, and get him with a long Spin-back Jumping Front Kick to the groin

As a last comment, please note that a high Flying Front Kick to the face is also an attractive possibility. We have not shown it in the examples presented above because it removes the height level aspect of the Feint. It still keeps the 'circular vs. straight' facet of the feint though. The Flying Front Kick being very powerful, this is still a very good technique for Artists who feel comfortable with it.

Illustrative Photos

Spin-back Flying Front Kick

Illustrative Photos (Continued)

Scissoring airborne for the Flying Front Kick

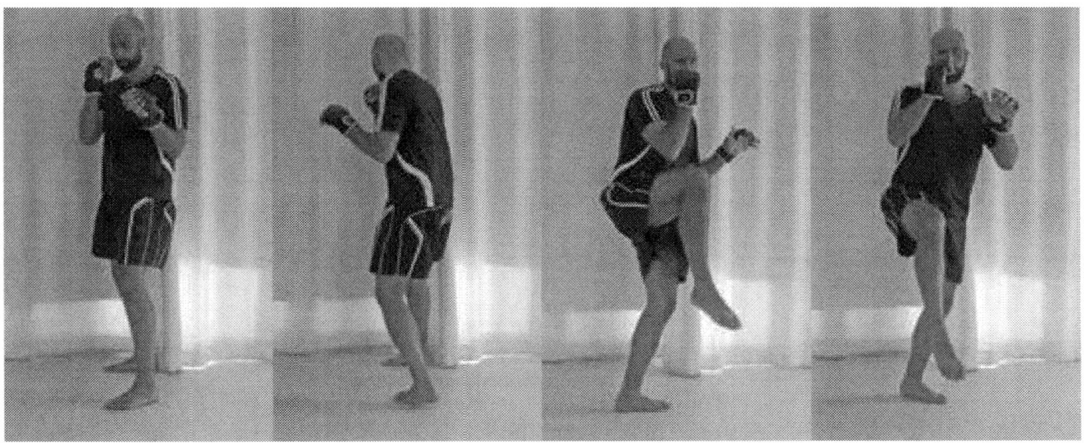

Front view of the Spin-back Flying Front Feint Kick

18. The Spin-back Roundhouse-chambered Side Kick

General

This a Complex Feint kick that could be considered a relative of the *Essential* 360 Spin-back Roundhouse kick and of the Stepping version of the Spin-back Front Kick, both of which are Feint Kicks by themselves. This could be dubbed a double-deception Feint Kick, once your opponent is not fooled any more by your 360 Spin-back Roundhouse Kick. If you are using this specific Roundhouse Kick a lot, then this Feint Kick will be very effective and easy to execute. You basically deliver the kick all the way to the Roundhouse Chamber and keep pivoting until it becomes a Side Kick chamber. Then you side-kick obviously. The feint works well because it looks like the original Circular Kick all the way, while in fact it ends up *straight and longer in range*. And you can even hop a bit while extending the Side Kick for even more range. An additional confusing attribute, is that the Roundhouse should be expected high, while the Side kick should in fact connect at lower mid-level. This is an especially good Feint Kick against opponents who tend to lean backwards to evade high kicks.

Description

The Figures below show clearly how similar the kick is to the original 360 Spin-back Roundhouse Kick (described in our book about *Essential Kicks*). As in the original kick, you spin-back and then step, and then start to develop a full rear-leg Roundhouse Kick that uses the momentum of the spin-back for more power. But in the case of this Feint Kick, you do not kick; you keep pivoting fully (as if kneeing) in chambered position. Your opponent has geared up for a high Roundhouse, but you 'stop pivot' with your side towards him, in Side Kick-chambered position. Side-kick him, preferably at mid-level, aiming for the ribs.

The Spin-back Roundhouse-chambered Side Kick

Key points

- The tightness of the chamber is dictated by the circumstances. It should look clearly as a Roundhouse at the beginning though.
- Keep your guard up.
- *Fully* stop the pivot at the end of the spin, just as you get into Side Kick Chamber position.
- Deliver after at least one 'conditioning' real high 360 Spin-back Roundhouse Kick.

Typical application

As illustrated below, execute a full powered 360 Spin-back Roundhouse Kick towards your opponent's head. Keep pressing him by repeating, but this time surprise him by delivering the Feint Kick ending with a *hopping* Side Kick at belt level. Follow up.

The 360 Spin-back Roundhouse Kick and the Spin-back Roundhouse-chambered Side Kick in series

Specific training

- Drill the basic 360 Spin-back Roundhouse Kick. Then drill it preceded with no pause by a full Spin-back Hook Kick; make sure that the start of the 360 Spin-back Roundhouse looks like a Spin-back Hook Kick. Use a mirror or a partner if possible. Then execute the whole series by capping it with no pause by the Spin-back Roundhouse-chambered Side Feint Kick. Drill this as a full Triple Kick series. See Illustrations at the top of next page.
- Work this Spin-back Stepping Kick on the heavy bag, with a chair forcing your high chamber; just like for the regular Roundhouse-chambered Side Kick described in section 3. Work from different ranges.
- Drill with a moving partner.

Front View of the Triple Feint kick combination; drill with no pause between the kicks

Self defense

The Figures at the top of next page illustrate a few variations on the same theme, and it also shows how effective this kick is against opponents who tend to evade high attacks by leaning back. The preparatory 'conditioning' Spin-back Kick is a *Hand-on-floor* version of the Spin-back Hook Kick and it is delivered as a *Stop Kick* against a hopping front-leg Roundhouse Kick attack from the assailant. And the final Side Kick will be delivered *low* to the knee. In this example, your kicking opponent succeeds, in extremis, to avoid the Spin-back Hook Stop Kick by leaning back while chambering back and retreating. From then on, you have just to keep the pressure by lunging immediately with a fake jab turning into a Spin-back. Your already flustered attacker will probably retreat while leaning back and lifting his guard, as he expect a remake of the Spin-back Hook Kick. But you surprisingly step deep and cause him even more retreating pressure. Your leg lifting into Roundhouse Chamber will cause him to lean back even more and fumble into retreat, in order to avoid a possible high Roundhouse. Remember that nobody can retreat as fast as you can advance. The high Roundhouse will not materialize, and in its stead, comes a crippling long-hopping low Penetrating Side Kick to the knee. You have now caught up with him, and can finish him off. In this example, you follow up, -after lowering the *low*-kicking leg-, with a real *high* Spin-back Hook Kick. You can land crouching low with a kneeling Swing Punch to the groin. You are then in ideal position for a sadly-neglected Shoulder Wheel Judo-throw (*Kata Guruma*). In a self-defense situation, you should lift the assailant as high as possible before throwing him down forcefully.

Conditioning Hand-on-floor Spin-back Hook Stop Kick, followed by Spin-back Roundhouse-chambered low Side Kick, and unconventional follow-up

Illustrative Photos

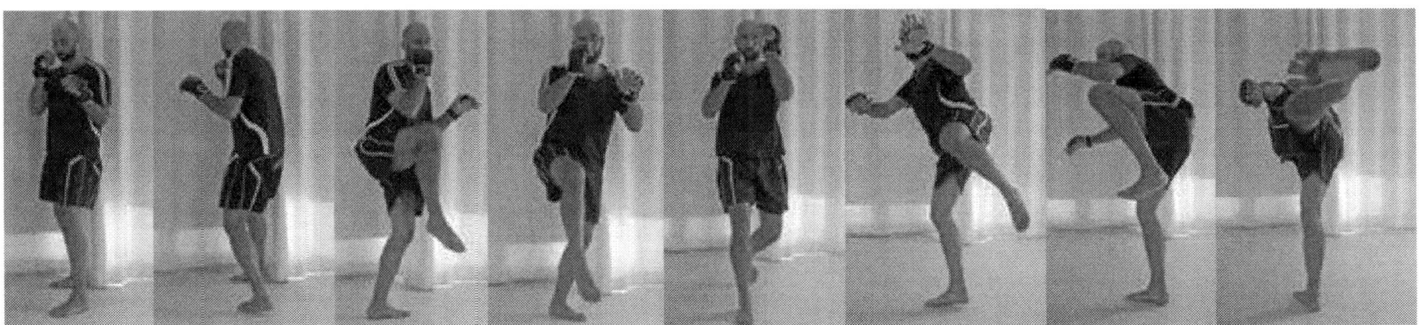

Spin-back **Outside Crescent** *Feint into Roundhouse-chambered Side Kick, front view*

Spin-back **Hook** *Kick Feint into Roundhouse-chambered Side Kick, front view*

19. The Low Kick Feint to Stepping Low Kick

General

This is another "<u>Kick turns into step</u>" maneuver, and a very effective technique. It is very specific though. You feint a low Roundhouse Kick that turns into a step that allows for a rear-leg Low Kick from the *other* leg and *to the other side*. This is a Side/Side feint-type of kick. This is a great practical Feint Kick, especially for hard close-combat work. And it is a must-practice combination: powerful, easy, naturally-flowing and still very surprising. The principles are identical to those of a **Switch Kick** (See *Essential Kicks*), but delivered slightly differently in a way suitable for Low Kicks. The switch between the Low Kick Feint and the subsequent Stepping Low Kick can be made *airborne* for speed; it can also be executed as a step for more power. Drilling the combination is important to learn to develop the power at final impact: it is not enough to simply drill the Low Kick alone; the combination requires some muscle memory for power.

Description and Applications

This Feint Kick being a flowing combination, we shall directly describe its typical application. As shown in the Illustrations and the following Photos (next page), you deliver a painful 'Low Kick' (Rear-leg Straight-leg Roundhouse Kick to the thigh) to your opponent and retract the leg back. This will be your 'Conditioning Kick' to prepare your subsequent feinting move. You then start another Low Kick from the same leg, but as a feint this time: you exaggerate the body movement, the pivot of the front foot, and the chamber. As your opponent reacts by lifting his front leg to block or smother the kick, you lower the lifted foot fast in front of you, and you make sure it lands tilted outwards (to better allow for the following kick from the *other* leg). Pivot forcefully and deliver a powerful rear-leg Low Kick from your other leg to his own rear leg. Follow up.

Simple, but effective: a conditioning Low Kick followed by the Low Kick Feint to Stepping Low Kick

Same kicking combination in photos

An interesting variation of this technique, very typical of *Kyokushinkai Karate*, is described in the Figures below; but this time it is starting from an opposite stances. After a first "Low Kick" to the *inside* of his front thigh to condition him to the move, you will feint a repeat performance. Make sure you move body and hips in the same manner, but take the half-chambered leg into a side step. As he has already lifted his front leg to smother or block the kick that is not coming, you can deliver a powerful Low Sweep Kick (See our book about *Low Kicks*) from your other (now rear) leg to his standing leg. This is akin to a '**Cutting Kick**'. Remember that this is a Kick first, not a sweep. Follow up as he falls down.

Low Kick Feint to **Stepping** *Low Roundhouse Sweep Kick*

Key points

- Most of the feinting is coming from the body and the front foot. Make sure it looks like a real Low Kick is coming.
- The rear-leg chamber and the step are one uninterrupted movement. If the body feint is well-executed, the chamber is minimal and flows into the step.
- Keep your guard up: you are close.
- The "Step" is a forceful move, nearly a stomping kick going straight into position.
- The foot lands directly into its final position, tilted outwards and crossing in front of the now-rear leg.
- Kick with full body and hip power, as becomes a Straight-leg Roundhouse Kick.

Specific training

- This is a special kick that needs drilling for power. Start by drilling the regular Low Kick for power into heavy bag, old tire, body shield, etc. Then drill the more complex Feint Kick to learn to execute the Feint & Step part with speed and the last part with full power; it requires training to get the blending right.
- Heavy bag training (See Illustration): Low-kick the bag as hard as possible, retract and rebound into the feint kick. Make sure your "chamber into step" move passes *just in front of the bag*, grazing it fast without touching it. Kick hard with the other leg. It is important to drill for power, as the kick is more complex to execute than the regular Essential Kick.
- Drill with a partner for speed and precision.

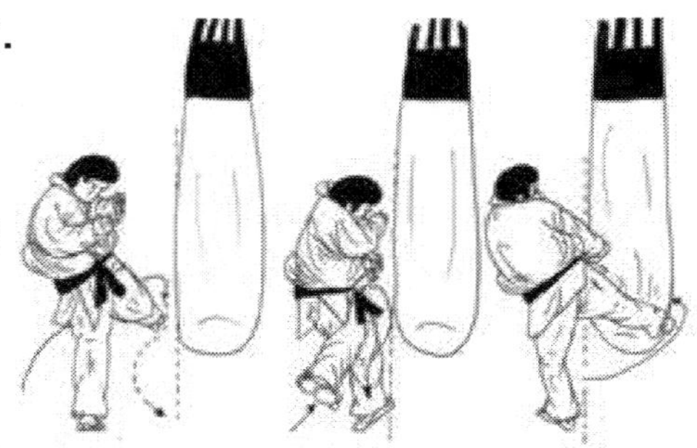

Use the bag to drill the chamber-to-step move; use the bag to learn to develop power at the end of the Feint Kick

Self defense

The Illustrations on the next page show a very useful variation of the kick: in the same application as before, the leg switch is done *airborne*. After a 'conditioning' Low Kick, you feint a repeat. From the fake chamber, you then *jump* for a faster transition to low-kicking from the other side. You can deliver the powerful real Low Kick to the inside knee or to the groin according to the circumstances of the encounter. Follow up; he is now yours to finish. This move is a close relative of the Scissor-jumping Low Straight-leg Roundhouse Kick, which allows to kick at longer ranges (See *Low Kicks*). The reader stands reminded that Flying Kicks are not necessarily to be executed high, but also often long and low.

The airborne scissoring version of the Low Kick Feint to Hopping Low Kick; the jump is slightly exaggerated for better understanding

The jumping Low Straight-leg Roundhouse Kick

Inside knee Low Kick Feint to hopping Straight-leg Roundhouse to the ribs

The Figures below show another variation, in which the concluding kick will be a *high* Roundhouse Kick, whether Straight-leg or regular; we'll also cap the example with an interesting follow-up to drill in.
This Feint Kick we are presenting being a Side to Side feint, the change of plane only adds to the confusing elements without diminishing the basic misdirection premise. Of course, this is a variation for the flexible fighter only, especially if the high kick is to be the powerful Straight-leg version (as executed in *Muay Thai* for example). As discussed in our book about *Essential Kicks*, the 'Low Kick' (Straight-leg Roundhouse) can be executed to the head of the opponent with much additional power coming from the torso and hips, but only if you are flexible enough and have drilled it seriously. In this example, you condition the opponent by at least two regular 'Low Kicks' to the knee of the front leg. You then repeat with a Low Kick <u>feint</u>, and step forward as long as needed, according to the opponent's reactions (previously discovered). From there, you deliver a high Roundhouse to his head. Once you have kicked trough his head or guard, it is natural to continue the strong circular momentum and execute a mid-body (or groin) Spin-back Short Back Kick. If you are a good grappler and the situation allows for it, you can then catch the opponent's neck and execute the Ju-jitsu takedown described (a sacrifice variation of *Kubi Nage* and *O Soto Gari*). You keep hold of him during the fall in order to get to the ground in a classic pin (*Hon Kesa Gatame*), from which you'll apply my favorite <u>double</u> Arm-lock. While keeping the pin, get his arm between your legs for elbow fulcrum; while he is so controlled, you'll have both your hands to apply a classic 'Bent Armlock' (*Ude Garami-Judo/Kimura-BJJ*) shoulder lock on his other arm. Apply pressure on both arms, as mildly or violently as required by the specific circumstances.

Conditioning Low Kicks, Low Kick Feint to High Straight-leg Roundhouse Kick, grappling follow-up

Illustrative Photos

The classic 'Low Kick' and application

Drilling the 'Low Kick'; notice the hip coiling before the kick

A Mid-level Straight-leg Roundhouse: the principles are identical to the 'Low Kick'

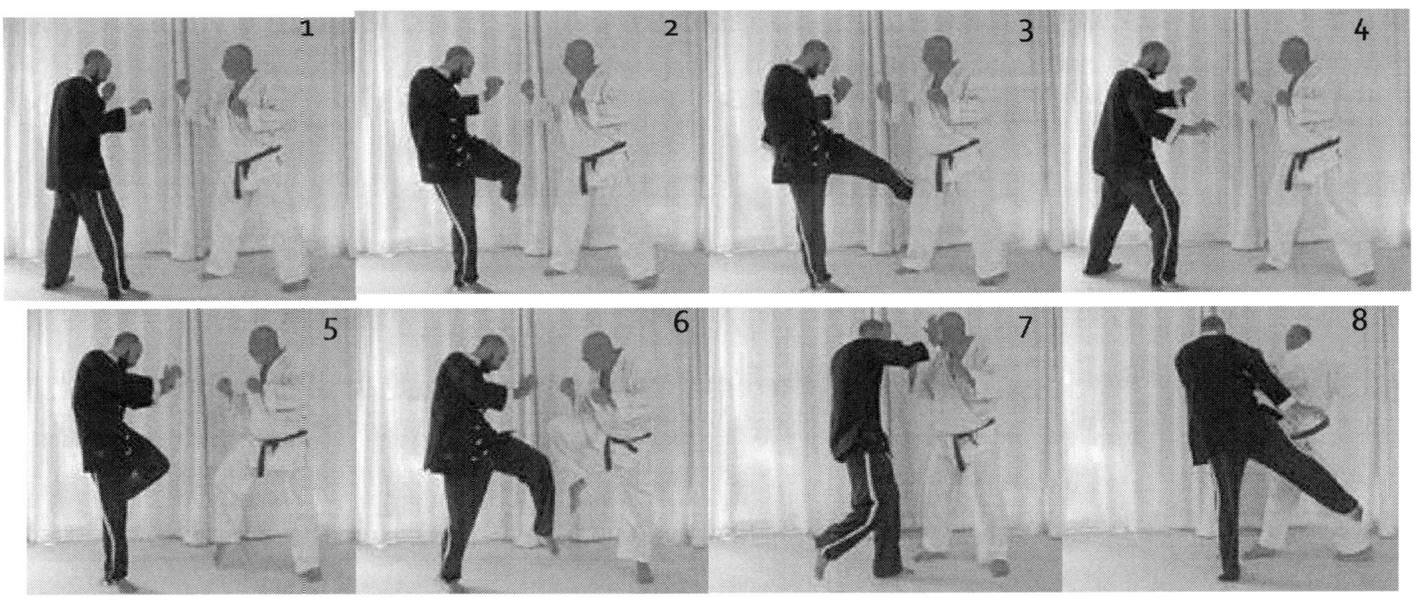

The classic Low Kick Feint to Stepping Low Kick

20. The Back Kick-chambered Downward Roundhouse Kick and related Hook Kick version

General

This is a very specific Feint Kick, narrow in its use and a bit special (in the good sense of the world). I did use to execute this kick quite often in my tournament days, as it is very effective if judiciously squeezed between a few real Back Kicks. If you are a fighter fond of using the offensive Front-leg Back Kick or the Back Stop Kick, this is a very effective feinting maneuver to complement your arsenal. The feint here is usually very convincing, because the position preceding a Back Kick is very typical and easy to spot. Furthermore, the following movement itself is very natural and the second (real) kick comes from a totally different and unexpected direction. The Downward Roundhouse Kick is certainly not as powerful as a Back Kick though, and you will always have to follow up. It is rather a sport Kick than a real life one, unless you are very proficient and have perfect timing. This Feint Kick is quite unique, is very specific and is relevant only in the context of previous Back Kick attacks; we shall therefore only present the typical application as its description.

Typical application

The following Photos series show the offensive application of the technique, from a Front view and from a Side view. The conditioning kick is an offensive Back Kick, but it should be clear to the trained eye that the technique works as well for a defensive Back Kick. As illustrated, you deliver a front-leg hopping Penetrating Back Kick to your opponent's lower abdomen. If he is protecting himself, you can kick powerfully into his arms and glean the same effect. Repeat the technique by hopping and pivoting into typical Back

Kick position to have him lower his guard and expect a mid-level straight Back Kick. But, this time, you do not extend the leg but lift it flexed until you find yourself into the classic chamber position of the *Essential* Downward Roundhouse Kick (Please refer to previous work). Kick downwards into his head or his clavicle while he is busy protecting his lower abdomen. Follow up as needed.

Conditioning Front-leg Back Kick followed by the classic Back Kick-chambered Downward Roundhouse Kick – Front View

Typical Application (Continued)

Applied Back Kick-chambered Downward Roundhouse Kick – Side View

Specific training

- Drill the underlying basic Essential Kicks: Back Kicks and Downward Roundhouse Kick.
- Then combine those kicks in sparring with a partner

Drill the Downward Roundhouse Kick, on the standing bag for example

Drill the basic Kicks and the combined Feint Kick with a moving partner

Self defense

As mentioned, the applied kick is pretty straightforward. In the example below, it is delivered as rebounding Feint Kick immediately after an orthodox Back Kick. You execute the first front-leg Back Kick at belt level. As you lower the kicking leg, you let the foot rebound on the floor to start the beginning of an identical Back Kick. As your opponent drops his guard and braces for the *mid-level* Back Kick, you lift the chambered leg and kick downwards in the classic Downward Roundhouse to his *clavicle* (**high**). Lower the kicking leg, still with your back towards him, and follow up with a *groin* (**low**) *Upward* Back Kick from your other leg (kind of a Spin-back version of the kick).

...You can then pivot back in the opposite and switch legs for a **high** (Spin-back) Hook Kick. Drill this combination in one uninterrupted go; it is an important *non-stop hi/lo* exercise.

Rebounding Back Kick-chambered Downward Roundhouse Kick, and hi/lo follow up

The Back-chambered **Hook** Kick mentioned in the <u>title</u> of this section is based on the same principles of making the opponent strongly believe that a Back Kick to the body is coming. This is a pretty easy thing to do because the Back Kick is a powerful hard-to-ignore Kick, and its set-up and chambering are very specific. In the example below, you

condition your opponent to a front-leg Back Kick attack; you then follow up immediately with a similar opening that will develop in a Hook Kick as late as possible. As the opponent lowers his hands and bends to smother the Back Kick, he gets hit by a high Hook Kick.

An applied Back-chambered high Hook Kick

Illustrative Photos

The Downward Roundhouse in free-fighting

The Downward Roundhouse Kick

21. Kick & Punch Feints

General

For the sake of completeness, we are adding a section about using Feint Kicks to set up a **punch**. As mentioned in the introduction, there are some times when punches are the right answer, not kicks. Also, what would be best than a surprising punch from an obvious kicking artist? Moreover, a punch after a kick-feint, could be just the mollifying start of a mean kicking combination... There are an infinite number of permutations and possibilities, and punching is somewhat out of the scope of this book. But we shall present a few typical examples and let the reader build on it by himself.
We shall present a few techniques only, to whet the reader's appetite, and these directly in their applied form. The interested reader is invited to explore further on his own and develop his own kick/punch combinations.

21.1 The Full Roundhouse Feint

The Figures and Photos at the top of the next page illustrate how to deliver a full-powered rear-leg Roundhouse Kick to the opponent's sternum. You then retract the leg rearwards and then repeat. But this time you will execute an exaggerated chamber with an exaggerated tilt sideways to convince him that another Roundhouse Kick is coming. As soon as the opponent starts reacting and gearing up to block the mid-level kick, you punch him directly in the face with your rear arm (Same as kicking leg). The punch is launched *even though* you are probably still with your knee airborne. This is not the strongest of punches, but it will put him seriously off-balance, both mentally and physically. Follow up, for example with a Low Roundhouse Sweep Kick of his front inside knee. If you are proficient, you could execute this follow-up kick without lowering the foot to the floor and by making full use of the momentum. As you land, you can deliver a reverse punch/front hook punch combination, and then take him to the floor with a front leg sweep.

→

The Full Roundhouse Feint (Continued)

Conditioning Roundhouse, followed by Full Roundhouse Chamber Feint to Straight Punch

Front View of the Full Roundhouse Feint to high Punch

Side View of the applied Roundhouse Chamber Feint to Punch

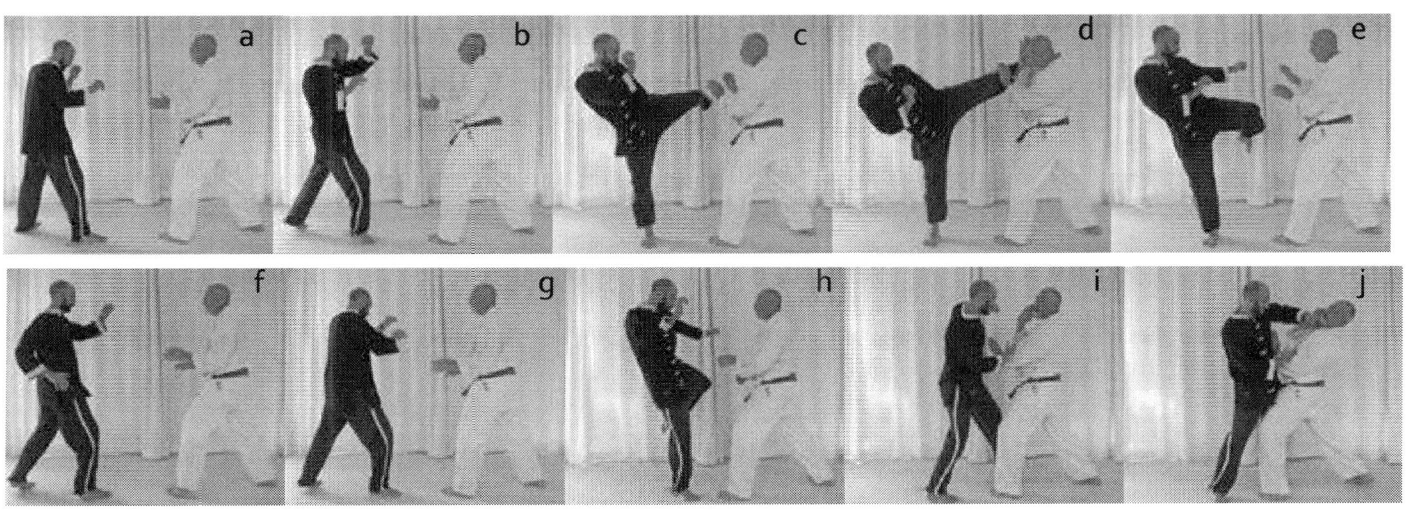

The Full Roundhouse Feint (Continued)

Of course, the Roundhouse Kick-feint needs not be rear-legged. In the example below, you have conditioned your opponent with one or more fast in & out **front-leg** mid-body Roundhouse Kicks. You have noticed that your opponent is a 'block-in-place' type. Repeat the same front-leg Roundhouse Kick attack until the chamber, but, then onwards, hop to land with a long Oblique Jab slightly outside of the centerline (*Nagashi Tsuki – Karatedo*). Continue smoothly with a Reverse Punch while grabbing his sleeve, collar or shoulder. A great follow-up would be a fast in & out Crescent Kick a few inches into his head, while keeping control of his arm (or shoulder). If you are a good ground-fighter, you could take advantage of his being stunned to take him down with a Side Sacrifice Throw (*Tani Otoshi – Judo*).

Front-leg Hopping Roundhouse Feint to Punch and follow-up

You can now stretch this Feint principle to delivering the Kick *all the way* while punching. Here comes an example of a rather dangerous Feinting maneuver to use against a 'leg-catcher' opponent. You deliver a mid-level Roundhouse Kick that you ***want*** your opponent to catch. It is kind of an unorthodox sacrifice move, but it can work very well if you have drilled it and if it suits your personal style and affinities. As soon as your opponent encircles your kicking leg, you hop and punch with all your body weight and momentum. If you are close to him when he catches your leg, or if the punch was not enough to have him release your leg, you can execute a Circular Elbow Strike instead (or after the punch, if it has not caused release). As you twist with the Elbow Strike you can wriggle and pull your leg out of his grab. Follow up with a return Side Elbow Strike (See next page).

Roundhouse Feint Kick **intended** *to be caught, and surprise Punch*

If you are close when kicking leg is caught, execute full-powered Elbow Strikes

21.2 The Front Kick Feint

This Feint Kick is somewhat related to the previous *Front-chambered Wide Step*, presented in section 5. The application presented below is self-explanatory; the technique is trivial, but it will usually work very well because of the atavistic instinct to protect the groin area. As illustrated below, you deliver a conditioning rear-leg Front Kick towards your opponent's groin. Retract the leg rearwards and repeat. But this time, you will jab him in the face as soon as he lowers the hands to react. Step long or hop if necessary. Follow up, ironically, with a real groin kick this time. Of course, in a sport context, you will not aim for the groin but for the belt knot; the general direction is identical and should cause the same instinctive response.

Front groin Kick Feint to Punch and follow-up

The Front Chamber Feint to Jab

Front Chamber Feint to Punch, after a conditioning real Front Kick

21.3 The Leg Tap

This is a very important tactical move of which I am very fond, because it works each and every time if it is not overused. You basically touch your opponent's ankle or knee with your front foot, in order to draw his attention down, even if it is only for a millisecond. You do not need to kick hard or sweep through, although it is always better if possible. What makes it a great Feint is that no power is needed: it is enough to extend the leg fast and just touch his front ankle; *but it should be done with minimum telegraphing.* In most cases, you can see how the opponent lowers his eyes for a millisecond. Start punching as soon as your leg makes contact, but not before. The key to the success of the Leg Tap is the no-telegraph-rule: drill the Tap in front of a mirror and make sure that there are no tell-tales and *that the upper body stays immobile*. The example illustrated below show such a Leg Tap in opposite stances, blending smoothly into a Back-fist Strike. To each one his preferred follow-up, but I think that the position is perfect for a fast kick-through Crescent Kick.

Leg-tapped high Backfist Strike and follow-up

The previous example starts in opposite stances, but the technique works as well in regular stances where you tap the inside of his front ankle or knee. The Illustrations below show a front-leg Low Roundhouse Tap, from regular stances, to the *inside knee* of the opponent. As soon as you touch the knee, you start an Oblique Jab while landing slightly out of the center-line (*Nagashi Tsuki – Karatedo*). You could follow up, ironically, with an inside sweep.

Inside knee Roundhouse Tap to **Nagashi Tsuki**

The Photo series below illustrate the fact that the Leg Tap is not only used to set up Punches, but can be the good opener for a subsequent Kick. The author was a frequent user of the Leg Tap in actual competition, as illustrated by the last photograph.

Low Hook Kick Tap to high Downward Roundhouse Kick

Low Roundhouse Tap to high Hook Kick

Low knee Roundhouse Tap to body Side Kick

Tap Kick in actual tournament – Marc De Bremaeker

21.4 The simultaneous Kick/Punch

This is a technique I am not particularly fond of, but it needs to be mentioned for the sake of completeness. Kicking and punching simultaneously defeats somewhat the purpose of both. It would be extremely difficult to be able to put the necessary body muscles in the best alignment for both actions at the same time.
To be fair, I must add that it can work in certain circumstances, and I have met, a long time ago, an Artist who had made the following applied technique his opening favorite move (*Tokyu Waza*). But it must be said that it was also relatively fast and powerful, because said Artist was drilling the move incessantly to make it second nature. And here is the place to repeat the basic principle: **Do what works best for you**. Every fighter must look for the techniques most suited to his personality, abilities and tactical preferences; after a lot of drilling, some of them should pop up naturally in free fighting and should hence on be drilled even more to become powerful sparring workhorses. We therefore present this section for the interested reader further exploration.

In a simultaneous Kick and Punch technique, neither the Kick nor the Punch are powerful enough to do real damage, even after lots of drilling. The purpose of such a strange Twin maneuver is to disturb the opponent's guard and *to set up a following more decisive technique*. The technique presented in the Illustrations below is an interesting one coming from a *Wadoryu Karatedo* school. As mentioned, I have seen it work quite well after serious training. Feint a Reverse Punch and then launch a simultaneous rear-leg Front Kick to the ribs/ Reverse Punch to the face. Your opponent will have to deal with both and will probably be hit by one. You the use the *pendulum* of your kicking leg going back to launch another high 'Superman" punch with all the power you can muster. As mentioned, the follow up is the important part of this exercise, as the kick/ punches are there mainly to unsettle him. Follow up, for example by catching his sleeve while low-kicking him in the knee; keep your grab while finishing him off with a powerful Reverse Punch.

Simultaneous Kick/Punch and follow-up

21.5 The simultaneous Leg Tap & Punch

Another section for reference mainly, as the author is not a big fan either. We mentioned in the Leg Tap section above, that the punch should start just as the Leg Tap connects. Obviously, not so for the simultaneous Leg Tap and Punch, which is more of a variant of the previous Kick & Punch technique. This time the kick is usually a Low Soccer Front Kick (See our previous book about *Low Kicks*) instead of a full Front Kick. The power that you can generate while simultaneously punching is such that it is more of a Tap Kick which purpose is to draw attention down while you keep attacking. But never mind the semantics; an applied example will tell it all.

As shown in the Illustrations, fake a Reverse Punch and then simultaneously soccer-kick his front shin while reverse-punching him in the face. Lower the kicking leg far and to his out-side while oblique-jabbing the side of his head in a typical *Wado-ryu Nagashi Tsuki*. Follow up with a Palm Strike leading to an Outer Reap throw (*O Soto Gari – Judo*).

Simultaneous high Reverse Punch and low Soccer Front Tap Kick; follow-up

21.6 The Side Kick-Step

This is very much in the line of the *Front Kick-chambered Wide Step* presented in section 5. It is much less in use, but is still a very valid technique; you'd go for a Back-fist Strike rather than a punch. And would have to follow up, of course. In the example presented in the illustrations below, you hop forward with a front-leg *Obstruction-like* Side Kick chamber to cause your opponent to expect the kick and try to catch the leg. As he lowers his guard, the kick turns into a large step while you 'high-backfist' him in the head. As you land and he lifts his hands back up, you 'shoot' for his legs. Take him down with a Double-leg Takedown, and follow up to the ground.

Side Kick-chambered high Backfist Strike, simple but efficient

All variations on this theme are welcome, and the reader is invited to go back to section **5** for ideas.

21.7 The missed-kick Trap

This is a very simple tactical maneuver, but extremely efficient if well executed and seriously drilled. You deliver a kick *with the purpose of missing* and of placing yourself in a vulnerable position that will blatantly invite a counter. Then, you'll be punching (or kicking) the unsuspecting opponent as he starts his provoked counter. Many examples of such Traps have been presented in our previous book about *Stop Kicks*, and the reader is invited to consult it and adapt some of these examples to his own preferences. These kinds of tactical moves work best after a previous 'conditioning' missed kick; and they work especially well against countering opponents. It is important to note that these moves stay valid if the kick in question has not missed on purpose; if you have missed with a kick you intended to score with, keep fighting and pre-empt the counter! That is why drilling these techniques is important, even if you will never use them by missing on purpose.
The missed-kick Traps are very good moves worth drilling and using, but they are outside the scope of this book; we shall present one example only, just to whet the reader's appetite.

In the example below, an overshooting kick-through Straight-leg Roundhouse Kick causes you to present your back to the opponent who has evaded backwards. Whether you have missed on purpose or not is not relevant to the rest of the sequence. Your opponent will come back forward to punch you from your back, but you are already moving towards him with a hip-powered Back-fist Strike (or Elbow Strike if he is closer). Follow up. Note that your stepping towards his counter is important to muddle his range calculations.

Missed kick-through Low Kick to high Stop Backfist **or** *high Stop Elbow, according to the specific range*

PART TWO

GHOST KICKS

PART TWO GHOST KICKS

INTRODUCTION TO GHOST KICKS

Ghost Kicks are very different from Feint Kicks because they do not seek to cause a reaction of the opponent. In fact, they seek to reach the target totally undetected and therefore aim at causing no reaction at all. Just like Stealth combat jets. Feint Kicks aim at causing a reaction from which you will take advantage: this is *misdirection*. Ghost Kicks are based on *dissimulation*; this is in the author's opinion the most sophisticated way to feint-kick. The Ghost Kick trajectory will aim at being out of the opponent's range of vision for utmost surprise. That is why, with notable exceptions, most Ghost Kicks target the groin and are executed with an immobile upper body. This will be easily understood with the first kick presented below, the Phantom Groin Kick, which is the archetype of Ghost Kicks and certainly one of my favorites. The Phantom Groin Kick is delivered from close up, and the foot is simply lifted directly into the opponent's groin with the knee opening up outwards. *All the while, the upper body does not indicate any preparation or execution*.

A Ghost Groin Kick

Of course, there are a few notable exceptions that we shall present, and there are more complex Ghost Kicks with some upper body moves. But the general principle is to hide the traveling kick for as long as possible.
Once a trainee has been acquainted with Ghost Kicks and starts to really understand the underlying principles, he can start to apply those same principles to regular Kicks to confer them *some* "ghostliness". In general, it would be drilling for an immobile upper body or it would be learning to position oneself on the blind side of the adversary. Aiming at some dissimulation for your normal kicks will help very much to hone your 'regular' kicking skills as well.
Ghost Kicks are not appropriate in all circumstances; but when they are suitable, they are extremely efficient. When well-executed, they generally come with total surprise. Ghost Kicking is a bit of a forgotten Art, and Ghost Kicks are therefore totally unexpected most of the time. Once you'll have mastered them, you should try them in free fighting. Once you'll have used them successfully, you'll certainly become a fan like me, and you will do your own research into other possibilities and variations. The dawning understanding of the Art of Dissimulation will lead you to your own research and personal training; it will certainly make you a better fighter.

Training for Ghost Kicks

The important skill to drill in ghost-kicking is the *dissimulation* part. The most important training tool will be the mirror. You'll have to drill endlessly the no-telegraphing and the unmovable upper body during execution. This requires a lot of patient work: do not be discouraged, because the result is certainly worth it. Once you have mastered the basic kick and improved your dissimulation qualities, you should train with a partner who will help you to keep the kick's trajectory out of his range of vision, and who will try to spot any tell-tale on your part.

Only after you have mastered enough of the dissimulation and specific trajectory, is it worth to work the bag for focused power delivery, but *always subordinate to good "ghost" form*.

Then use the kicks in free fighting to slowly improve them in realistic combat.

Training for Ghost-kicking is as much a thing of the mind as it is of the body. The Artist will have to concentrate, imagine, role-play and look for the best fit to his personality and style. This is a process that takes time and that is very gradual. No quick fixes; Martial arts are about patience, hard work, perseverance, not instant gratification. This training also requires meditating and visualizing the kicks and the various situations. The author thinks that is Martial Arts at their best, with emphasis on the word 'Art'.

Drilling the Phantom Groin Kick for power, **only after mastering correct form**

22. THE PHANTOM GROIN KICK

General

This would be, in the author's opinion, the archetype of the Ghost Kick. It is delivered with an unflinching upper body and with 'as-if' disconnected legs, it is targeting the groin, it is executed from very close where a kick is not expected, it is totally out of the opponent's field of vision, and it is extremely fast. In the right set-up and if well-mastered, it is a kick that is impossible to miss; and the groin being the target, the results are guaranteed.
It has never failed me, and I love it.
As I have mentioned it in previous work about *Essential Kicks*, the **Phantom Groin Kick** is my preferred *Bunkai* (Kata Form move interpretation) for the very typical move of the traditional *Tekki Shodan Kata* in *Shotokan Karatedo*.

Description

You simply lift the foot *directly* from where it is, in a straight line towards the opponent's groin. In order to do so, you do bend the knee and open the hip outwards, so as to adjust distance. You also twist the foot inwards, so as to present the inside blade towards the target for a better reach between the legs. During the execution you keep your upper body totally disconnected from the lower body, and as immobile as possible. Remember that any change of the height of your head will be the first tell-tale of something coming; avoid it at any cost. The illustrations are better than a thousand words.

Front View of the Phantom Groin Kick

The Phantom Groin Kick should be automatic when getting in close range

Side View of the Phantom Groin Kick

Key Points

- Do not look at the target
- Keep the upper body relaxed and your hands high
- Make sure there are no tell-tales of the incoming kick

Typical applications

This Stealth Kick works even better if you simultaneously pull the opponent's attention up with a high hand feint; or even better if you use it as a follow-up to a high punch. The photos below illustrate the fast combination 'Jab/Phantom Groin Kick'.

The Phantom Groin Kick swiftly following a Jab

The Classic Phantom Groin Kick is usually executed with the front leg for shortest possible trajectory. But it can also be delivered with *the rear leg*. It is then more powerful, but also easier to detect. Once you have fully mastered the classic front-leg version, you should start to drill the rear-leg version along the same principles. With serious training, the unorthodox rear-leg version can be as stealthy as the front-leg one; it is, though, usually more used as a follow-up or simultaneous attack together with a high punch. As it is more powerful, it is a redoubtable attack if well mastered.

The powerful ***rear-leg*** *version of the Phantom Groin Kick, after a high Jab*

The kick is also a great Counter Kick or even a Stop Kick. In the illustrations below, the front-leg Phantom Groin Kick closely follows the block of a classic stepping Lunge Punch. This is a good drill for the situational use of the kick. As the opponent bends over from the groin pain, you could follow up with a Downward Circular Elbow Strike and a Knee Strike.

Block and groin-kick

Targets

The groin, mainly.
Also the face, if the opponent is bent-over. The illustrations below show a double Phantom Groin Kick: to the groin first, then to the face! We have shown both options for the second kick: the same front-leg option and the rear-leg option.

Double rebounding Phantom Groin Kick, groin then face **with the same foot**

Double Phantom Groin Kick; front-leg to the groin, rear-leg follow-up to the bent-over face

Specific Training

- The most important aspect to drill first and foremost is the 'stealth' of the technique. Train in front of a mirror for complete dissociation of upper and lower body and for no tell-tales.
- Only once you have fully mastered the Stealth Kick, should you start to train to add power to the move, with no sacrifice of the 'Ghost' execution. You can drill with a partner holding a focus pas or with a bag hanging at groin level.

Drill the Phantom Groin Kick with a focus pad

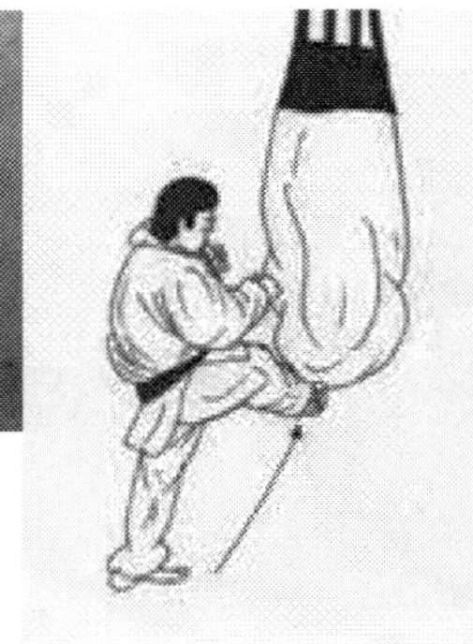

Drilling the Kick on the hanging bag; train for power but with no upper body move

Self Defense

The use of this kick is generally offensively pre-emptive. Sometimes you'll have to control or block the start of an attack or of a grab, while (or just before) executing the kick. In the example illustrated below, you check the extending hand of a close assailant, and execute the Phantom Groin Kick. You could follow up with a Hammer-fist Strike to the back of his head, a slap to his exposed neck and an Essential Upward Hooking Back Kick from which you can start walking away from your chastised would-be assailant.

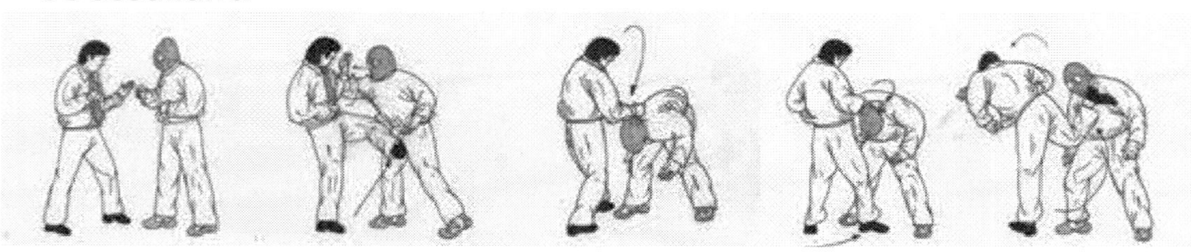

Control a suspect hand-move from close-up while executing the Phantom Groin Kick

The last example, will show the use of the kick after you have been grabbed in a standing front choke. It is in fact a kick to boost a classic self-defense release; an unexpected groin kick should definitely help loosen the assailant's grip. The kick should precede the release maneuver by a millisecond. You could then follow up with a mean *Krav Maga* series: Knife-hand Strike, Low Kick, Elbow Strike.

The use of the Phantom Groin Kick in a classic front choke self-defense release

23. The Lift Kick

General

This Kick is a close relation of the previous Phantom Kick. It is based on the same principles but executed with the straight leg, because the opponent is further away. There is no bending the knee outwards. The Lift Kick is therefore less powerful and more difficult to execute stealthily. But, as it targets the groin, it does not need that much power; and a powerful delivery can be achieved with focused training. The stealth delivery also needs more training, but it can be achieved. In fact, this is an important kick to drill in order to be able to deliver a Stealth Groin Kick from all ranges: from a close Phantom Groin all the way to a further Lift Kick.
The Kick is best delivered from a weightless front leg-stance, -like Karatedo's *Ko Kutsu Dachi* and *Neko Ashi Dachi*-, but the stance should not be obvious. In fact, as already mentioned, drilling the stance is at least as important as drilling the kick.

Description

The classic way to start drilling the Lift Kick is to start from a stance in which the front leg bears little body weight. This allows for a smooth and fast lift of the leg with no telltales. Simply lift the foot directly from its position directly into the opponent's groin.

The Lift Kick with a partner

The classic Lift Kick

Key Points

- No telltales. Start lifting without preparation.
- Dissociate upper and lower body.
- Hide the fact that your front leg is originally relatively weightless.
- Kick fast a few inches into the target, and retract fast; it must have some 'whipping' effect.
- Do not look at the target.

Typical applications

A rearward evasion that causes your opponent to overextend is a good opportunity for a Lift Kick, especially if you retreat just enough to "pull him in" and if you keep his attention upwards with hand moves. In the example below, you retreat gradually from a deep lunge jab, while placing body weight on the rear leg. It helps to lift a hand in an empty block. When your assailant arrives at the end of his move and *before* he starts to recover, you lift the front foot to his groin. This is a typical '**Attack on Recovery**' (as described in our previous book about *Stop Kicks*). You could follow up by scooping his front leg as he reels from the groin pain, and take him down in a nasty fall with a variation of *O Uchi Gari* (Large Inner Reaping Throw – *Judo*).

The Lift Kick in an **Attack on Recovery,** *and follow-up*

But, still the best application for the Lift Kick is to execute it stealthily as soon as an opponent gets in range. Wait for him in place, and lift in!

The best application for the kick is wait and execute

Targets

The groin, exclusively. The execution of the kick as a Stealth Kick, -with the leg straight-, is unnecessary to hit a bent-over face: a regular Upward Front Kick with some chambering will be as fast and much more powerful!

Specific Training

- Again, training must first and foremost concentrate on the stealth qualities of the Kick: no telltales, no body moves, no glancing down,... Drill in front of the mirror and with a partner
- It is important to also train to hold the preparatory stance with a relatively weightless front leg. This is also mirror work and application in free-fighting.
- Only when you have mastered the Stealthy Lift Kick, should you drill it for power focus on the hanging bag or a focus pad held at groin level by a partner. A more powerful kick is better, as a concussion effect in the groin area is very efficient if you have missed the testicles, but it should never be on account of the stealth quality.
- Straight-leg lifts repetitions are a very good muscle builder for a more effective Lift Kick. Alternate longs sets of as many repetitions as possible; it will have tremendous effect. *Plyo-Flex* training is also warmly recommended.

Straight-leg Lifts drilling will help build a fast and powerful Lift Kick

Self Defense

As mentioned, one of the common use of the Lift Kick is after an evasion leading into a weightless front leg-stance, like the well-known 'Cat Stance' common to many Martial Arts (*Mao Bu* in *Kung Fu*, *Neko Ashi Dachi* in *Karatedo*). As illustrated below and on the next page, the evasion can be rearwards, sideways or in between.

Lift Kick after Side evasion into Cat Stance

Lift Kick after rearward evasion

The Lift Kick is also a great Stop Kick against a kicking attack. As your assailant starts to develop his kick while expecting you to flee rearwards, you stay in place and surprise him by simply lifting your foot in his opening groin.

Lift Kick against a Roundhouse Attack

Lift Kick against a Front Kick

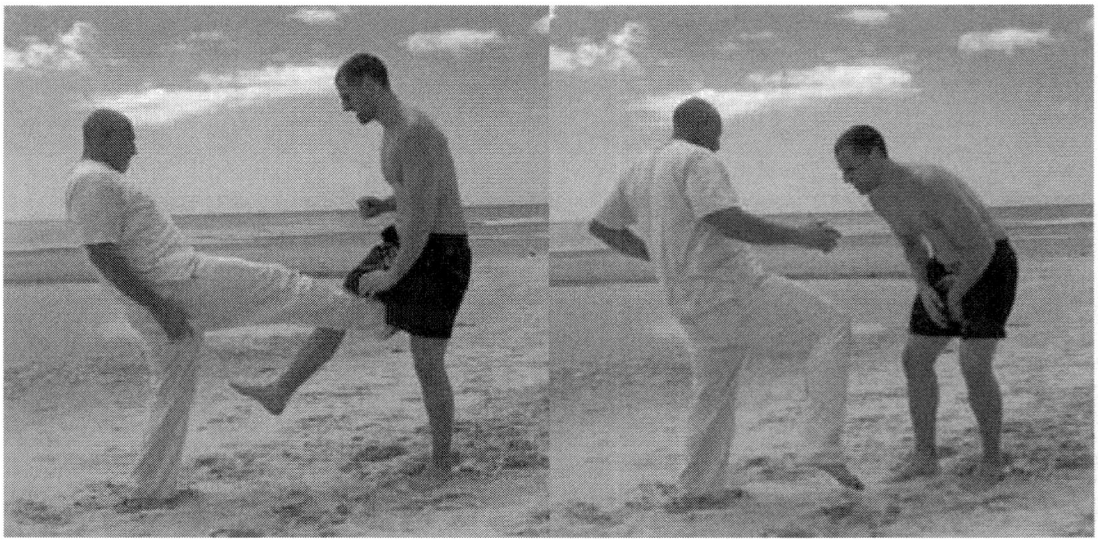

24. The Stealth Upward Back Kick

General

This could be described as the Stealth delivery of a hybrid between two classic Essential Kicks: the *Uppercut Back Kick* and the *Upward Hook Back Kick*. The Stealth aspect means no chambering and minimum upper body involvement. The Kick itself is simply a short Back Kick delivered upwards. Like all Back Kicks, this Stealth Kick can be delivered directly rearwards if it is where the opponent is, or after pivoting in a way that makes believe you are fleeing or scared. The execution of the kick itself is not orthodox and is highly dependent on the respective positions of the protagonists. It can be simply a near-straight-leg Lift Kick (See '*The Back Ghost Lift Kick*' in our previous work about *Essential Kicks*) or a full-powered 'hooking' Uppercut Back Kick with leg extension upwards. Various examples will be provided, but the reader must remember that he should concentrate on the **Stealth** delivery.

Description

The Stealth Uppercut Back Kick, *unlike* the classic Essential Uppercut Back Kick, is delivered without chambering. As illustrated, you simply lift the bent leg upwards directly into the groin of the opponent standing behind you. Try to keep the upper body as immobile as possible, though it takes training and flexibility. If you are not flexible enough, stay with trunk immobile for as long as possible and bend forward only when the leg is already on its way. How much you bend the leg depends on the range to your opponent.

The Stealth Upward Back Kick delivered directly behind you

A longer Stealth Upward Back Kick

Of course Back Kicks are not only delivered to opponents standing or approaching behind you; they can be used against front assailants by turning you back on them. Many such Back Kicks are described in our previous book about *Essential Kicks*.

Description (Continued)

...In the context of Feint Kicks, these Back Kick variations take a special meaning: turning your back on your opponent should look like you are fleeing and cowering. This would serve a double purpose. First, you so give a false sense of security to your opponent while he gets closer and in range for your Stealth Kick. And Second, it justifies in his eyes your bending away: he will think you are afraid, while in fact you so help the execution of the Back Kick. The reader should realize that the '*turn-away-to-flee*' Feint is an extremely efficient technique that will lure even trained opponents. It plays well into human psychology and what your opponent wants to believe. Your job is to make it look as real as possible. From there on, the Back Kick blends naturally and easily into the move and is very difficult to detect. The illustrations below show such Twist away & Kick-techniques, with a short Uppercut Stealth Back Kick and a longer straight-leg Ghost Lift Back Kick.

The fleeing Feint into Uppercut Stealth Back Kick

The fleeing Feint into Ghost Lift groin Back Kick

Key Points

- Keep the upper body immobile for as long as possible during the execution of the kick. Bend only when and if you need to.
- Lift the plant of the foot directly upwards.
- Kick a few inches into the target and whip the foot back.

Typical Applications

The simplest and most useful of applications, is the twisting away Stealth Upward Back Kick on an opponent attacking you or stepping into dangerously close range. The illustrations at the top of next page show clearly how you show your reluctance to fight, and lift your hands in a cowering gesture that has the added advantage to keep the aggressive assailant's attention up. As the opponent steps in nonetheless to punch you, you lean back with your hands up while starting to twist, looking as if you are about to turn and flee. As your assailant gets in range, you front foot simply lifts directly up into his groin, with some 'hooking' if possible. He is now at your mercy, and you can follow up. If you are a good grappler, you could for example grab your flustered attacker and take him down by twisting into a Sacrifice Shoulder Throw (*Soei Otoshi – Judo*). ➡

Typical Applications (Continued)

Make an aggressive assailant believe you are going to turn away harmlessly, and execute the Stealth groin Back Kick as he steps in range

Of course, the Kick works as well if you are attacked from behind. When an opponent tries to grab you or punch you from behind, you simply lean forward and back-kick him up in the groin.

Stealth Heel Uppercut Back Kick up into the groin of an attacker behind you

This Stealth Kick works also extremely well at the end of an offensive combination attack that has got the opponent's attention up. Remember that the twisting away move will signal retreat to the unconscious mind of the opponent, making the stealth effect more effective. In the example below, you start your offensive combination with a Front Kick to the body and a (very) high lunge punch as you land. Twist smoothly into the unexpected Ghost groin Lift Back Kick.

The Ghost Lift Back Kick in an offensive combination

The Stealth Back Kick is also a Stop Kick of choice against a kicking attack, with the same idea of luring the assailant in by looking like a frightened fleer. In the photos below, the opponent attacks you with a Roundhouse Kick in spite of your cowering away. The example shows the groin kick delivered with the leg further away from the opponent this time, something akin to a 'Spin-back' variation of the Stealth Upward Back Kick.

Spin-back Stealth Upward Stop Back Kick against a Roundhouse

Opposite View of the Kick's impact

Targets

The groin obviously. But also the head of a bent-over opponent; it is not then fully a Stealth Kick, but still a very unexpected fast little kick that usually is not seen coming. It is usually, but not always, executed as you push down the opponent's head with your hand. The technique illustrated is also great against a bobbing/weaving opponent: a fake Hook Punch wil make him bend blindly into the Kick.

Applied Upward Back Kick to an opponent's face

Specific Training

- These Kicks must be drilled first and foremost for Stealth, in front of a mirror or with a partner.
- Only once you have mastered the Stealth part, is it worth drilling the move for speed and for precision (range) as well. Use a heavy bag or a focus pad held by a partner.
- Once you can execute the kick fast and without any telltale, you should start drilling its power on the heavy bag (hanging at groin level). Kicking hard means *while staying fully faithful to the Stealth delivery acquired*: Stealth and Speed are definitely more important than Power.

Once Stealth form is mastered, drill for Speed and Precision

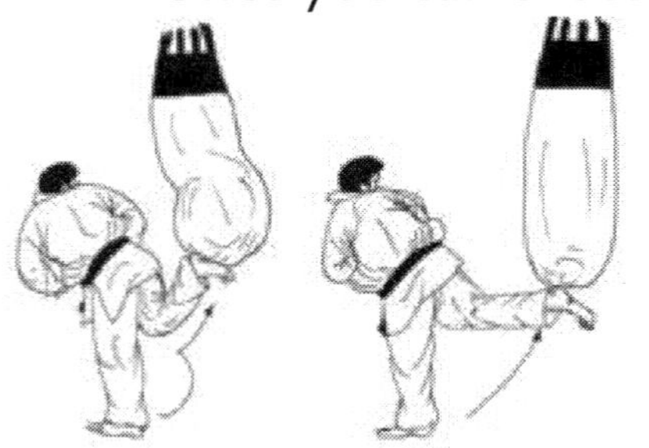

Drill all variations for Speed, Precision and Power on the heavy bag; but no compromise on Stealth delivery!

Self Defense

The photos below illustrate a Spin-back delivery of the Uppercut Back Kick after a classic release from a standing Front Choke attack. The Kick is delivered after you have turned away, and look like you are leaving the area after concluding your release with a double eardrum Palm Strike. **Deception and Stealth go hand in hand.**

Front choke release, double eardrum Strike, 'twist away to flee'-Feint, Spin-back Stealth groin Back Kick

Another good use of the kick, -as a Counter Kick this time-, is presented below. Against a serial user of the high Roundhouse Kick, you can typically smother the attacks by using your shoulder. In doing so, you twist away to present said shoulder while crouching slightly and protecting your head. What is more natural than deepening this move into a full twist-away? As your opponent starts to retract his kicking leg, you pivot and lift the front foot into his groin. You can follow up very naturally on this Stealth Uppercut Back Kick with a powerful Scissor Kick Takedown (*Kani Basami* – see previous book about *Ground Kicks*)

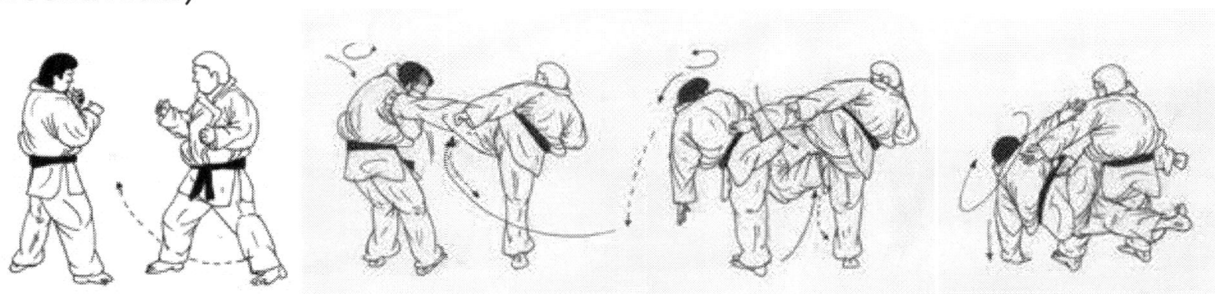

The Stealth Uppercut Back Kick as a fast counter to a shoulder-blocked Roundhouse Kick

But the optimal use of the technique is still as an undetected lift while a menacing opponent thinks you are cowering away. In the example below, you feign fear as a stick-holding assailant confronts you. As he lifts his stick to strike or to threaten, you twist away, -as if preparing to flee or "shell in" under the blow-; but you are simultaneously lifting your front foot into his groin. As he bends up in pain, you twist back forwards, -with all your body weight and hip power-, into a horizontal circular Back Elbow Strike to the head. You could follow up by naturally letting your striking arm enveloping his neck for a Guillotine Choke. Submit him, or go to the ground by simply sitting down.

Twist-away Ghost Upward Back Kick against an overhead stick attack

In the same vein, you can look like cowering away after blocking a punch, all the while keeping your hands up for further misdirection. In the example below, you evade out a lunging Jab while controlling it with the rear hand. Cross-step while starting to look back and 'cower' away. Your hands stay clearly up to keep his attention there. The cross step allows you to execute the Stealth Upward Back Kick to the opponent's groin from close up enough to hook with the heel.

Groin-hooking Stealth Kick after block; the cross-step or hop gets you in range

We shall close this section with two examples of Stealth Upward Back Kicks *to the head*. Although less stealthy than the Groin Kicks, the head Kicks are still unexpected and their trajectory is mostly out of the opponent's range of vision. During execution, your upper body is relatively erect and straight while the kick climbs too close to the opponent's body to be easily detectable early. Those kicks are surprisingly efficient and are worth mentioning here. This is again an opportunity to remind the reader that Stealth is also a matter of the mind and a matter of intention during delivery...

The first example below is the drilling of a 'hooking' Heel Upwards Back Kick while pushing the opponent's head down towards the kick.

The second example in the Photos below is an applied full Uppercut Back Kick to the chin of an unsuspecting opponent. You set up the Stealth Kick with a low Jab to evading-out Swing Punch. For the surprise kick, you are staying as straight as possible *on the out-side* of the opponent and you let your foot climb up as close as possible to his body to avoid detection. Remember that knock-outs are more the result of surprise than of power.

Hooking Heel Upward Back Kick to held-down head

Offensive combination ending with a Stealth Uppercut Back Kick to the chin

25. The Ultra-close Hook Kick

General

This is a fantastic little kick that I have unfortunately had to use once in a cramped space (an underground carriage), in real life. I can therefore fully guarantee the overwhelming surprise effect and the chilling efficacy of the technique if well-mastered. This is simply a head Hook Kick, but delivered from extremely close to the opponent while bending down. The photos below will do better than a thousand words. It is to be noted that the 'bending down', not only causes surprise and allows for easier high kicking, but it also removes the upper body from immediate danger. This is a great kick; and its drilling is by itself conducive to better general kicking proficiency and the ability to deliver all kinds of kicks from all kinds of situations.

Training for the Ultra-close Hook Kick: from shoulder-to-shoulder

Description

This Kick is simply a classic **Hand-on-floor** Hook Kick, -as described in our previous book about *Essential Kicks-*, but stretched to its extreme. From a natural Side Stance, you bend explosively sideways while lifting the opposite leg in a high Hook Kick, something like a front-leg Hook Kick while letting your hand touch the floor. For further Stealth, the trajectory of the Kick should be close to the opponent's body in order to stay 'under the radar. Only when getting close to the target, should the foot take a little range out before 'hooking in' (The general principles of the regular Stealth Hook Kick will be presented in further detail in the following section; they *do* apply to the Ultra-close version as well). The kick is more efficient if you 'hook' into the target: you kick a few inches into the target before chambering back, but as you make contact, you bend the leg slightly for more local power delivery. The illustrations below illustrate the simple way to drill the kick, but this is a Kick that needs to be delivered from all possible positions close to the opponent. The reader is invited to search for his own preferences and set-ups. In any case, this is a fun kick to train for.

The Ultra-close Hook Kick

This Kick should be drilled from all possible positions and situations: Various examples of applied Ultra-close Hook Kicks

Key Points

- The simultaneous bend-down and leg lift must start explosively and with no tell-tales.
- The foot goes to the opponent's head with a slightly curved but very direct trajectory.
- Kick a few inches *into* the target while 'hooking' and pull the leg back: this is a 'whipping' kick.

Typical Applications

My exploration into the Ultra-close Hook Kick started a long time ago when introduced to the '*Scorpion Kick*' in a seminar by the great Shotokan Karate master **Kanazawa**. The Scorpion Kick illustrated below, is a hybrid of Back and hook Kick delivered while bending forward and leaning on the opponent's leg for support and control. This is also a Stealth Kick and certainly a relative of the Ultra-close Hook Kick. It is a surprising technique, and even more surprising is the fact that it came from a *Shotokan-ryu* high-ranked master; Shotokan Karate is not known for extravagant kicks. In any case, I started drilling it and using it in free-fighting, which led me gradually to stretch it to the Ultra-close Hook Kick.

The Scorpion Kick after a high Back-fist set-up

As mentioned the Kick can and should be used from all kinds of situations. In the example below, it is used as a dynamic long-hopping front-leg kick after a Roundhouse Kick set-up. After a rear-leg Roundhouse Feint Kick to the opponent's kidneys, you immediately hop forward <u>and out</u> to get very close to him and to disturb his sense of range. You so jam his punching counter. You start bending and lifting the kicking leg already *while hopping.* Execute the Hook Kick.

A dynamic offensive Ultra-close Hook Kick

The Ultra-close Hook Kick is even stealthier if delivered from outside the opponent's vision range. For example, if you have got control of his arm from his out-blind side, as illustrated by the photos below. This is a relative position to be achieved by the classic *Tai-Sabaki* (circular evasion) moves of *Aiki-Jitsu*.

A very stealthy Ultra-close Hook Kick

Target

This is a head Kick exclusively. The element of surprise comes from the kick being a high Kick while executed from very very close. An *undetected* kick to the head will generally cause knock-out.

Specific training

- Drill the kick with a partner standing side-to-side with you. Start with some distance between you and drill the kick in its pure Stealth form. Then gradually get closer to your partner until you can execute the kick from a shoulder-to-shoulder position.
- Drill the regular Stealth Hook Kick presented in the next section. Especially concentrate on the trajectory close to the opponent's body.
- Drill on the heavy bag, just as you did with a partner: start explosively from close to the bag; the climbing leg razes the bag from close by.

Drill the kick with a partner and start from a position gradually closer to him

Example of a drill; hug the bag close and explode into the kick

Self Defense

It is now clear to the reader that the Ultra-close Hook Kick is a technique of choice when you get near the opponent and want to surprise him. In the illustrations below, you get very near the assailant with a classic 'roll-in' Spin-back Horizontal Elbow Strike, very typical of *Muay Thai*. You can do so after blocking a jab or the beginning of a lunge Punch. You then follow up with the surprising Stealth high Hook Kick. A good finish would be spinning back after lowering the kicking leg for a Double Outer Reap Takedown (*O Soto Guruma- Ju Jitsu*) while getting hold of his chin or throat.

Get close with a Spin-back Elbow strike, then execute the Ultra-close high Hook Kick

The Kick is also an excellent technique when you are surprised at close range from behind or from the side. Remove the body from immediate danger by bending away, and surprise him by kicking in spite of being at *ultra-close* range. In the example illustrated below, you are surprised from behind by a potential assailant who grabs your shoulder menacingly to pull you around to face him. Do not turn in the direction he wants you too: he could be waiting to sucker-punch you. Meld into his pull, judo-style, by going with it slightly and then gradually change direction. Use your whole body weight and hip power to bend down away from him and in the other direction. Execute the Hook Kick. If relevant, you should try to hit his elbow with the explosive twist and get control of his grabbing arm; for safety and for an eventual follow-up. Drill this technique fast and in a focused way: look over your shoulder and then explode down into the kick.

The Ultra-close Hook Kick against a rear shoulder grab

Of course, the Ultra-close Hook Kick is basically a simple Hook Kick but delivered from very close, and therefore, all Hook Kicks *variations* and applications are valid. It is just that the kick will be executed surprisingly from closer than expected. In the Photos below, a Front Kick is evaded forward and out to allow for counter with a Spin-back version of the Kick. Now that the principles have been made clear, the reader will look by himself for his preferred applications and variations.

Spin-back Ultra-close Hook Kick against a Front kick attack

26. The Stealth Hook Kick

General

In my heyday, this was definitely my favorite technique for tournament fighting, mostly as a Stop Kick. This is a fantastic kick I used to drill incessantly and to perfect painstakingly. Once you have mastered it, and if it is compatible with your personality and physiology, it simply...works. The Stealth Hook Kick is simply a high Hook Kick executed while keeping the kicking foot close to the opponent's body and therefore *out of his vision range*. I did tend to use this kick mainly as a 'timing' Stop Kick, but it can be used as a normal Offensive or Counter Kick.

The idea is very simple. By letting your kicking foot climb close to the opponent, you keep it unnoticed for the beginning of the maneuver. You then start to bend back to allow for the high kick; this should be started as late as your flexibility and proficiency allows for. Your opponent will then start to realize that something is happening, but he will not see a kick yet. It is probably too late anyway. Just before reaching head level, your kicking foot will take some range for an effective kicking impact: the trajectory will take the foot a little bit further from your opponent before whamming back into the target. The illustrations below will make all this convoluted explanation easier to understand.

The experienced Artist will immediately realize that the valuable stealth of the Kick seriously encroaches on its power. And here comes the rest of the story. For one, this kick needs serious drilling, especially power development into its perfect Stealth form. For two, the Hook Kick is a whipping kick which effectiveness is based on speed and whipping pull back. For three, knockouts and knockdowns are the result of the surprise of the hit more than its power. Even in light-contact karate bouts, I used to score many knockdowns with this kick. In spite of the knockouts, I nevertheless usually gleaned the points because I made sure to connect visibly with the plant of the foot and not the heel. The shock to the brain causing knock-outs comes from the fact that the hit is not expected and that there has been no 'preparation' to absorb it. I can assure the reader that it works. And in real life, you can also connect with the heel, eventually even in a hard shoe.
In a word, a *great* kick!

Description

For the general principles of the Hook Kick, the reader is invited to refer to the dedicated whole Chapter in our book about *Essential Kicks*. The trajectory of the Stealth version of the Hook Kick is described above and illustrated below. It is pretty easy to understand: lift the leg straight up with minimum body move. Then take some range away from the head at shoulder level to gather speed and power for impact. If it is well executed, the opponent will have no inkling before it is too late.

There is not much to add. This is a kick best 'felt' by drilling. Practice diligently, and all will become clear.

The special trajectory of the Stealth Hook Kick

Key Points

The Stealth comes from minimum upper body movement at the start of the kick. Then later, it results from the kicking foot climbing up as close as possible to the opponent's body.

Typical Applications

There is not much very specific in terms of applications for the Stealth Hook Kick. All applications of the regular Hook Kicks and its variants are relevant: the kick is simply delivered as per the Stealth Principles. As mentioned, the author feels that the optimal embodiment is as a Stop Kick; this does not necessarily suits all temperaments and styles, but I think this is highly suitable to the Stealth delivery. The reader may experiment in other set-ups like offensive and counter situations. The examples given in this section will be very close to those presented in our book about Stop Kicks, but with slight adaptations to Stealth. The reader should practice the example given in the spirit of **maximum dissimulation!**

Typical Application (Continued)

We shall present the classic '*timing*' Hook Stop Kick against a punch, with the Hook Kick delivered to the face or the back of the neck according to the circumstances. It should be clear to the experienced Artist, that delivery to the back of the head is even stealthier than to the face, as the foot travels along the opponent's back.
In the first example, in regular stances, you simply lean back to evade the opponent's jab while lifting your hands. Your leaning back liberates your front foot from your body weight. You can therefore start to lift the leg along your opponent's back without moving your upper body further. Keep your hands high and visible to help keeping his attention up. Do not lean further away before the lifting leg requires it, as per your flexibility. As your foot reaches the opponent's shoulder level, let the foot take slightly more distance away for extra range when slamming back into the head. You could follow up with a Stomping Side Kick into the back of the opponent's knee. It should be noted that the execution of this technique in regular stances, as presented, requires more proficiency and more flexibility than its counterpart in opposite stances: it is important to kick higher and avoid any possibility of a smothering of the kick into the opponent's shoulder.

Stealth Hook Stop Kick against Jab, in regular stances

The version in opposite stances is easier to execute, requires less flexibility, but it supposes a better mastery of stealth. You simply lift your front leg straight and close to the opponent's body as you lean just enough to evade his jab. Again, lift your hands up and keep them there to further keep attention up. Execute the Stealth Kick as already described several times. You could follow up with a Spin-back Short Back Kick, for example.

4 5 6

Stealth Hook Stop Kick against Jab, in opposite stances

Of course, the Kick works just as well against a Reverse Punch, and other attacks; just keep it stealthy.

Stealth Hook Stop kick against Reverse Punch

A great example of the Stealth principles is given in the following application: not only the kick is executed by climbing close to the opponent's body, but it is also delivered from his blind side and in between other techniques. This is a stunning kick, because totally unexpected, and it does really soften the opponent for the coming typical *Aikido* throw. In fact, original *Aikijitsu* techniques were always executed with hard hits (*Atemi*) to ensure their success. In the specific example below, you evade the lunging jab/cross of your opponent and catch his reverse punch while palm-striking him. Keep your hand up while kicking him with a passing Front Kick that will allow you to pass below his caught wrist. From the opponent's back, you can launch a nearly invisible hooking Hook Kick and throw him with a classic Aikido throw as illustrated.

Stealth Hook Kick from blind side before Aiki takedown

Targets

This is a head Kick exclusively, with the hope that the surprise effect will cause a knockdown or a full knockout.

Specific Training

- One must first concentrate all training on the trajectory; focus on Stealth and Speed.
- One must then train in front of a mirror and with a partner, to focus on no-telltales before and in the first stages of the kick.
- Only once the kick is mastered as a Stealth Kick, should one start working on developing power; use the hanging bag and the standing bag. Of particular interest are the bean-shaped bag for trajectory emphasis and a medicine ball on top of a standing bag for pure power (kick as far as possible while keeping the Stealth trajectory).

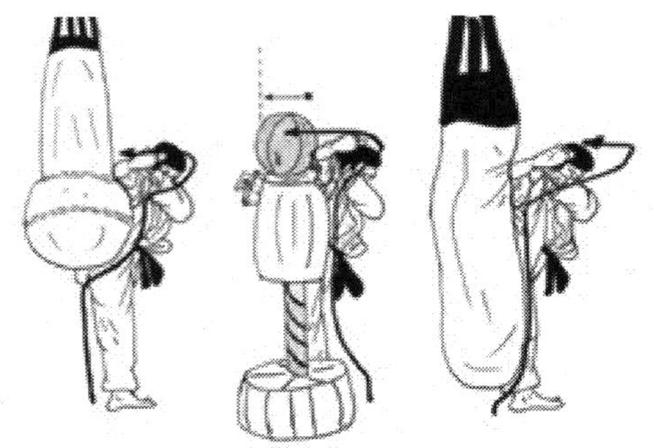

Drilling the Stealth Hook Kick

Self defense

Our first example again illustrates a Stop Kick, but against a Front-leg Hopping Kick this time. As your assailant starts his hop into a front-leg Side Kick or Roundhouse Kick, you stay in place instead of retreating. You lift your hands to pull the attention up, while starting to lift your front leg along the assailant's back. As he progresses in the execution of his kick, you bend away while finishing your own kick according to the Stealth principles. The reader of my previous book about *Stop Kicks* understands that staying in place, or even inching forward to stop-kick an attack jams all the range calculations of the opponent and is even preferable to retreating; the principles of stop-kicking must be respected here, with the additional twist of a stealthy delivery that will postpone even more the opponent's realization that something is off. A good follow up could be a full-powered Straight-leg Roundhouse Kick to both his legs.

The Stealth Hook Stop Kick against a Hopping Front-leg Kick attack

The second example is also a Stop Kick, as we think it is the optimal use of this technique; but this Stop Kick is delivered after causing the opponent to counter a feint of yours. This is a classic **Offensive Trap**, in which you feint a certain attack against an opponent whom you expect to counter. In the example, you deliver a credible but too short reverse punch to the body, with some leaning forward; go as far as needed to cause a reaction. As soon as your opponent launches his own punching counter, you twist back and bend away from the punches while starting to lift your front leg in a stealthy manner, close to the opponent. Connect with head and follow up. The finish of this technique, as you let your kicking foot land after hooking a few inches into the target head, lends itself naturally to a *Kani Basami* Scissor Throw. Keep kicking on the ground.

Stealth Hook Stop Kick against a counter

The last example will be a full offensive technique, capped by a Stealth Hook Kick. This is very simple and useful combination that I have found effective if used parsimoniously. The opening of the combination is a combined high Back-fist Strike evolving into a Jab. The idea is to keep the opponent busy with your hands at head level, as both strikes are not really dangerous especially in this 'feinting' set up. The arm retracts partly after the outside Backfist Strike to come around the blocking hand into an inside Jab. The inside jab keeps the opponent busy on his high inside gate while you have cross-stepped forward and start lifting your front leg in his back. For further dissimulation, you keep your upper body straight for as long as possible while keeping your hands up and moving: this will keep his attention up and restrict his range of vision. Once the Stealth Hook Kick has connected with full surprise, he is yours. Once you have retracted and landed the foot, you can follow up with a fully powered Spin-back Hook Kick of the other leg. Here is the place to advise you not to underestimate mindless hand moves for distraction: the simplest things work usually best. Just do not overuse it, and remember that with more skilled opponents, you would need to be more subtle to be realistic.

Offensive Stealth Hook Kick Combination; simple, but effective

Illustrative Photos

It is extremely difficult to illustrate the Stealth principles in photographs. The Stealth aspect of this kick is as much mental as physical; it requires subtlety and adaptation to the circumstances. Here follow a few photos of Stop Hook Kicks with some Stealth properties.

Marc De Bremaeker

Marc De Bremaeker

Itay Leibovitch

Marc De Bremaeker

Dotan De Bremaeker

A few applied Stealth Hook Kicks

27. The Stealth Roundhouse Kick

General

This is the counterpart of the previously described Stealth Hook Kick; obviously coming from the other side. The idea is obviously the same: the leg is extended from the start and the foot climbs up close to the opponent's body so as to be undetected. When the foot reaches about shoulder lever, it takes a wider trajectory in order to gather range for some momentum-gathering. It then slams into the opponent's head, hopefully as a total surprise. Unlike for the corresponding Hook Kick, the Stealth Roundhouse Kick requires some retracting back (bending the leg slightly) before connecting. This happens together with the widening of the trajectory and provides some power and 'whippiness' for the kick.

This delivery may, again, look strange to some. I can guarantee that this simply works. It may differ in degrees of stealth from one Artist to another, it may suit one more than the other, but it is a fantastic kick. Of course, it is not a powerful delivery; but the effect of surprise, when well executed, more than compensates. This kick does tend to cause less knockdowns and knockouts than the previous Hook Kick, because it is often not a total surprise. Because of the need for some cocking before impact, and the fact that it is best used on the face, the kick 'pops up' in front of the opponent, too late to block but long enough to let the brain expect impact. It is still a great kick though, especially if you make sure you follow up with a powerful technique on the flustered opponent. It can certainly be executed with complete stealth and surprise to the back of the head, but you then need to be very flexible in order to come high and avoid the shoulder; in that case, knockdowns are common.

In fact, I did develop my Stealth Roundhouse Kick well before my Stealth Hook Kick, and I was able to cause many knockdowns by hitting the back of the head. It was mainly because a lot of flexibility work that allowed me to easily kick very high and because I was delivering a slightly downward version of the kick.

All this said, this is not a kick for everybody, but it is well worth trying for and drilling towards.

Description

After the detailed general introduction, the following illustrations will easily make it clearer than another additional thousand words. Each Artist will adapt the principles described to his preferences and develop his own version by trying and training.

Description (Continued)

The Stealth Roundhouse Kick – Front View

The Stealth Roundhouse Kick – Side View

Key Points

Just like for the Stealth Hook kick:

- Keep upper body immobile for as long as possible.
- Try to keep opponent's attention up.
- Let foot climb close to the opponent's body and out of his vision range.
- Kick a few inches into the target and retract forcefully

Typical Application

Just like for the Stealth Hook Kick, the preferred embodiment of the Stealth Roundhouse Kick is as a Stop Kick. Of course, it also helps the Stealth to have the opponent concentrating on his own attack while you lift your leg. In the example below, you deal with an opponent fond of jab/cross combo openings. You retreat just enough for the opening jab and keep your hands up to keep him interested. While he develops his Reverse Punch, you execute the classic Stealth Roundhouse Kick and catch him totally unaware.

Just like for the Stealth Hook Kick, there are not many specific applications: any applied Roundhouse Kick can be executed with more or less Stealth. Refer to our previous works about *Essential Kicks* and *Stop Kicks*, and try all high Roundhouse Applications with a Stealth emphasis.

A Stealth Roundhouse Stop Kick

Target

There is no other relevant target than the head to the Stealth variation of the Roundhouse Kick. This is all about surprising with a high Kick.

Specific training

- The good execution of this kick requires flexibility. *Plyo-Flex* training is warmly recommended, as well as the assiduous practice of the regular high Roundhouse Kick.
- The unmovable upper body at the start of the kick must be drilled in front of the mirror and with a helping partner.
- The trajectory, and the power of delivery, can be drilled on the heavy bag. Especially good is the round-bottom bean bag hanging at the right height, as illustrated: it really forces the required trajectory.
- The best exercise I have used to develop power at impact is the kicking of a basketball. The ball is stuck at head height on a yoga block, that is on a tire, which itself is on top of a standing bag. Kick a few inches into the ball with the purpose of sending it as far as possible. The tire will force the right trajectory change after you have razed the standing bag. We shall not underline enough that the drilling of power for Stealth Kicks comes only after full mastery of all other qualities: stealth, speed and no telltales,...

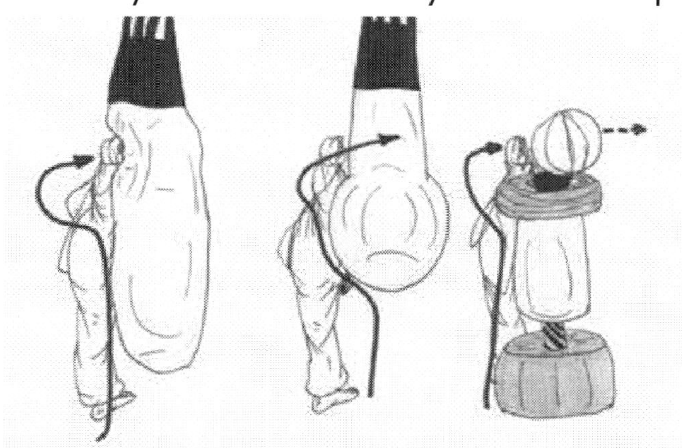

Drilling the Stealth Roundhouse Kick

Self defense

The photos below try to illustrate an offensive version of the Stealth Roundhouse Kick. In this example, you open with a high crossed-stepping Back-fist Strike which will keep the opponent's attention up. The cross-step with the rear leg going behind is also minimizing the expectations of a Roundhouse Kick. The Backfist then turns into an arm grab which will divert the opponent's attention even more, while the leg is climbing close to his body for the coming Roundhouse.

The development of an Offensive Stealth Roundhouse Kick

A similar example is presented now, with a Spin-back Back-Fist Strike opening. The idea is the same; and, in this case, the Spin-back Strike conditions the opponent for further attacks coming from the same side. In their stead, comes a Stealth Roundhouse Kick coming even more surprisingly from the 'wrong' side.

Offensive Spin-back Backfist to Stealth Roundhouse Kick

We mentioned earlier that the Downward version of the Roundhouse Kick is even better suited for the Stealth delivery. If you are flexible enough, it is certainly a version worth drilling: it has even a more surprising trajectory and it makes irrelevant the problem of a kick being smothered or even blocked by a shoulder. One of my old favorite combinations is presented below: an outside leg tap with high hands, followed by a slightly Downward Stealth Roundhouse Kick. The whole offensive is capped with a Spin-back Back Kick to the midsection. The pictures have been taken out of a video in order to try to show as well as possible the actual Stealth trajectory. It has proved quite difficult and we apologize for the quality of the ensuing pictures. Best understanding for the reader would be to try and drill the Stealth delivery by himself on the tatami.

Offensive combination with a slightly downward version of the Stealth Roundhouse Kick

We shall cap this collection of applied examples with a set up for the kick that I used a lot when I was competing in 'points' Karate tournaments. It is, in fact, a compounded misdirection: not only the Roundhouse Kick does follow a stealth trajectory, but the opponent's attention is also purposely drawn down while the starting position for the Roundhouse Kick can seem illogical. The start of the combination and the set-up for the Stealth Kick is a classic very deep and low punching attack. The high lunging Jab/ body reverse Punch is the bread and butter of Points Karate; it is generally delivered with an explosive long lunge, nearly suicidal. In this execution you lunge long and land so low that your Reverse Punch is executed with a knee on the floor. The last thing your opponent will expect is a high kick executed from this starting position. For maximum surprise, you will deliver the stealth version of the kick after pulling the rear foot forward in a hop as you stand back up. This technique may seem fancy and difficult: it is not. The transition from knee down to hopping front-leg Roundhouse is relatively easy to execute for a trained Artist. The surprise effect is extraordinary, and I strongly recommend drilling this maneuver. The Roundhouse Kick needs not be the Stealth version for success, but the double misdirection ensures better odds at scoring.

Front-leg hopping Stealth Roundhouse Kick from knee-down position

Illustrative Photos

Just as we mentioned just above and in the section about the Stealth Hook Kick, it is very difficult to illustrate in real photos the Stealth of these Kicks. Practice will make for a better understanding. Below are a few examples of more or less stealthy deliveries of Roundhouse **Stop** Kicks, the preferred application of Stealth Kicking.

Examples of stealthy Roundhouse Stop Kicks

28. The Stealth Small Heel Back Hook Kick

General

This is a fantastic kick to surprise an opponent behind you or on your side; and, unlike most Stealth Kicks, it is a kick that can deliver loads of power. It is therefore not only directed at the groin, but it can also target the solar plexus, the lower ribs, the kidneys and even the outer thigh.

The kick is kind of a hybrid between a very short Back Kick (See the *Essential Book of Martial Arts Kicks*) and a Hooking Close Hook Kick. It is delivered behind you with minimum upper body movement and straight into the target from the starting position. With some training, you can learn to use the hips to power the Kick without compromising the Stealth properties. As it is short and fast, you will then have at your disposal a redoubtable weapon, and the only thing left to drill will be the setting up of the right situations for use. This work is well worth it, for the results are spectacular: fast, powerful and undetectable.

Description

Side View of the Stealth Small Heel Back Hook Kick

The hybrid characterization above is probably the best description in words. Have a look at the illustrations below and try to practice it for a full understanding of the move. It must be said that different physiologies or personalities will tend to execute the kick slightly differently, and it is perfectly OK. Some will emphasize the hooking, and some the straight upward trajectory. Just make sure you concentrate on proper and reproducible Stealth form. At impact, make sure you kick with the *heel* a few inches *into* the target while '**hooking**' in (= pulling in towards you).

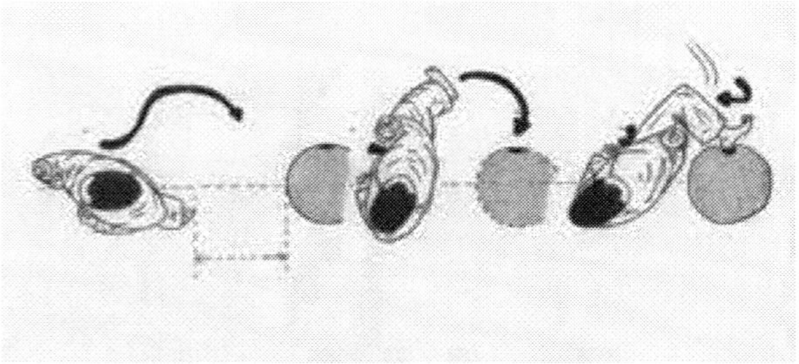

Top View of the Kick

Back View of the Stealth Small Heel Back Hook Kick

Description (Continued)

The illustration above (previous page) do describe the classic way to get acquainted with the technique: you kick back with the front leg, which gives you more range to cover and to gather power. It is the right way to drill Stealth, because it requires more dissimulation. Once you have mastered the Kick, you should start to train from all possible postures: drill from regular standing posture or execute the kick from the rear leg.

Back View of the rear-leg Stealth Small Heel Back Hook Kick

A rear-leg kick rearwards will be less powerful, but much faster and undetectable. It will be your job to train for power without compromising the Stealth, even for very short kicks.

An important point to make here is that you can execute the kick without looking at the opponent, or at least starting it without looking. This will have the effect to reinforce the Stealth of the kick. You can also look briefly, then look away. Or you can make sure to look away as if preparing to flee. Stealth kicking is a specialty in which the axiomatic 'keep eye contact with the opponent' can eventually be disregarded to further the misdirection. In this example, it is possible because the kick is very short and fast. This said, the experienced Artist knows that it must be weighed against the possible downsides, and only the specific situation will provide an indicative answer. Looking away from your opponent or your assailant is dangerous, obviously!

Key Points

As mentioned above:

- Keep upper body immobile for as long as possible. All the way, if you are flexible enough.
- Go straight up and into the target.
- Kick into the target for a few inches while hooking in; then only chamber back.
- Do not train for power before you have mastered Speed and Stealth

Typical Applications

Once the kick is mastered, it is all about the setting up of the right conditions for an offensive application. Training to get to suitable relative positions will also ingrain those set-ups for instinctive defensive use. Being close enough, having the opponent's attention up, and presenting at least partly your back; those are the optimal prerequisites for the kick. ➔

...In the first example below, you get close and get his attention up with a classic Back-Fist Strike attack. A fast kick into his exposed ribs will be undetectable. Follow up, preferably high.

Backfist to Stealth Small Heel Back Hook Kick

Of course, most spin-backs will place you in the same position. And, *if you are close*, the opponent does *not* expect a Spin-back **Kick**

Backfist to Spin-back Stealth Small Heel Back Hook Kick

Targets

The groin, the outer thigh, the lower ribs, the solar plexus, the kidneys.

Specific training

- Drill the stealth and trajectory with a spotting partner.
- Drill speed and precision on the heavy bag. Make sure you mark a spot on the bag at required level (groin, solar plexus or other) and hit it precisely.
- A great way to drill the 'not-looking' version of the kick is to touch the bag with the hand and kick from this position.

Drill the Kick on the heavy bag

Self defense

As a defensive kick, this is a technique of choice when you are confronted or attacked from behind. Act fast, and keep your hands up, both for protection and for misdirection.

In the example below, you detect that you are being attacked from behind. Let your front foot go straight for the assailant's groin in classic Stealth Small Heel Back Hook Kick; hook into his groin. During execution you have kept your hand up to keep his attention up, and to eventually smother an incoming blow in case you have not been fast enough. Even if you have missed the testicles, the power of the kick and its reverberations are enough to have him reel in pain and in fear. But you have continued your twisting momentum to hit his face with a full-powered Back-fist Strike as you lower your kicking foot. If you can, land on his foot and toes. Remember that you have been attacked from behind and with a stick: do not stop until the assailant has been fully vanquished and poses no threat. Follow up, for example, with a naturally-flowing fully-hipped Upward Palm Strike to his chin; you can then grab his head for a Knee Strike. If you are a good ground fighter, you could follow then bring your mellowed assailant to the ground with a sacrifice takedown: in this case, throw yourself to the ground under his bent-over body and twist to pull him over you for a nasty fall. This is the classic *Yoko Wakare* of *Judo*, or its older *Jiujitsu* versions. You should then stick to him for submission by choke or lock.

Defensive rearwards Stealth Small Heel Back Hook Kick to the groin and detailed follow up

Of course the kick is also great within an offensive situation, especially if you have concentrated opening moves high around the opponent's head. In the illustrations below, you attack your opponent with a high Front-leg Hook Kick, eventually with a preceding or simultaneous high Back-fist Strike. Lower the kicking leg while keeping you front hand menacingly high; or, even better, execute an additional high Back-fist to keep him busy in the higher gates. Your landing kicking foot rebounds on the floor for an undetectable Stealth Small Heel Back Hook Kick to the groin or solar plexus. This is a very serious technique because of both the surprise and the fact that the opponent is fully opened, and it should be used carefully. After you kicking foot lands back, you can follow up with a full powered high Spin-back Hook Kick coming from the other side. All in all, a surprising high in/low in/high out-combination; highly recommended. Make sure the Stealth Kick is delivered as such and follows all the rules.

Rebounding Stealth Small Heel Back Hook Kick in the midst of a good combination; keep his attention high for the Stealth Kick

As a last example, we shall remind the reader that this fantastic little kick can be used: when you are sideways to your opponent; with your 'front' leg; while you make your upper body look like you are cowering away; and with the kidneys as a target. All those are important opportunities and they are bundled together in the following application. On a separate note, it should be noted that it is important to drill this kick as an instinctive response to an attack from the side.

In the example illustrated at the top of next page, you are suddenly confronted by an assailant on your side and you cower away *with your hands up* while freeing your front leg from body weight. The Stealth Kick is executed as soon as possible and according to the rules of dissimulation. In this example, the assailant stands in a position that allows for a kidney strike and you should make sure to project power, to connect with the heel and to 'hook' into the target. [Should the assailant stand in opposite posture, it would be wise to target the groin.] As he reels from the painful kidney hit, a good follow up would be to neutralize any response by crowding him, while delivering an Elbow Strike to the head. From there, a Twin Outer Leg Reaping Throw (*O Soto Guruma - Judo*) is a no brainer. Finish him off with a Stomping Kick to the ribs.

Front-leg Sideways Stealth Small Heel Back Hook Kick to the kidneys from fake cowering posture

Illustrative Photos

The following photographs have been extracted from a video to try to better illustrate the trajectory of the Stealth Small Heel Back Hook Kick. It also shows the use of a body shield hold at the right height by a partner for power drilling.

Drilling for power while concentrating on right trajectory

29. The Outward Ghost Groin Kick

General

I love this Kick! It looks like nothing, but it is very powerful, hard to detect and easy to execute. It also has the possible advantage of being the logical start of a moving away maneuver: the natural continuation of the vector after the kick takes you behind the opponent and ready to step further away. If all this is not enough, it also can be executed from nearly any standing position. It should be used nearly automatically whenever the situation is right. It is a close-combat Kick targeting the groin. As it is very powerful because of the hip twist, it delivers a concussive blow. Even if you miss the testicles of your assailant, the shock waves of the impact in the general area will do the trick. I'll finish this round of praise by saying that any experienced Artist exposed will immediately understand that it is a Stealth Kick par excellence. Look below!

A power delivery of the Outward Ghost Groin Kick

Description

It is a difficult technique to describe in words: you lift your knee and bend your leg to get the heel close to your glutes; you also pivot forcefully with your hips to bring the side of your foot into the opponent's groin. All this is done with an upper body as disconnected as possible from the legs. Pictures and drawings will make this much clearer!

Outward Ghost Groin Kick from classic stance

The development of the powerful Outward Ghost Groin Kick

Key Points

- Keep upper body immobile and disconnected from lower body for as long as possible. Especially make sure the head does not pop up even slightly.
- Use the hip twist for power. You kick with the *hips*, not the leg.
- Remember that the closer your foot to your hip, the more power can be applied.
- Kick *trough* the target.
- Keep moving after the kick.
- Keep your hands up, both for protection and to keep the opponent's attention up.

Typical applications

One of the most classic of applications is after evading out of a jab attack in opposite stances. Evade and kick, nearly simultaneously. As shown in the photos below, kick the abs in training; it is counterproductive to kick at groin level with no-touch control as it breeds bad habits.

Execute the Stealth kick while evading out

The following application illustrates two points: 1. This kick can be delivered from normal stances and should be drilled as such; no need to go through a combat stance, kick directly from the stance you are in. 2. The momentum of this kick takes you behind the opponent in a way that is conducive to further movement; you can kick and follow up, kick and go away, kick and twist.
In this example, you are confronted by two assailants. As the first one closes in menacingly, you execute the groin kick going forward into his momentum, Stop-kick-style. You land behind the first attacker, but easily facing the other way. You are ready for the second assailant coming towards you, for example with a Front Stop Kick.

The Outward Groin Ghost kick in a two assailants-situation; kick and move

It is certainly the place for a little off-subject comment: the example below is a drill and an illustration. It will ingrain good reflexes and techniques. But the Artist should always remember that fighting multiple attackers is a difficult proposition, very unlike what it seen in motion pictures. Even an experienced artist will find it exhausting and very complex; it should be done in real life only if you have no choice or if the athletic and technical abilities of the assailants are very poor. The upper Black Belt examinations in the Shi Heun school of Karatedo do include multiple opponents free –fighting; it is enough to go through those once to be convinced of how much it reduces your odds. Try it and be forewarned.

The kick can be also used offensively within a combination, preferably when getting close and just after a high attack that will block the opponent's range of vision. In the example below, the Stealth Kick comes at the end of an overwhelming classic Reverse Punch/Rear-leg Penetrating front kick/Reverse Punch combination.

The Outward Groin Ghost Kick to cap an offensive combination

A great application of this Stealth Kick is, surprisingly, as an all-out *'fire-and-forget'* **Stop Kick**. After you have mastered the technique and have drilled the instillation of power in it, I suggest you try it a few times as a Stop Kick. In that application, you must consider this a kick-through kick to which you commit without hesitation: once started, there is no going back. The kick is executed fully in the Stealth mode, but you give it everything you have while protecting your head with your forearms in "shell" mode. In this 'sacrifice' context, the kick can be used against any forward move or attack; but it is best used after your opponent is convinced that you are about to retreat.

In the example illustrated *at the top of next page*, you retreat exaggeratedly several times against your opponent's front-leg kicks. Once your opponent has been conditioned and will probably overextend his closing hop, you go forward (in high protective guard) with all your hip power to catch him in mid-move. Kick through. As you land behind him, you could follow up with a mean Spin-back Upward Hook Kick to his bent-over face, and then a naturally flowing Scissor Takedown if you are a good ground fighter (*Kani Basami – Ju Jitsu*).

I cannot recommend this application enough: this is a very surprising and very efficient move when used judiciously, but you have to dive in with no hesitations.

A great Application: the all-powered Outward Groin Ghost Stop Kick

Targets

The main target is the general groin area. In some cases, the head of a bent-over opponent or his kidneys can be a worthy target for the full-powered kick.

Specific Training

- You must first master the technique and its Stealth fine points by working in front of the mirror or with a helping partner.
- Work on your hip joint flexibility (refer to *Plyo Flex*). The more flexible you are, the faster, the more disconnected from the upper body and eventually the higher will the kick go.
- It is a kick that definitely gains by power drilling. Use the body shield and the heavy bag, as illustrated throughout the section.
- In order to get familiar with various set-ups and to gain the necessary automatisms for its intuitive use, it must be used in dedicated free fighting (proponents need to wear testicle protection). Only free-fighting will let you master the necessary sense of distance for this kick.

Use also the hanging bag to develop power for the kick

Self defense

Here is an example of the kick as a '**facilitator**' for a wrist grab release and subsequent arm-lock. The release and the following arm-lock technique are classic (*Gyackute Tori Ikkyo - Aiki Jitsu*), but the kick will definitely soften the assailant and make the release much easier. As the opponent menacingly grabs your (same-side) wrist, you side step slightly while encircling his own wrist from the outside. You are in perfect position for a fast and powerful Outward Groin Ghost Kick. Twisting back into arm-lock position will now be much easier. You can now further soften him up with an Upward Front Kick to his offered face. From there, you can either control him in classical *Ju-Jitsu/Aikido* fashion; or, if you are not the grappling type, you can push him away and crush him with a Downward Heel Kick.

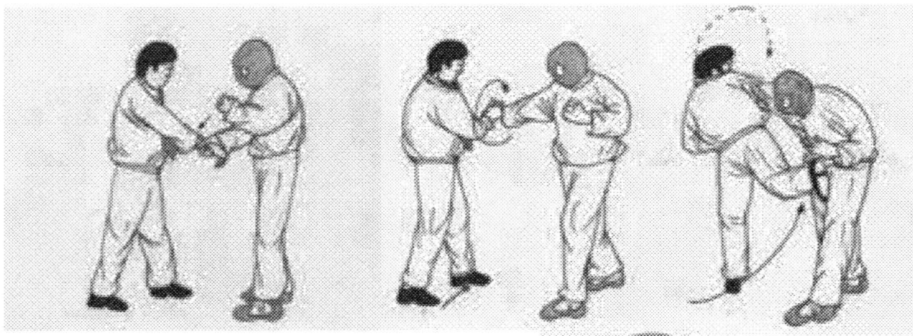

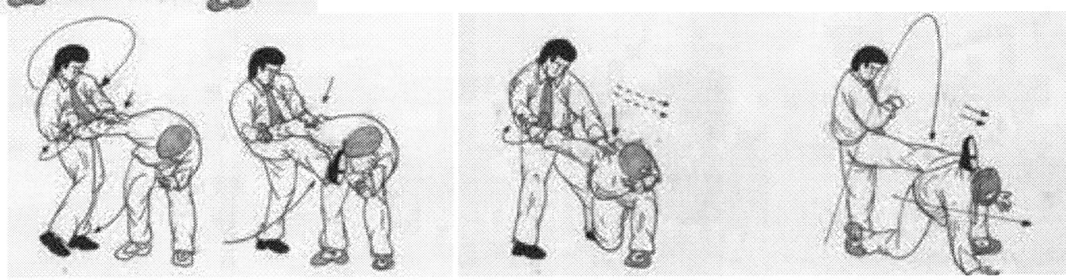

The Outward Groin Ghost Kick can help in a classic wrist grab release

As mentioned, the power of this kick, because of the hip twist and the proximity of the foot to the body center, makes it great to target the head for a *finishing* blow. Also as mentioned, this is a great kick to hit and immediately take distance from the confrontation. This is therefore a great follow up to any groin kick that causes the opponent to double over and put his head in range. In the example below, you stop a threatening assailant with a Groin Upward Front Stop Kick. As he bends over in pain, you let your kicking foot rebound on the floor for an Outward Ghost Kick to the head. Kick powerfully *through* his offered head, and use the momentum to start walking away.

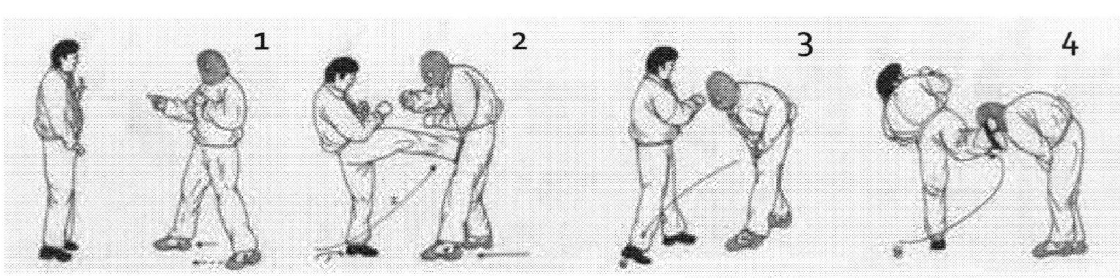

The Outward Head Ghost Kick as a finishing blow before moving away

This is a very versatile and useful kick, and it befalls each Artist to find his own way to set it up. The last series of photos just tries to illustrate the development of the kick, and especially the finish behind the opponent. The kick is executed here by *Sensei Roy Faige* after the classic offensive combination already encountered.

Offensive Outward Groin Ghost Kick landing behind opponent

The opportunity to secure ourselves against defeat lies in our own hands, but the opportunity of defeating the enemy is provided by the enemy himself.
~Sun Tzu

30. The Stealth Soccer Low Front Kick

General

The reader is invited to consult our previous work about *Low Kicks*, where a full chapter is dedicated to the Soccer Low Front Kick. The Soccer Low Front Kick and the classic Low Front Kick are by themselves near-Stealth Kicks: they are delivered fast and very low, generally at the knee or below, and they can be executed without moving the upper body.

It has already been mentioned, and it will be mentioned again, that Stealth is a matter of the mind as well as of the body. Many kicks can be executed with more dissimulation and more misdirection, and it is the intention that is the key difference. The Stealth Soccer Low Front Kick will be delivered with extra care about the immobile upper body, and eventually with a misdirecting high hand move. It will be delivered with a strong and purposeful *stealth mindset*, and so will it become the Stealth version of the classic kick.

Description

Your foot simply goes straight, by the shortest route, to the target: the knee or the mid-shin. Make sure nothing moves above the belt. Especially make sure that your head does not pop up even slightly and that your hand position does not change brusquely. Try to kick a few inches into the target ; this is basically a Soccer kick, but instead of the ball, you kick into a shin. It may seem trivial, but the shin and the knee are very sensitive targets, and the pain caused will certainly allow you an easier path to the follow up.

The Stealth Soccer Low Front Kick; keep the upper body straight and the head at constant level

A trivial, but very efficient way to improve the **stealth** is to lift the open palms to draw attention while the kick is delivered. It is childishly simple... *but it works.* This is misdirection added to dissimulation.

Lifting your open hands while kicking will help the kick to go undiscovered

Key Points

- Keep the upper body immobile and disconnected from the kick.
- Do no lift your head height even slightly: this is the first alert signal discernable to an opponent.
- Kick a few inches into the target.
- Keep your hands up and follow-up; you are very close.

Keep the body straight and the hands in the original guard

Typical Applications

The most obvious applications of the kick are offensive: explode into the classic kick with no frills, or execute the kick with a high hand feint like a jab or a cross.
The punching misdirection works even better if the punch looks innocuous; for example you can condition the opponent to an ineffective punch once or twice before using it to disguise the start of the Soccer Kick.

In the first example illustrated below, you purposely deliver a too short and too high Jab Punch. When you repeat the punch, the opponent will be less threatened. As he still watches the punch, your Soccer Kick is already underway.

In the second example, *illustrated at the top of next page*, the idea is similar, but you base the misdirection on a more common and believable Jab/Cross classic opening. After one or two such openings coming too short, you will have your opponent conditioned. You can then repeat, and let your cross punch pull your rear leg smoothly into the invisible Soccer Kick. It will catch your opponent, even if he is in the midst of his own counter punch. Your opponent will be painfully flustered and you can easily follow-up with your own concluding Reverse Punch.

Stealth Kick under a fake Jab

Stealth Soccer Kick under the guise of a classic Jab/Cross opening combination

You can also add to the misdirection by executing the kick after retreating in a way that builds your opponent's overconfidence. The kick can then be just an *Offensive Kick* to an overconfident opponent, a *Rebounding Kick* to an opponent moving forward, or a *Stop Kick* to an attacking assailant. The example below can be drilled in all **three** versions:

- You can step back, stop to break the rhythm, and then kick.
- You can step back and let your foot rebound on the floor to kick forward.
- You can retreat and gauge the distance, then kick as the assailant starts initiating his own attack.

The illustrations, *at the top of next page*, show how you retreat deeply as a threatening assailant steps towards you. You are far enough to consolidate your guard and be ready; as your opponent starts or keeps moving forward to attack, you kick powerfully into his shin. As he expected you to keep retreating, both surprise and pain will stop him in his tracks and subject him to your follow-ups. You should keep hammering him, preferably in an alternating hi/lo fashion; for example, with a high punch and then a groin attack.

In the example, we have chosen to present an interesting follow-up move that would be ideal for a cunning ground fighter. This is a move I personally like very much, as it is very surprising and very efficient. This is a maneuver that adds the feeling of doom your opponent will have: 'with you, nothing can be expected and everything goes'. This is also a very good exercise for stamina, for legs conditioning and for general kicking proficiency.

In the example, you let your kicking foot rebound from the assailant's shin directly deep behind you while kneeling down. Nearly simultaneously, you use your front fist to punch his groin. All this is one uninterrupted smooth move! You diving down is also an evasion from any possible high counterpunch; though you should keep your other hand up to protect your face. You then keep the momentum by spinning back on your front leg for a Ground Spin-back Back Kick to the opponent's midsection. If you are a good ground-fighter, stay on the ground and get him there with you.

Retreat and stealth-kick hard; drill the interesting follow-up

Targets

To stay stealthy, this kick targets the lower leg from the knee down. The knee can be attacked from any angle. The shin must be attacked frontally to be effective.

Specific training

This is a very useful and versatile kick, but it definitely requires drilling for power. You must train to kick powerfully while keeping the stealth properties of the execution. If you drill it seriously, you will have in your arsenal a crippling kick that is also fast and difficult to spot; what is not to like? So drill it regularly and with purpose.

- Drill the good Stealth form first in front of a mirror
- Only when form has been mastered, drill with a partner wearing serious shin guards. He will help you by trying to spot the telltales. You can then start adding power to the kick, gradually. In the example below, you drill the stop-kicking version of the Stealth Kick with a protected partner.
- A great prop is the medicine ball; kick it as if it was a shin. Kick a few inches into the ball and try to kick it as far as possible. You can increase the weight of the ball gradually and place it higher on a training block. You can also have the ball held in place by a partner as illustrated on the next page.
- For muscle tone development, you should use a restraining elastic band and execute the kick. Remember to always execute a few kicks free from the band at the end of each set. You can then compound the exercise by kicking a medicine ball while restrained by the elastic band, as illustrated on the next page.
- For impact and penetration training, there is no substitute to the long hanging bag and the old tire held in place. You have to kick powerfully and *into* the targets.

A protected partner will be of great help

Compound drilling: medicine ball and restraining elastic band

Drill for power, penetration and impact! But keep the Stealth

Self defense

Most examples following are extracted from our previous works about '*Low Kicks*' and '*Stop Kicks*'. The Stealth Soccer Low Front Kick is first and foremost a Low Kick, and it also lends itself particularly well to **stop-kicking**. *Stealth-kicking* is a <u>state of mind</u> and requires small adaptations of the classic underlying kick. Most examples in the previous books are relevant and the reader is invited to consult them for more applications.

There is a notable exception to the 'immobile upper body' rule, and it is in the case you lean back to evade an attack. In this case, your Soccer low Front Kick will be even stealthier, as your opponent is concentrated on his attack and will not take your backward leaning as a threat.

Evade a slap by leaning back, while executing your undetectable kick

It should also be noted that in very close combat, any low kick will be, by definition, stealthy; but the stealth aspect can be further improved by the right mindset. The example *at the top of next page* reminds the reader that getting into a clinch should automatically call in the Soccer Kick. If you have trained hard, this small kick can be devastating and change the whole fight instantly. The series below illustrates a great follow up: the "<u>Scrape, Stomp & Push</u>". After kicking *into* your assailant's shin, you let your foot scrape down his shin by pushing *down and into* the shin. You then let your foot land forcefully onto the opponent's toes. Keep your foot firmly on his by placing all of your weight, while pushing him backwards violently. The push while his foot is immobilized will cause him to fall down. If you keep his foot stomped while he falls (**<u>Something that you should never do in training!</u>**), it will result in serious ankle injury.

The Stealth Soccer Low Front Kick in clinch, followed by the Scrape/Stomp/Push

We already mentioned that this kick, -in spite of being potentially a crippling attack with enough training-, needs a follow up. We present here two combination series starting with the Stealth Soccer Kick.

The first example is also a misdirecting trap, which goes well with the sneaky Stealth Kick. You execute a simple direct Stealth Soccer Low Front Kick according to all the rules (Note the straight upper body in the photo). After kicking into the opponent's shin, you pull the leg back deep and turn slightly away, as if you were afraid of the payback. The message that your body language should convey is: "I am scared of what I have done; please do not come after me". When your opponent then opens up to counterattack, you hop back in with a front-leg Penetrating Side Kick. Surprise.

Stealth Kick opening and luring opponent into a Stop Kick

The second offensive example is a simple but very effective **hi/lo/hi/lo** series that includes two Stealth Soccer Kicks which will send your opponent home with sore shins. You open with a high Jab Punch and a very closely following low Soccer Kick; you then lower you kicking foot on the outside for a rear-leg high Roundhouse Kick. The landing-back kicking foot *rebounds* on the floor for another low Soccer Kick. Ouch!

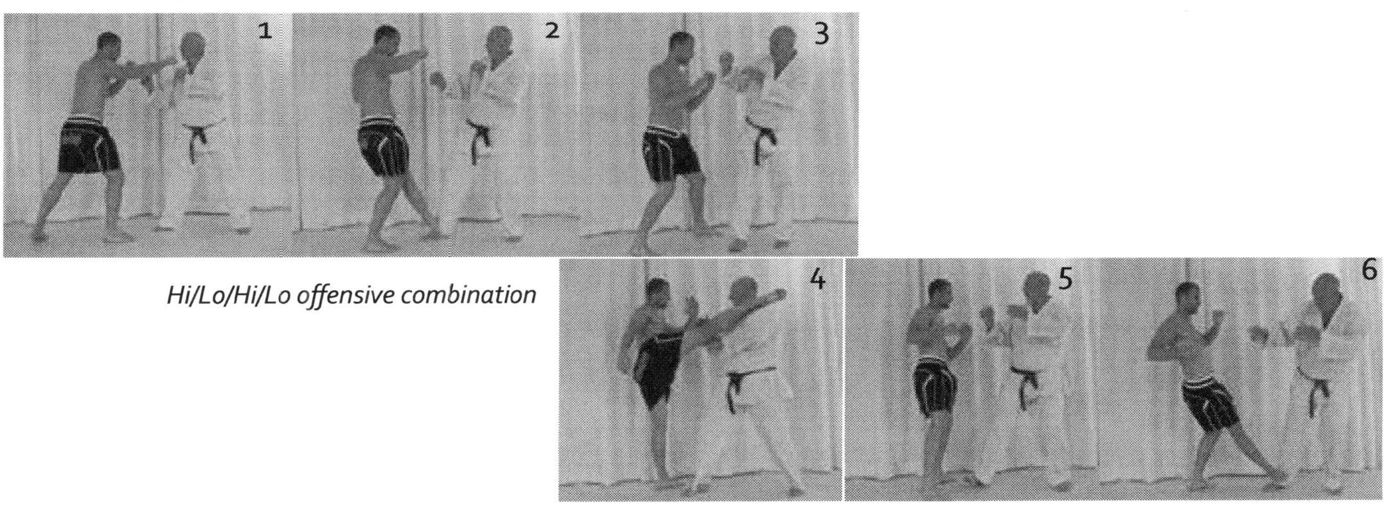

Hi/Lo/Hi/Lo offensive combination

Stealth-stop-kicking is the last general application to review here. It is so easy to stop a stepping, a hopping or a kicking opponent while keeping the upper body immobile! In previous books I have told the anecdote of my being creamed by *Savate* fighters when I took them up with their fighting rules. The Soccer Low Front Kick, common in *Savate-Boxe Francaise* and called '**Coup de pied bas**', was unknown to Sport *Karate* fighters because forbidden by their rules. It took me several months to get used to this fantastic Stealth Stop Kick and adapt. A great lesson in humility too for the cocky competitor I was. To sum it up, it is a great Stop Kick, as well as an **Attrition Kick**, especially against fighters who have not encountered it before. And it takes time to get used to it, to learn to avoid it and to start taking it into account.

The first example below show a typical 'stop-the-kick' maneuver: you powerfully kick the shin of an incoming rear-leg Front Kick early, while keeping all the rules of Stealth. Kicking the shin of a kicking leg is extremely efficient, as it adds the speed of the incoming kick to the power of impact. Lower your kicking foot forward to smother the surprised assailant, and deliver a Palm Strike to his face, followed by a full-hipped Elbow Strike from close up. In the proposed follow-up, you could knee is offered groin to bend him over and catch him in a *Guillotine Hold*. You can then knee his immobilized head, even a few times if you so wish. If you are a good ground fighter, you could then take your weakened opponent down with a combined Groin Kick/Sacrifice Throw, as illustrated (Belt holding *Sumi Gaeshi* variation – *Ju Jitsu*).

'Stop-the-kick'
Stealth Soccer Low Front Stop Kick and follow-up

The second example illustrates, *on the top of next page*, a '**stop-the-step**' Stealth Stop Kick: as your opponent steps in to attack while expecting your retreat, you stop-kick his shin in the middle of the step. Lower the leg and evade out while punching in a classic *Nagashi Tsuki* of *Wadoryu Karatedo* that takes you out of the centerline. After a natural high Roundhouse to the head of your still-flustered assailant, you can take him down by grabbing him while letting your leg lower directly into Sacrifice Throw position (*Yoko Otoshi – Judo*). Follow up on the ground.

'Stop-the-step' *Stealth Soccer Low Front Stop Kick and follow-up*

When stop-kicking, it is always good to let the opponent build his (over)confidence first by letting him nearly score with his favorite attack. Next time he'll try, painfully stop kick him.

Condition the opponent before stop-kicking him; the Stealth Soccer low Front Stop Kick in application

31. The Lotus Kick

General

We did present the 'Lotus Kick' as a basic kick in our book about *Essential Kicks*, under the name 'Instep Angular Front Kick'. But in fact, and especially in this work, the kick could simply be named: the **Stealth Outside Crescent Kick**. It is basically a high Outside Crescent Kick with a stealthy trajectory very close to the opponent; just like the Stealth Roundhouse Kick and the Stealth Hook Kick that we have encountered before. In previous work, we described it as an hybrid between an Upward Front kick and an Outside Crescent Kick; but we have here to underline the Stealth trajectory aspect. The classic Outward Crescent Kick starts with a straight leg and has a much wider trajectory. To make it stealthy you have to make it start with a somewhat bent leg and therefore with less body movement; and with a very narrow undetectable trajectory.

The concept is pretty easy to grasp, but the maneuver takes time and training to master: you need to get the necessary automatisms to set it up, and you definitely need to drill for *stealthy power*.

I personally love this little kick, and there was a time when I used it a lot in free-fighting for its speed and its sneaky surprising effect.

Description

The classic kick is taught as a rear-leg kick. It starts as an Upward Front Kick with some chambering, but not necessarily full chambering. The upper body stays immobile. The kick then develops up and to your inside, like an Outward Crescent Kick, but very close to the opponent's body. At head level it then starts traveling outwards into the opponent's face. The illustrations below show the execution of the classic version, and also a comparative trajectory to the corresponding Essential Outward Crescent Kick. An applied Kick is also shown for better understanding.

The Lotus Kick, or Stealth Outward Crescent Kick

Compare the trajectory of the Lotus Kick to that of the classic Outward Crescent Kick

Applied Lotus Kick

Key Points

- Keep the upper body immobile and especially head height.
- The hands must be high and stay in place
- The trajectory is a narrow arc ending at the head
- Leg extension and lifting are simultaneous
- Kick fully through the target.

Typical Applications

The classic execution of the kick is a rear-leg one; but the preferred embodiment is probably the front-leg version: it is faster and stealthier. Of course, each fighter will have his own idiosyncrasies; just practice both and you will feel what works better for you.
In the example below, you offensively 'crowd' your opponent with a high jab which purpose is to get his attention up and to close the distance. You then hop forward while making sure to stay low: this is a forward discreet move, not a jumping kick. The fast Lotus Kick will go through his guard and catch him by surprise. Follow up with a Palm Strike as you land. You could then very naturally keep pushing his chin back while taking him down with a Big Inner Reap Throw (*O Uchi Gari – Judo*). Whether you go down with him or not is a function of how good a ground-fighter you are.

Offensive Front-leg Lotus Kick

Another offensive application starts with *Karate*'s classic high *Kizami Tsuki/Gyacku Tsuki* opening (Jab/Cross combo). By punching deliberately high and keeping your hands there, you will keep the opponent's attention up while the kicking (rear) foot is climbing. You could follow up with another high Reverse Punch as you land.

Offensive Lotus Kick after Jab/Cross opening

Targets

This kick, in the Stealth version, is to target the head exclusively.

Specific Training

- The Stealth trajectory must be drilled in front of the mirror or with a partner holding a focus pad.
- Once the basic Stealth version is mastered, it is imperative to start drilling the *front-leg version* as well: this kick should be available to you from any foot position.
- This kick must then be drilled for **power** while keeping its **Stealth** properties: use the heavy bag or the standing bag. As it is a kick-though kick, it is also important to drill kicking powerfully *through* a focus pad or a basketball held by a partner at head level. Keep the kicking stealthy throughout though!

Drill for stealthy power with a partner holding a focus pad; pictures taken from a video, not of high quality but showing clearly the kick preferred development

Self Defense

Our first example will again be a fast front-leg version, but this time in a defensive context. As your assailant steps in to punch you, you inch forward and slightly out in a protective 'shell' guard instead of retreating as expected. Immediately hop forward (and low!) while executing the front-leg Stealth Lotus Kick. Kick through his head and lower the leg deep out; use the full power of your hips for a Hook Punch follow-up (*Mawashi Tsuki – Karatedo*). You could finish him up with a dangerous Spin-back Downward Hook Kick to the neck, very appropriate in this set-up.

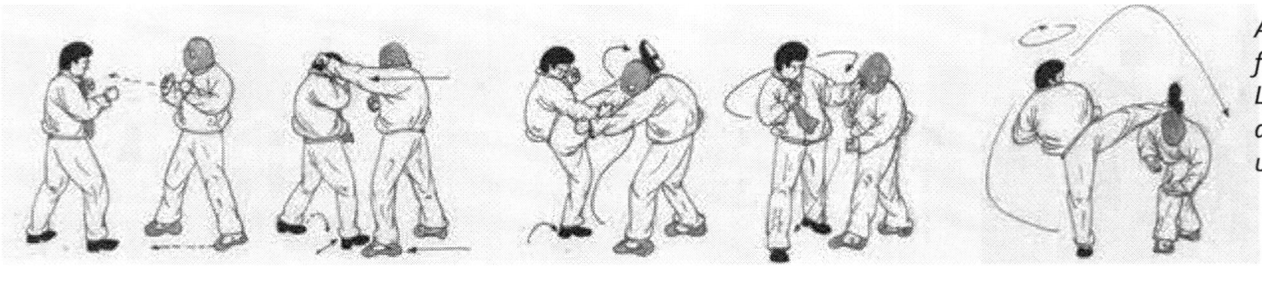

A defensive front-leg Lotus Kick, and follow-up

The classic rear-leg defensive application of the Lotus Kick is presented below. In this case, the kicking leg is released from body weight by the hip twist of the rear-hand block (*Gyacku Soto Uke – Karatedo*). The kick is then coming from the opponent's blind side and therefore even stealthier. The experienced Artist understands well that, in fact, the block (or check) and the kick are nearly simultaneous.

Twisting rear-hand Block and Lotus Kick

The next example illustrates a *Near-Stop Kick* (as defined in our previous book); it could be also named a Counter-Kick or an Offensive-defensive Kick. It is also kind of a trap, as you retreat under attack, but just enough to let your opponent over-extend slightly. As your opponent chambers back to settle back in guard, you execute what we described in *Stop Kicks* as an <u>Attack on Recovery</u>. You follow the chambering back of your assailant with a low forward hop and a front-leg Lotus Kick. Kick through his head and reverse-punch as your kicking foot lands. You could follow up with a sweep of his front leg, pulling **forward** (*De Ashi Barai – Judo*); and a Stomp Kick as he lands on the floor (See *Low Kicks* for the Stomp Kicks).

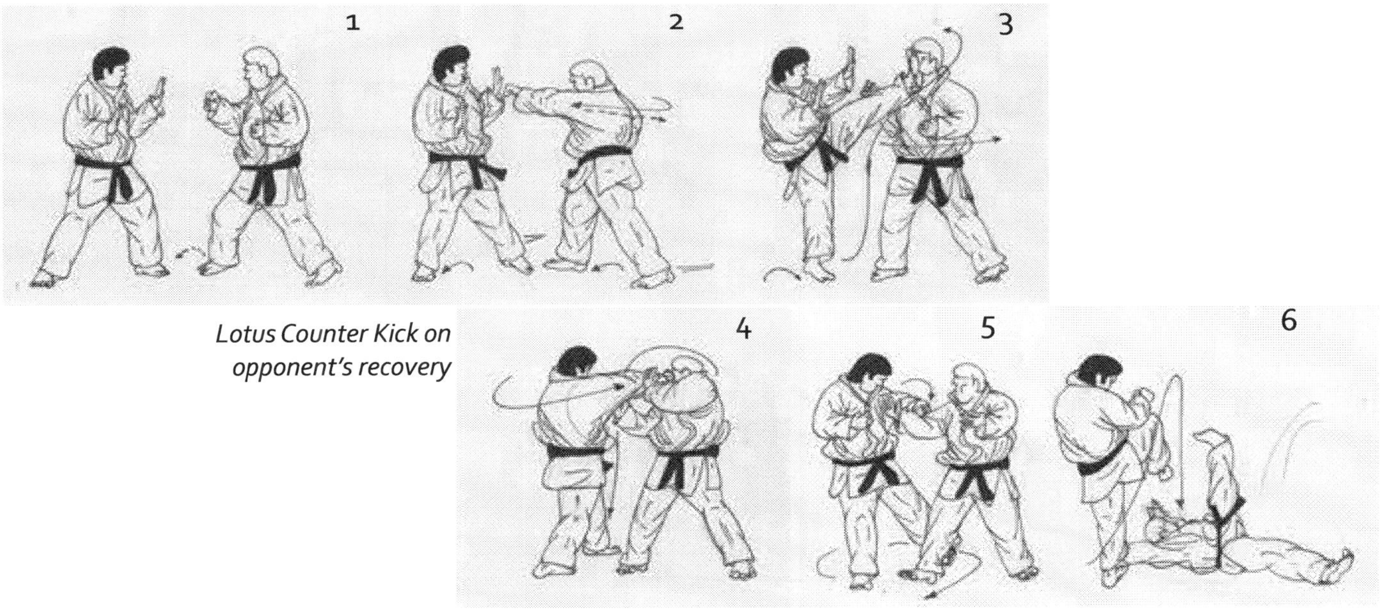

Lotus Counter Kick on opponent's recovery

Last but not least, we shall again show an offensive version of the front-leg variation, starting with a Progressive Indirect Attack which purpose is to better pull the attention upwards to conceal the lifting of the leg. In this example you start a jab towards the opponent's midsection. This Jab Punch must be convincing enough to cause a reaction, but it will then on evolve into a *high* jab. The movement is a smooth gradual circular retraction and extension; it is a classic **PIA** (Progressive Indirect Attack). By going first down, then up, you do attract even more attention to the higher gate than with a simple high feint. The photos, extracted from a dynamic video, show the development of the kick, not a kick-through this time. The follow-up proposed is a Palm Strike with the landing and a Hooking Upward Groin Back Kick. The experienced fighter will notice that the final position is perfect for an *Uchi Mata* or a *Harai Goshi* Judo Takedown (Not illustrated).

Front-leg Lotus Kick after Progressive Indirect high Jab

It's not whether you get knocked down; it's whether you get up.
~ Vince Lombardi

32. The Downward Back Kick

General

The last two kicks that we shall describe as **Ghost Kicks** are somewhat different and are presented as illustration of a sub-category of 'Surprise' Kicks. These are certainly Ghost Kicks, but more based on a mix of surprise and dissimulation than on dissimulation only; these are not preceded by misdirecting feints, but they have none of the 'immobile-upper-body' principles.
Both these 'Surprise Ghost Kicks' have been described in previous work as *Essential Kicks*; and so we shall only present them in brief. As mentioned numerous times, Stealth is about intention and nuances, not only technique. These **Surprise Kicks** could have been just as well presented in the following chapter about **Near-Feint Kicks,** with a note encouraging an emphasis on dissimulation during execution.

The first presented Surprise Ghost Kick is the Downward Back Kick, a.k.a **Scorpion Kick** or *Sasori Geri*; that we characterized in Essential Kicks as "sneaky and deceptive". It surprisingly comes from *Shotokanryu Karatedo*, a style not know at all for extravagant kicking. It is also present under various versions in the sneakier Art of Capoeira where it is sometimes named 'Scorpion' as well (*Escarpiao*), or Mule Kick (*Coice de Mula*). The kick is very unexpected in close quarters, and therefore very efficient if not overused. It works best as a Stop Kick, but can be great after a closing-in offensive combination. It has the particularity of lending itself naturally to following up with the fearsome Leg Scissors Takedown (*Kani Basami*), giving together a great fight-ending combination. The idea is very simple and easily understood by looking at the photos below: you bend deep and outside your close opponent, place your hand(s) on the floor and lift your leg up and forward to kick over your own body into your opponent's head.

The surprising Scorpion Kick, a special Ghost Kick

Description

As illustrated below, you simply bend over and place one hand on the floor and then lift your rear leg nearly straight up and diagonally. You keep bending the body forward and drive the foot *into* the surprised opponent's head, face or clavicle. The last leg of the trip is often slightly downwards; hence the name 'Downward Back Kick'. The Scorpion's tail analogy is very clear from the execution, which explains the convergence of the name in both Japanese and South American nomenclature. The bending of the upper body can be done and is preferably done on the *outside* of the opponent as illustrated above; it also can be executed on his inside as illustrated below.
As it is an unorthodox kick, it needs to be drilled for speed and ease of execution, but it is fact quite easy to master after some training. If you intend to use it, it is then wise to drill for power.

The Essential Downward Back Kick

Bending over on the opponent's **inside**

Key Points

- The bending and lifting of the rear leg are smoothly simultaneous. They must be executed with speed, not power.
- In the spirit of ghost-kicking, the bending must look like a frightened evasion or a cowering into shell defense. It is best done protected with the hands guarding the head.
- You must forcefully kick a few inches *into* the target.
- Try to connect with the heel.
- The power of the kick comes both from the leg lift (Glutes and lower back) and some leg extension at contact (Quadriceps).

Typical Applications

As mentioned above, the preferred use of the kick is as a Stop Kick. We shall present the classic drillings against a punch and against a kick for familiarization with the technique.

Stop-kicking a high punch with the Scorpion Kick

The first example shows the simple stop-kicking evasion against a committed Jab. You evade out and down while kicking in one single smooth move. Of course, -as always in stop-kicking-, it is all about timing. And the opponent adds the energy of his own forward movement to the impact.

The second example is a near-Stop Kick after blocking a Front Kick. The last thing your opponent will expect is see you dive outwards instead of coming with a conventional counter. The kick from above will be totally unexpected. With good timing, the same technique can be drilled without the block: you then evade the Front Kick by going forward and out of the centerline to execute the kick in step with no interruption and no block.

The Downward Back Kick, ***Sasori Geri****, as a counter, after blocking a Front Kick attack*

To cap this section, we present the simple straight use as a surprising offensive technique. You simply dive in front of your befuddled opponent and execute the kick. Of course, sudden explosive speed is of the essence. As hinted in the photos below, the opponent looks like wondering: what on earth is he doing? This could be reminiscent of some Chinese *Kung-Fu* sneaky schools like the Drunken Fist style or the various Monkey styles.

Offensive straightforward Scorpion Kick

Targets

Essentially the top of the head, the face or the clavicle.

Specific training

- The first step is to become familiar with the awkward technique itself, and this is best done on the heavy bag. Do not try to kick hard at first.
- Familiarization with a partner, static at first, will help you set up the technique. Make sure you dive both inside and outside the partner's guard.
- Once the technique becomes natural, you should work on speed and the sudden start of the kick with no tell-tales. In front of a mirror.
- ONLY when you can kick well, fast and suddenly, should you start working on power. Drill that with the heavy bag and a partner holding a focus bag.

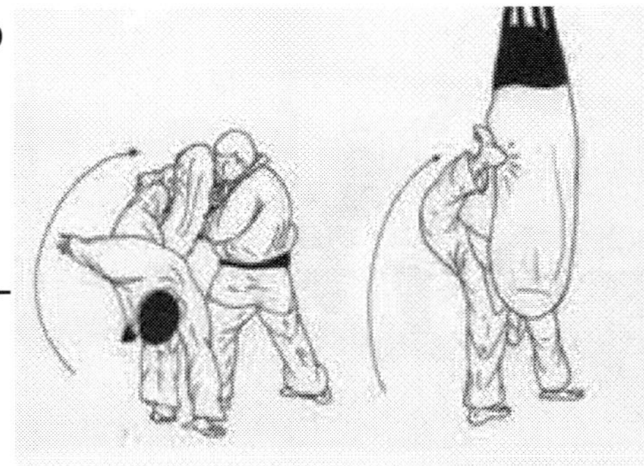

Drill with a partner and on the heavy bag

Self defense

The best offensive application of the kick is after a move that places you on the outside of the assailant. A good example would be a lunging Backfist Strike taking you out of the centerline. In the example below, you are threatened by an assailant and further misdirect him by raising open hands in a despondent move. As he approaches further, you unexpectedly lunge from your cowering stance forward and out, while executing a high Backfist that he will have to block. As he counters, you are already bent over behind him and your rear leg is travelling up. After the Surprise Ghost Kick hits him, you need to follow up; it is relatively easy as you are behind him. We shall present the classic Scissor Takedown follow-up in a further example and we shall illustrate another 'kicking' way to follow with instead: the Groin Hooking Back Kick with the other leg. You can execute this while staying bent over or while straightening up; just make sure that you 'hook' into the assailants groin and pull your foot back forward.

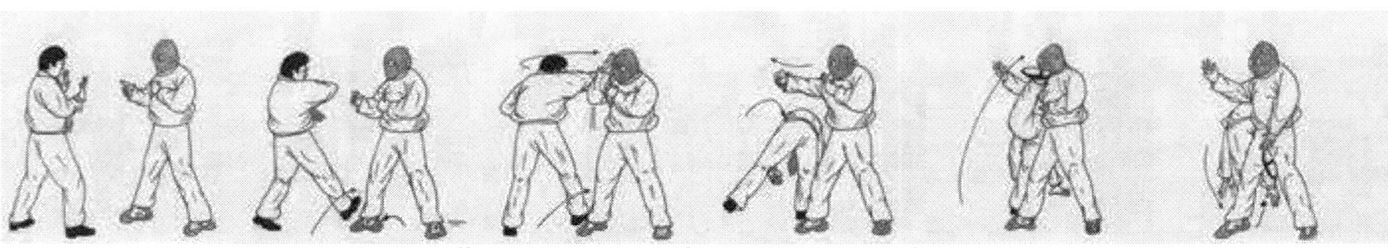

Offensive Sasori Geri after an opening Backfist

Of course the preferred use is as a *Stop Kick*, for example as the opponent steps forward while extending his hand to grab or strike.

Inside Downward Back Stop Kick

Last, but certainly not least, we shall finally illustrate the preferred Scissor Takedown follow-up that we mentioned several times in the section. The examples below are drills in classic orthodox stances and settings (*Ippon Kumite – Karatedo*). Once the technique is fully mastered, the Artist is invited to drill in more modern and relaxed stances, and to try the moves in light free-fighting.
The first sequence is against a classic Full Stepping Lunge Punch (*Oie Tsuki – Karatedo*). You step **forward** while evading **out** and bending forward; the Scorpion Kick is a Stop Kick. As soon as the kick has connected, you spread the other leg behind the opponent's front leg while keeping the kicking leg in place. You are in perfect position for *Kani Basami* (Scissors Throw – *Jiu Jitsu*). As he lands hard, you can heel-kick him in the face. Of course, the techniques are all executed in one uninterrupted move with smooth transitions.

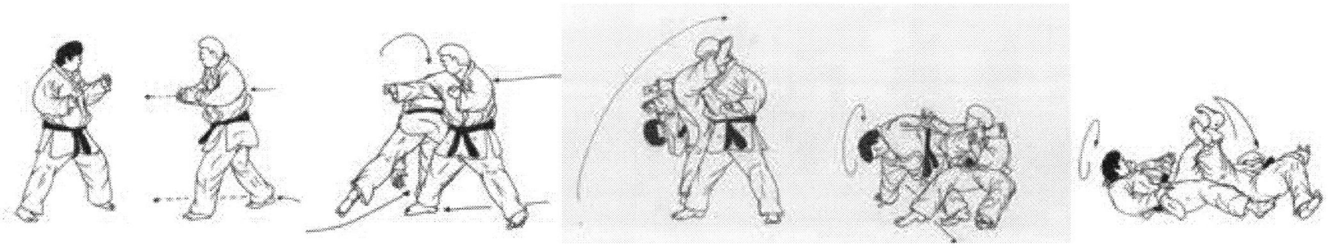

Classic Ippon Kumite drill: Uke executes Oie-Tsuki; Tori evades with Sasori Geri and concludes with Kani Basami and Kakato Geri

The last example is again a classic-type drill in which you handle a rear-leg full Penetrating Front Kick with an orthodox stepping back Downward Block (*Gedan Barai – Karatedo*). As soon as the kick is blocked, you initiate the Scorpion Kick and roll smoothly into the Scissor Throw and Downward Ground Heel Kick.

The Downward Back Kick and preferred follow-up against a Front Kick Attack

33. The Drop Overhead Back Kick

General

The Drop Overhead Back Kick is the second example we shall give of a ***Surprise Ghost Kick***. Its Ghost classification comes from the fact that it is impossible to see coming until very late, its Surprise middle name comes from the fact that it is very unexpected, in view of its convolution and acrobatic appearance. It is though, quite easy to execute; it just requires a sense of timing. This kind of kick is very typical of the misdirecting Art of Capoeira. It may be looked down upon by some who will consider it unnecessarily showy and quite inefficient; I can assure the reader that it is extremely harsh, especially as a Stop Kick. I even have had the chance to see it cause a knockout singlehandedly in a MMA bout.

The surprise effect comes from your disappearing down by bending forward in front of the opponent, just to have you feet popping up towards him from a handstand. The trajectory of the feet is mostly out of the adversary's field of vision. If you use it sparingly and as a Stop Kick against a high punching attack, it will be easily executed and will usually score. The kick lends itself naturally to a one-two with the other foot; you can then land back on your feet from where you came from, or you can decide to crowd your opponent and take him down by rolling forward onto him. It is quite a versatile technique.

The Drop Overhead Back Kick

Description

This is certainly not a static kick starting from a set position; it is a dynamic kick suddenly springing from an adequate moving set-up. But the classic execution for drilling its basic form starts from an orthodox guard. You then step forward while bending, which gives you momentum. This is done as if you are doing a handstand, which you basically are. As your hands touch the floor and start getting some of your body weight, your rear leg lifts off directly towards your opponent's face. Ultimately, this move will also pull up the other leg at some point. You kick powerfully a few inches into the target, and then, - in the classic version-, you chamber back by pulling back the legs to where they came from. In some cases, you can double-kick: once you have connected, you chamber back while kicking with the other foot! And some more acrobatic styles will have you kick through, roll forward and fall onto your struck opponent. It is advised to master the classic version first though.

Description (Continued)

The classic Drop Overhead Back Kick; drilled on the heavy bag

1

2

The classic Drop Overhead Back Kick is a great equalizer

Key points

- This is a timing kick only, best used as a Stop Kick.
- The downward drop must be sudden and fast.
- Kick at least a few inches into the target.
- You must be fully committed: no hesitation and no way back.

Typical applications

As mentioned, this is a 'timing' kick and therefore mainly a Stop Kick. You have to start the execution as early as possible once you have discerned a committed attack. As disserted in *Stop Kicks*, this is mostly based on intuition; intuition is itself based on experience and committed training. Your Surprise Kick could then start as early as the opponent's unconscious decision to launch is attack (*Sen No Sen*), and as late as making the bending forward an evasion from the actual strike. The *first* series of photos below shows a late '**evading**' version of the kick, still very surprising. The *second* series illustrates an early '**Sen No Sen**' start of the maneuver and the execution of the interesting *One-two Double-impact* version of the Kick.

1. Evading execution of the Overhead Back Stop Kick

2. Starting the kick as soon as the opponent commits to start his attack, executing the double version of the Overhead Back Kick

Typical Applications (Continued)

An example of stop-kicking use with extra surprise effect is the use of the kick against high Spin-back attacks. The opponent loses eye contact when spinning back, kicks or punches in the void, and the gets kicked high from down below. Surprise indeed!

The very unexpected Overhead Back Stop Kick against a high Spin-back Outside Crescent Kick

Targets

The face, throat, clavicle and upper sternum. You should aim to connect with the heel and penetrate a few inches into the target.

Specific training

This kick is relatively easy to master, but it needs familiarizing with *before* drilling for speed and power. Drill the kick from various positions, drill with and without a preceding step, drill the single and the double version of the kick, drill chambering back and drill kicking through into forward roll.

- Drill on the heavy bag as illustrated early in the section.
- Drill on the wall, preferably padded.
- Drill with a partner for fast set-up.
- Drill on the beach to counter any possible apprehension from falling down.

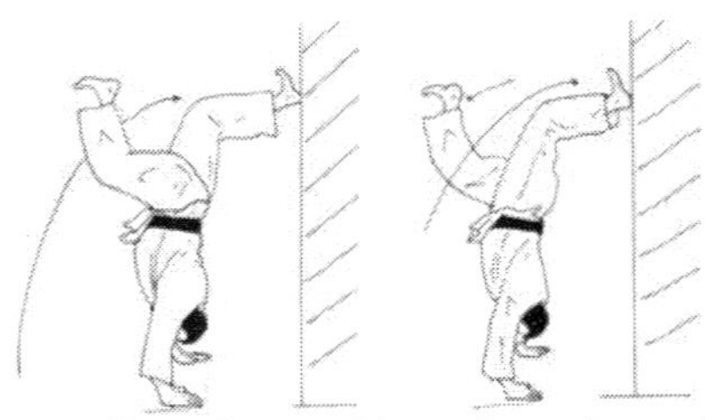

Drilling the Double Kick on the wall

Getting safely familiar with the Overhead Back Kick by drilling on the beach

Beach-drilling of the kick-through version of the Overhead Back Surprise Kick – Dotan De Bremaeker

Self Defense

The first example we shall present here will illustrate the fact that there are many ways to go down, and that could be a natural set up for this particular kick (The wide array of 'going down'-techniques is also a theme of our previous book about *Ground Kicks*). In this case, the kneeling down-evasion is a technique I love for Self-defense: it is sneaky, surprising and very easy to execute. Against a committed or rushing punch, you simply kneel down to evade while punching the assailant's groin. This is a great starting position for our Overhead Back Kick, especially in light of the fact that the opponent will most certainly lower his hands and leave his upper gate open. This is a fantastic opening that every Artist should know and drill; and, should you like the fancy Overhead Back Kick, this is an ideal

A fantastic Stop-Punch set up for the Overhead Back Kick

set-up. Our last example will make the connection with Ground Kicks. The Overhead Back Kick is a great kick to initiate from the ground against a standing opponent. The kick should be executed after some opponent conditioning: your opponent should be made used to some Ground moves that lead to nothing else than movement, and once he becomes reassured of his safety, you suddenly let a Ground move evolve into the kick. The reader is invited to refer to our previous book about Ground Kicks for Ground moves, Going-to-the-ground techniques and Standing-up maneuvers. He can choose a few and experiment. In fact, the kick could be at the end of a convoluted going down and ground-moving around combination.

The example below is a fantastic drill in itself for overall kicking proficiency, for all-terrain kicking awareness, for stamina and for ground movement. It is an interesting combination that can be adapted to your own preferences and to the specific situation; for example, you could start the combo from standing and going down one way or another, to roll into the kick as described. The flurry of moves is a misdirection in itself and reminiscent in the sneaky principles of the Art of Capoeira. The specific context for the move is an opponent unwilling to join you on the floor and giving you space to stand up safely in order to continue the fight standing. The kick will work even better if it has happened already earlier in the fight. You roll back to gather momentum for a forward roll all the way to a crouch, a natural way to get back up standing. But you use the full momentum to keep lunging forward from the crouch with one foot. From the deep lunge you execute the kick. This is a good set-up for keeping rolling onto him and get the fight on the ground where he did not want it.

The 'Roll-through' Overhead Back Kick from a Ground Guard

PART THREE

NEAR-FEINT KICKS

PART THREE NEAR-FEINT KICKS

Introduction to Near-feint Kicks

It has been argued several times in the course of this work that feinting is very much a thing of the mind and that many kicks can be executed with *some* level of feinting or stealth. In this third part of the book, we shall present briefly kick variations that do not make the grade to Stealth Kicks, but still are close; they all have some element of **unexpectedness** and **surprise** that could be emphasized by the proficient Artist and/or modified when needed.

These Kicks have all been presented before in our previous books, and will only be briefly presented as a basis for further research by the reader. It will hopefully get the reader thinking and help him realize that there could and should be some ***Stealth*** and ***Misdirection*** in nearly every technique.

Should one of those Surprise Kicks be of particular interest to the reader, it would then be up to him to dig deeper, to drill it and to make of it his own special Feint Kick with his own personal twists and emphasis.

Here come the Near-feint Kicks, organized in three general categories:

- Hopping Kicks
- Drop Kicks
- Trajectory-modified Kicks

34. Hopping Kicks

Hopping Kicks are basic kicks *during* which execution occurs a hop of the standing leg to close more range than expected. The hop occurs as late as possible in the execution so as to fool the opponent; in any case, it happens well after the chambering. To further fool the opponent, such a Hopping Kick is best executed after one or several too-short attempts of the regular (non-hopping) version of the kick. The emboldened opponent will retreat just enough to avoid the kick which will then turn out to be much longer in his reach. This is clearly Misdirection, with the hop itself being somewhat stealthy!
Our book about *Essential Kicks* presents the **Hopping Front Kick** and the Hopping Roundhouse Kick, but all Kicks basically lend themselves to this sneaky maneuver.
A good way to train for hop-kicking is to do dojo length of kicking *without lowering the kicking leg* and with simultaneous hops and kicks (from the chamber position).
The principles of Hop-kicking will be clear from the illustrative photos below. The Artist wanting to make those misdirecting Kicks will take the pains of 'preparing' the opponent with short kicks and will make sure that his hop, when it happens, is **long, late** and with **no** tell-tales (like the popping up of the head!).

The Hopping Front Kick; look at the reference on the floor

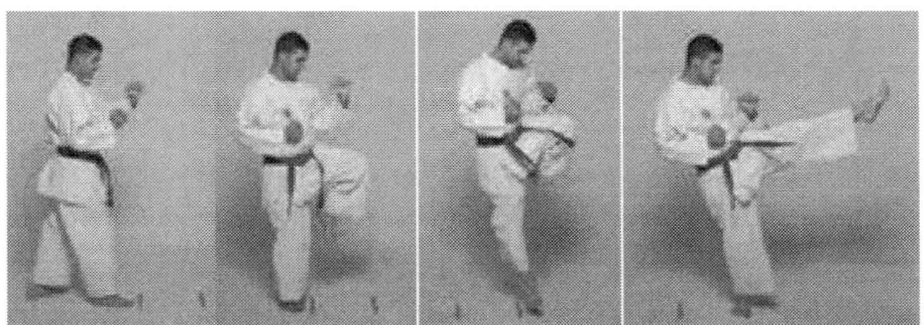

An exaggerated hop for better illustration of the Hopping Front Kick

The following two Photos series illustrate the surprise effect of the longer-than-expected Front Kick, executed by *Sensei Roy Faige*.

Applied Hopping Front Kick

When the opponent realizes the threat, it is already too late to flee

One of the uses of the Hopping Front Kick would also be closing of the distance on an opponent *whom you are pushing away*! In the example below, you counter a front bear hug by striking your assailant's ears, kneeing his groin and pushing him away forcefully. He may feel he is out of range for a follow-up, but he is certainly close enough for a Hopping Penetrating Front Kick. Finish him off with a Palm Strike and a 'Low Kick' (Straight-leg Roundhouse Kick to the outside knee).

Applied Hopping Front Kick to an opponent being pushed away, in a self-defense situation

The same principles apply for the **<u>Hopping</u>** version of the **<u>Side Kick</u>**. The later the hop, the more surprising the kick's reach will be to the opponent.

An applied execution of the kick is presented below. The Hopping Side Kick is executed just after a too-short regular Side Kick that will instill false confidence in the opponent. The Hopping Side Kick starts directly from the chamber-back position and scores. As the opponent bends over in pain, he is easily finished off with a Punch to the head.

The Hopping Side Kick: the development of the kick and the hop are simultaneous

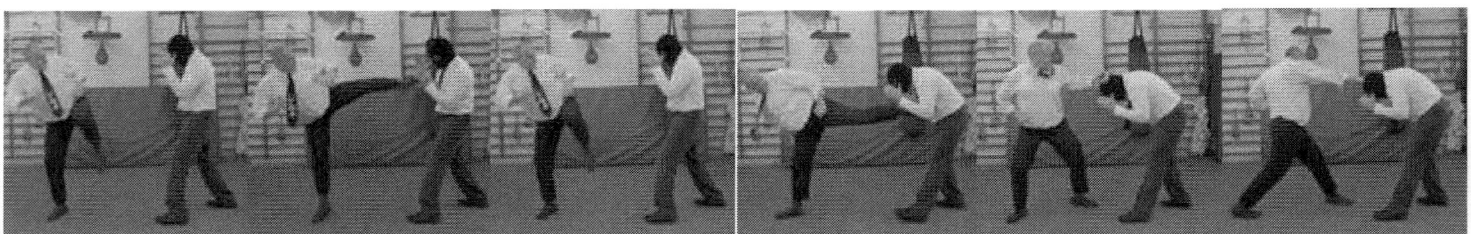

Applied Hopping Side Kick from chamber-back of conditioning regular Side Kick

The **<u>Hopping Roundhouse Kick</u>** is usually even more surprising than the straight kicks presented above. Being circular, they seem inherently shorter and limited by the maximum circumference. Not so if you stealthily move the center of the circle forward during execution with a low but long hop.

The Hopping Roundhouse Kick – Shay Levy

The stages of the Hopping Roundhouse Kick

In many cases, a short hop is enough to surprise, as illustrated below.

A small in-kick hop should be used to close on a retreating opponent

The Hopping Roundhouse Kick to the groin should be a fixture for self-defense situations in which the assailant feels you are too far to 'get' to him. It can then be a surprisingly fast Stop Kick, especially if used very early in the opponent's decision to attack (*Sen No Sen*). In the example below, you groin-kick an assailant lifting a stick to attack you. A Hammer-fist Strike to the head and a 'Low Kick' will terminate the confrontation.

A groin Hopping Roundhouse Stop Kick

The secret of getting ahead is getting started.
~Mark Twain

35. Drop Kicks

Drop Kicks have been covered in all our previous books. They are basically Ground Kicks delivered while or just after letting yourself fall suddenly down. There are many ways to go down to the ground and they have been covered in *Ground Kicks*. The purpose of Drop Kicks is to surprise and/or evade. Especially when used as Stop Kicks, they can be very efficient as the opponent tends to impale himself on them. A kick delivered while falling to the ground travels usually on a trajectory that stays long out of sight. The change of plane is also extremely surprising and unsettling to the opponent; it is especially unexpected in view of the negative connotation of falling to the ground. Hence the misdirection. But one must only fight a good ground-fighter once to understand that it could be just the opposite: the ground can sometimes be the preferred "high ground" for the skilled fighter. We will just show a few examples, and the reader is invited to consult our previous work. The basic Drop Kicks and Ground Kicks can then be drilled with a 'Feinting' frame of mind. The reader is invited to whet his appetite with the photos below, and to then start his own experimenting.

The simplest Drop Kick and the one which should be mastered first is the **Drop Front Kick**, aiming for the groin or knees. Drop at the last possible moment for maximum surprise.

The Drop Front Kick

More phases of the classic Drop Front Kick

The following series shows an applied Drop Front Kick against a committed stepping Lunge Punch; it shows clearly that the attacker is flustered in mid-step by the dropping opponent. Too late though.

Applied Drop Front Kick as a timing Stop Kick against a classic full-step Lunge Punch

In self-defense, the drop can be an evasion and the groin makes a perfectly legitimate target. The example below illustrates the use against a committed stick attack.

Groin Drop Front Kick against a full-powered stick diagonal strike

A more exotic version is the **Drop Twin Front Kick**, in which you kick with both legs simultaneously, in front-kick-fashion. This is a less practical kick, but very good against an opponent who cannot control his momentum or his developing kick. This 'breaking-the-open-door'- type of assailant will impale himself on the Twin Kick.
The kick is easy to understand.

The basic Drop Twin Front Kick

The phases of the Drop Twin Front Kick against a committed kick

The series below illustrates perfectly the preferred use of this kick against an opponent losing his balance forward as he tries to push you violently. As an assailant typically tries to bully you by pushing you on the chest, you drop just as he starts pushing (or *pushing again*) and let his momentum drive him into you Twin Kick. Simple but very effective. The drop must be sudden and at the last possible moment. The series below is concluded with a Ground Scissor Kick to the (hurt) opponent's leg.

The self-defense use of the Drop Twin Kick against a 'pushy' assailant

The principles are identical for the other Drop Kicks, like the **Drop Side Kick** illustrated just below. The Drop Side Kick is especially good against the groin of high kickers, whom your downward evasion will have literally kick into thin air.

The Drop Side Kick against a high kick

Clear illustration of the drop in a classic Drop Side Kick

Drop Side Kick in self-defense situation, with Scissor Kick follow-up

The **Roundhouse Drop Kick** is more common, because of the inherent speed of the Roundhouse Kick. But, as it cannot stop a forward momentum, it will generally target the groin only. It is, of course, another great Stop Kick against high kicking attacks. There are two basic ways to execute a Roundhouse Kick while dropping or on the ground: the rear-leg version and the front-leg version. The front-leg version is faster, stealthier and more in use, but it is good to drill both sides for versatility. The 'Drop' principles are the same, and are the same as for other Drop Kicks.

The more difficult rear-leg Roundhouse Drop Kick

The faster and more common front-leg Roundhouse Drop Kick

A front-leg Drop Roundhouse Kick against high kick

Another front-leg Drop Roundhouse Stop Kick with Takedown follow-up

Self-defense Groin Drop Roundhouse Kick against a jabbing knife; followed by twisting Ground groin Hook Kick to takedown

An applied rear-leg Drop Roundhouse Kick against a high kick

In the spirit of the previous Twin Drop Kick (Front), there is also a quite useful **Drop *Twin* Roundhouse Kick**, which importance is in the *concussion* effect it has on impact. It is a fully-committed kick-through kick that uses all the body weight, and it is therefore very powerful on impact. It is therefore enough to target the general area of the opponent's groin to have groin pain results from the impact waves; and the kick-through in that area is generally enough to also cause the opponent to fall down. Both feet can impact at different levels, and the Solar Plexus can also be a worthwhile target.

A high-target Drop Twin Roundhouse Kick

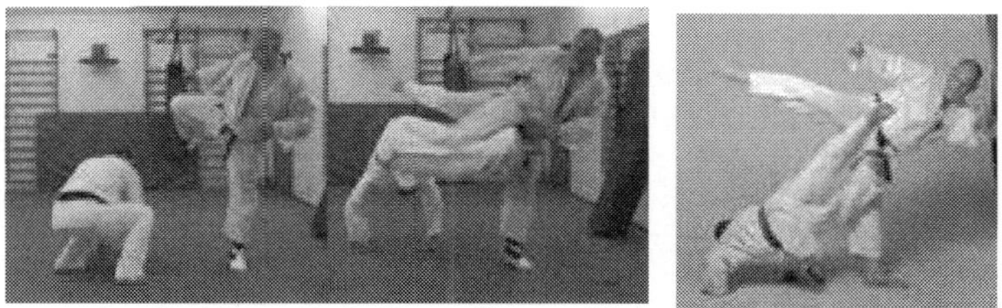

Applied Drop Twin Roundhouse Kicks against high kicks

Self-defense Drop Twin Roundhouse Kick as downward evasion from a committed knife jab

The **Drop Back Kick** can be used against a facing opponent or an assailant coming behind you; in the first case you pivot half-a-turn while dropping down. You can either stay on one knee and hands to kick with the other leg; or you can stay on both hands and kick back with both feet, donkey-style. All versions are very powerful because of the back muscles involved.

Drop Back Kick against an opponent behind

Half-drop Back Kick against rushing punch attack from behind

The chamber and development of the Drop Back Kick

The powerful Drop Twin Back Kick against front attacker

The dropping principles are the same for **Drop Hook Kicks,** of course. A few examples are illustrated below.

An offensive Drop Hook Kick to the outer thigh as the start of a Ground Kicking attack

Classic Drop Spin-back Hook Stop Kick against a high kicker

You want to know the difference between a master and a beginner? The master has failed more times than the beginner has ever tried ~Yoda

36. Trajectory-modified Kicks

The Trajectory-modified Kicks are basic kicks that look like they will not reach the opponent but which trajectory is tweaked to surprisingly do so. By emphasizing the first part of the kick, you can transform these kicks in to true Misdirecting Kicks. The examples will shed light on this definition, and the idea will immediately be clear. Some of those, sometimes called 'Special Positioning Kicks' are also the result of evading footwork that takes you to uncommon set-up situations from which a regular kick is totally unexpected and/or invisible. Again, examples will be self-explanatory

The simplest example would be the **Side Front Kick**, a kick to the side that is executed just like an orthodox Front Kick but in the 'wrong' direction. This kick is anecdotally called a Side Kick (*Yoko Geri*) in *Wadoryu Karatedo*. It is quite surprising though, and especially in self-defense situations where you are attacked from the side or by two aggressors. The surprise/feint effect can be reinforced *by looking intently forward while kicking sideways.*

The classic Side Front Kick

The Kick needs not be fully sideways, but can be diagonal, like in the classic Tai Chi form

The Front Side Kick is very useful after a deep forward diagonal evasion

The kick is great for multiple assailant self-defense, but it would be better to look at the opponent you are not kicking for more surprise effect

Typical Wado-ryu style: An example of a kick-evading ***front-leg*** *Side Front Kick and mean follow-up takedown*

The **Outward-tilted Front Kick** is very useful kick that can also be executed in a near-feint way. This is a technique that I used much in my tournament days against opponents feeling safe from straight kicks because of their Side Guard positions, presenting their well-protected narrow side only. This kick is a classic *Essential Kick* in many curriculums which underlines its importance and practicality. It is the '*Gyacku Mawashi Geri*' of many Karate schools and the '*Dragon Kick*' of Okinawan styles. It is basically a hybrid between a Front Kick and a small Outside Crescent Kick, but it starts clearly as a Front Kick from a Front Chamber. It will go around the Side Guard though to connect with the unprotected front of the opponent. The later the start of the curving of the trajectory, the more a Feint Kick it will be. The rest is mind-games.

Opposite views of the Outward-tilted Front Kick

*Applied Outward-tilted Front Kick: surprise-kicking from **outside** after blocking an incoming kick to the inside*

The Kick's principles are easily understood from hitting a diagonally-hold focus shield: deliveries from opposite views

The **Inward-tilted Front Kick** is the opposite of the previous Outward-tilted one, but based on the same 'curving' principles. It is now more of a hybrid between a Front kick and a Small Roundhouse Kick, attacking from the side an opponent expecting a straight kick. The kick starts from a Front Chamber and curves inwards as late as possible. The groin of a Side Guard opponent is the preferred target.

Applied Inward-tilted Front Kicks

The **<u>Oblique Front Kick</u>** is a classic Front Kick executed *<u>while</u>* pivoting on the standing foot; the pivot is generally on the in-side and can go all the way to a 90 degrees pivot according to the circumstances. This can be a very surprising kick because the pivot starts after the chamber and the change of trajectory is not expected. This is an important kick to drill for general kicking proficiency, and so is it described in our book about *Essential Kicks*. It is a very useful and versatile kick in dynamic situations where everything moves. (An additional example in compounded use is also provided in the section below about Oblique Roundhouse Kicks) Besides the surprise offensive use from unexpected position, this versatile kick is good to use after strongly deflecting a momentum-driven straight-kicking opponent, whether blocking to the inside or to the outside.

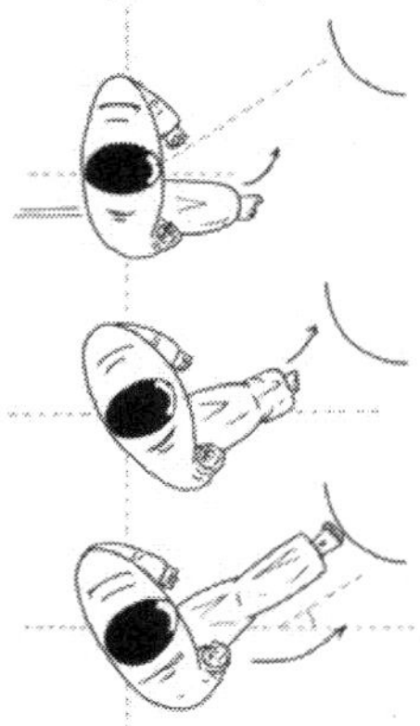

Top View of the Oblique Front Kick: well-worth drilling

The Oblique Front Kick: easy to understand

Oblique Front Kick after **Inside** *Block of Incoming Front Kick*

Oblique Front Kick after **Outside** *Block of Incoming Front Kick*

Switch Kicks are also classic kicks, but delivered just after switching rear and front legs more or less in place. In fact, the former front foot rebounds on the floor in its now-rear position, in order to allow for a powerful rear-leg kick. The trajectory modification consists in the front foot going back to rebound into a chamber, instead of going straight up into the chamber. All kicks can be executed this way, and the switching allows for: distance adjustment, rhythm break, use of most powerful leg, *misdirection* and *surprise*. It can be executed with a lifting of the hands for further flustering of the opponent. We shall only present the **<u>Switch *Front* Kick</u>** and the reader can refer to our previous books for other applications.

The Switch Front Kick

Exaggerated *hop in Switch Front Kick, for illustration only. The head does not go higher during hop!*

A great use of the Switch: evade a Low Kick to the front leg; the foot then rebounds at the rear for a powerful **rear-leg** *Front Kick!*

The **Front-chambered Side Kick** could have been presented in Part One about fully-fledged Feint Kicks, in the spirit of the Front-chambered Roundhouse or of the Front-chambered Hook Kick. But it is quite a trivial classic kick, and is as such described in our book about *Essential Kicks*. In fact, the front-chamber is the way the basic Side kick is delivered in some styles. With the right emphasis and state of mind though, it can become a Feint Kick and it is therefore worth mentioning briefly. The trajectory of the foot to the Side Kick Chamber is purposely angular and long, instead of round and smooth. The rhythm is broken and the path is longer, in order to emphasize the fake Front Kick that will not be coming. Of course, it will work best after a few 'conditioning' Front Kicks. With the right mind-set, this can become a full Misdirecting Kick.

The Front-chambered Side Kick

Applied Front-chambered Side Kick: the Side Kick is longer than the Front kick

The complex chamber of the Front-chambered Side Kick can also be a Leg Block to Side Kick maneuver

The **Oblique Back Side Kick** is one of those *Special Positioning Kicks*, using evasion for a set-up in which the trajectory of the kick is not orthodox. You step out and forward obliquely to find yourself on the in-side of your opponent; instead of completing the step, the rear leg lifts into a Back Side Kick. Pretty simple but confusing if well-executed. The misdirection is emphasized if you look like you are fearfully fleeing sideways. The 'Back' in the name of the kick refers to the kick being delivered slightly as a Back Kick because of the set-up; refer to the *Essential Book of Martial Arts Kicks* for more about the 'Back' Side Kicks.

The classic Oblique Back Side Kick

The Kick is best used as a Stop Kick

But the Oblique Back Side Kick can also be used offensively; you can, for example, lunge forward diagonally while delivering a high Back-fist Strike. The Kick will follow naturally.

An offensive Oblique Back Side Kick and painful follow-up

The *Kneeling-up Kicks* are definitely surprising kicks, deeply ingrained in Chinese and East-Asian Arts. They have been presented in our book about *Essential Kicks*, but they definitely have their place in a work about misdirection, feint and surprise. They may seem convoluted, but are quite effective, on top of being excellent drills for stamina and kicking proficiency. The change of plane is as unsettling as that of Drop Kicks or Flying Kicks. We shall present the **Kneeling-up Side Kick** only, as the principles are identical for the Kneeling-up Roundhouse. Understanding will be pretty straightforward, but only drilling will make this natural and effective.

The unexpected Kneeling-up Side Kick

The **Oblique Roundhouse Kick**, in the spirit of the previous Oblique Front Kick, is a technique that must be drilled, regardless of whether you are going to use it as a Near-feint Kick or not. It is a fantastic drill for situational kicking and general proficiency. The idea is pretty easy to understand: you are, or *you do place yourself*, in a situation in which your Roundhouse Kick needs to travel *more than 180 degrees* to hit the target. This is obviously unorthodox, unexpected, and has the additional bonus of delivering more power (Coming from acceleration on a longer trajectory). See the illustrations below.

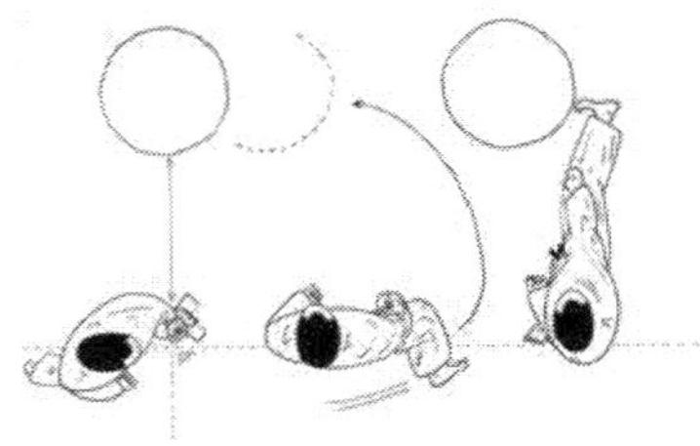

Drilling the classic Oblique Roundhouse kick

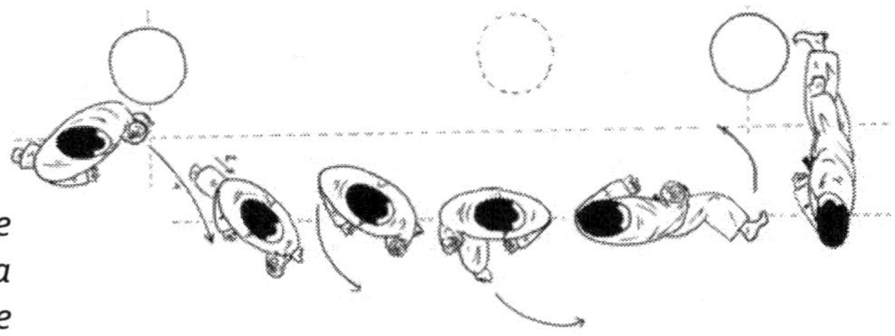

Evading forward to place yourself in position for a surprising Oblique Roundhouse Kick

Forcefully blocking a straight kick can place you and your assailant in relative positions requiring an Oblique Roundhouse Kick as a counter. Evading out places you in the same situation (The Photos in the second series below unfortunately do not catch the Oblique Roundhouse at impact).

Oblique Roundhouse Counter-Kick and follow-up

Evade out, Oblique Roundhouse-kick; follow up

A classic offensive use of the Oblique Roundhouse Kick is after a deep-lunging high Reverse Punch, as often executed by points-karate fighters. You lunge fast to catch your opponent's lead hand and deliver a high Reverse punch; the hand catch helps preventing flight and acts as a great diversion. Instead of pulling your back leg straight forward, you pivot sideways while keeping hold of the opponent's front hand. You are in perfect position for a body Oblique Roundhouse Kick, as you opponent expects further straight high punches! A great technique, to be executed smoothly and fast.

Oblique Roundhouse Kick in a fight-tested classic offensive combination

Another offensive use is after the fantastic *Backfist Diagonal Lunge* opening move. As illustrated, you lunge **long, forward and out** and launch what should be then an unexpected kick.

The second series, below, shows a compounded move after the Backfist diagonal lunge out of the centerline: execute first an *Oblique* Front *Kick* , but which will turn after impact and chamber-back into a *Roundhouse* Kick from out of the opponent's vision range.

Oblique Roundhouse Kick after Diagonal Backfist Lunge

Double *Oblique Kick: Front to Roundhouse after Diagonal Lunge Backfist opener*

For the sake of completeness, we also present two more Near-Feint *Roundhouse* Kicks.

First comes the ***Front-leg*** **Oblique Roundhouse Kick**; also a surprising Oblique Kick, but with a different footwork pattern.

An offensive Front-leg Oblique Roundhouse Kick; different approach, same results

Then comes the shorter-trajectory **Evading Roundhouse Kick**, which is very simple but embodies much the misdirection and dissimulation principles of feint kicking: the set-up makes your opponent react in a desirable way that will open him for a kick difficult to detect. In the example below, you feint a high reverse punch together with a front kick chamber. As your opponent reacts with a block, your chamber turns into a deep evading step that takes you out of the opponent's vision range. You block the expected Backfist counter while starting a difficult-to-detect Stealth Roundhouse Kick to his opened ribs.

A trap: the evading Roundhouse Kick

The **Oblique Hook Kick** is a favorite of mine, based on the same principles than the previous Oblique Kicks. It is very fast, and I have found it very unexpected. You simply step forward and out of the centerline to evade an attack and kick with the rear-leg; the trajectory is longer than for a regular Hook Kick because of the relative positions of the protagonists.

Oblique Hook Stop Kick against a Lunge Punch

Oblique Hook Stop Kick against a kick

A good offensive application of the Oblique Hook Kick is after a long Reverse Punch/ High Jab attack. The straight line deep attack gets the opponent's attention on the centerline. The high jab covers half-a-step from which you will lunge diagonally, and then launch your rear-leg Hook Kick. This is a very practical technique with high scoring potential.

An offensive application of the disconcerting Oblique Hook Kick

The **Half-pivot Hook Kick** is a fantastic little kick based on a different evading step. It is easy and sneaky, and it definitely should be drilled by all. The kick start with a 90 degree pivot on the front leg and out of the centerline, reminiscent of the *Tai Sabaki* of *Aiki Jitsu*. From there on, the kick is delivered easily and sneakily; it is recommended to execute from the opponent's blind side for Stealth. It is illustrated below against a full step lunge punch; it can be executed with a block, or as a no-block evading Stop Kick. In any case, a great and sneaky technique.

Half-pivot Hook Stop Kick, no blocking

Evade, block, grab and execute the Half-pivot Hook Kick

A classic offensive use of the Half-pivot Hook Kick is after a classic lunge jab/reverse punch: you pivot out, to hop forward with an undetectable front-leg Hook Kick.

An offensive application of the Half-pivot Hook Kick

The **Oblique Spin-back Hook Kick** is another simple but hard-to-detect kick with fancy footwork: your front foot steps forward and in. It is faster than a regular Spin-back Hook Kick because of the shorter trajectory; it makes it a good Offensive Kick. The principle is in line with previous Oblique Kicks and quite easy to grasp. Go and try.

The Oblique Spin-back Hook Kick; the oblique step is very clear from the line on the floor

An offensive Oblique Spin-back Hook Kick, starting with an Angling Back-fist Strike

Afterword

Be extremely subtle, even to the point of formlessness. Be extremely mysterious, even to the point of soundlessness. Thereby you can be the director of the opponent's fate.
~Sun Tzu

We have come to the end of our imperfect research about Feint Kicks and Ghost Kicks. As mentioned many times, and as concretized by the 'Near-feint Kicks' part, it should be clear to the reader that this book present a certain classification and a certain outlook that is by no means absolute. This is the way the author feels about Stealth Kicking, in a general way suited to his experience and morphology.
In no way should the reader feel that this is an orthodox presentation set in stone. It is, in my eyes, the basis for a personal exploration and research suited to each Artist in its own way.

Always be yourself, express yourself, have faith in yourself, do not go out and look for a successful personality and duplicate it
~Bruce Lee

Another message this work has tried to impart is the following: Any kick or technique can be somewhat stealthy or misdirecting, or it can be set up in a way that is. If your personality is compatible to such a way of fighting, it will be in your interest to drill the techniques presented in this book, and then to look for similar 'angles' in your regular preferred techniques. Drilling the techniques as presented in this book, even if they do not 'feel' right for you, will open your eyes and intuition to variations of your own that will give you an additional 'misdirecting edge' that can only help. Train in the way intended here before wandering on your own; some complex things need getting used to at first, but they will soon feel natural.
Pure Dissimulation and Misdirection are not for everyone, but they can certainly give an advantage to all fighters. Training in the techniques illustrated here will also give the fighter an insight of what could be coming his way one day or another from sneaky adversaries.

Some Arts are based on some of those principles of surprise, cunning and sneakiness. *Ninjitsu* comes to mind as an archetype of misdirecting fighting. The Chinese Arts of **Drunken Man** and **Monkey** Style *Kung Fu* are based on erratic movements which purpose is to trick the opponent into complacency and set him up for unexpected strikes. *Capoeira* emphasizes 'trickiness' (*Malandragem, Malicia* in Portuguese) and its constant dancing move is the taunting that dissimulates the start of real attacks.
If feinting and tricking your opponent is a way that suits your personality or your fighting style at a certain phase, you then have to make it a way of looking at things. For every technique you execute, think how you could dissimulate it for longer, or how could you get the attention of your opponent away from the real thrust of the attack.
Remember that misdirection is not limited to the complex kicks presented in this book: a body move, a hand move, a glance, a word, a shout, a stumble, an appearance of fearfulness, any of those and many more can be enough to have your opponent miss the fraction of a second he would have needed to see your real attack coming.
Many times in this work have we reminded the reader that keeping his hands high will always attract attention, even for a critical millisecond. This is very much the misdirecting principle used by illusionists. These hand moves can be of all types and it befalls to the reader to explore and choose what is most suitable. For example, pushing into the (too) tight guard of an opponent will both disturb and misdirect attention, allowing for a groin kick.

Lunge to push-in a tight high guard into the assailant's own face and groin-kick

The example below is presented, again, to remind the reader that everyday objects should be used in self-defense situations. Throwing your keys or anything you hold towards an assailant's eyes will allow you to kick him, and/or more. And it could be your bag, dirt collected from the ground as you seemingly cower in fear... anything goes. That's cunning, that's sneakiness, that's misdirection.

Throw your keys towards the eyes of an assailant and kick him as he instinctively lifts his hands

And here is to make you think further at nearly the same thing. Your mind should roam free of banalities and be ready to add layers of misdirection.

...The illustrations below show how you can add an additional serving of cunning at throwing something towards an assailant's face. Instead of throwing it directly from your hand, as would be expected and as maybe your assailant is aware, you can let it fall on your foot while looking in panic. You can then kick it up towards him while brandishing open hands to keep his attention up. In the example illustrated, you let your bag fall down to be kicked towards his face. Of course, it could be any other object. Kick immediately as he lifts his hands instinctively, and follow up fiercely. That's cunning. That's misdirection. That's feinting.

Letting an everyday object fall on your foot to be kicked towards the assailant's eyes

Think about doing the same thing with a walking stick or an umbrella. If you hold a walking stick or a long umbrella, the assailant would expect you to use it as a weapon, wouldn't he? Imagine his surprise if you let it fall down (on your foot) and lift your hands in fearful surrender. Of course kicking it towards his eyes will surprise him even more... (not illustrated). Layer upon layer of misdirection.

Everyday objects can be used as weapons, as well-known to experienced Artists. But you are invited to broaden your mind and look for the use of those as diversion and misdirecting moves as well. To each his own affinities, just think about it. If you do, my work is done.

This reminds me of a high school friend who used to walk around in wooden clogs; it was strange looking fashion-wise, but quite comfortable according to him. I grew up in Central Africa where personal security was a big problem back then, and where we had to be alert and careful. My friend used to train to powerfully kick one of his clogs away with precision, using a bow and arrow target. He could hit bull's eye nearly every time at 10 meters. I do not remember if it has ever been used in self-defense, but imagine the surprise of a would-be mugger getting hit in the face with a wooden shoe....

In the absence of props, hand and body movements will do. And you can reinforce them by talking, shouting and even singing. The old: "Look behind you!" may seem childishly stupid but it can work long enough to dissimulate your launching your attack. Doing something crazily unexpected will also surprise. Of course, the whole art of *Kiai Jitsu* (Energy shouting from the belly) is related to this topic: A sudden shout (*Kiai*) does paralyze the opponent for a fraction of a second.

...Even childish hand wavering as misdirection will work: remember that you only need a millisecond of inattention to get you real attack on the way. It is interesting to note that the *Kuji-Kiri* hands signs of *Nin Jitsu* were also used to misdirect while also playing on the superstitions and supernatural beliefs of the time.
In fact, *Nin Jitsu* has many prop-less techniques and series that aim to drill moving the body and hands to misdirect the opponent; one such drill is presented below. Remember all those, be on the lookout for new ideas and research on your own all that can be done in the spirit of Stealth and Feinting. Even if you are a more straightforward fighter, your Art will only be better for it! ***Good Luck!***

Childish hand moves with verbal misdirection will befuddle your opponent and allow for an undetected first attack

Examples of Nin Jitsu esoteric hand signs

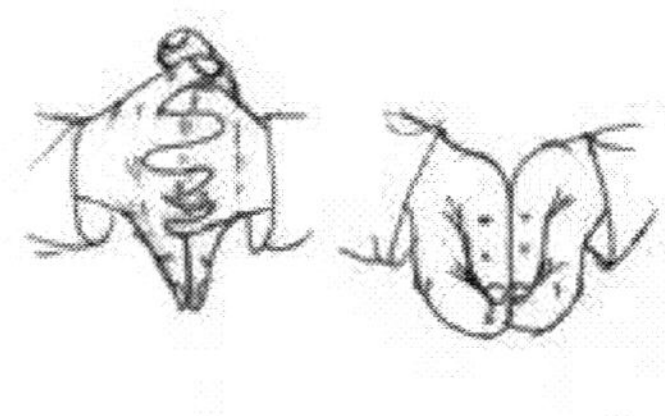

Nin Jitsu drill, body and hand moves draw attention away from incoming kick

"Misdirection is the key to survival, never attack what your enemy defends, never behave as your enemy expects, and never reveal your true strength,..."
~'Romulan' Quote

<u>If you have enjoyed the book and appreciate the effort behind this series, you are invited to write a short honest review on Amazon.com.</u>..It has become extremely difficult to promote one's work in this day and age, and your support would be much appreciated. Thanks!

All questions, comments, additional techniques, special or vintage photos about Feint Kicks, or other Kicks, are welcomed by the author and would be introduced with credit in future editions. Just email:**martialartkicks@gmail.com**

The author is trying to build a complete series of work that, once finished, could become an encyclopedic base of the whole of the Martial Arts-Kicking realm, a base on which others could build and add their own experiences.

In his endeavors the author has already penned:

- **The Essential Book of Martial Arts Kicks** – *Tuttle Publishing* (2010)
- **Plyo-Flex** - Training for Explosive Martial Arts Kicks (2013)
- **Low Kicks** - Advanced Martial Arts Kicks for Attacking the Lower Gates (2013)
- **Stop Kicks** – Jamming, Obstructing, Stopping, Impaling, Cutting and Preemptive Kicks (2014)
- **Ground Kicks** – Advanced Martial Arts Kicks for groundfighting (2015)

In the same frame of mind, the following works are in preparation:

- Suicide Kicks
- Combo Kicks
- Joint Kicks

Only one who devotes himself to a cause with his whole strength and soul can be a true master. For this reason mastery demands all of a person.

~Albert Einstein

LOW KICKS are often neglected by Martial Artists: they seem easy to execute and are not especially spectacular. Big mistake! Low Kicks are probably the most suitable techniques for real-life combat and self-defense. It is not by chance that the Martial Arts closest to their martial roots and furthest from modern sport often spurn high kicks for low ones. This makes them all the more valuable and surprising when used.***LOW KICKS*** need training just like any other Martial Arts maneuver. Once you have learned them and drilled them seriously, you will have in your arsenal some of the most useful of fighting techniques. This book codifies the different possible Low Kicks in categories and goes on to describe their variations and applications with examples taken from various Martial Arts.

Plyometrics and Flexibility Training for Explosive Martial Arts Kicks and Performance Sports presents a system of plyometric exercises and intensive flexibility training designed to increase your kicking power, speed, flexibility and skill level. Based on scientific principles, ***PLYO-FLEX*** exercises will boost your muscles, joints and nervous system interfaces to the next performance level. After only a few weeks of training, you should see a marked improvement in the speed of your kicks and footwork, the power of your kicks, the height of your jumps, your stamina and your overall flexibility. Hundreds of illustrations and photographs will guide you through the basic plyometric and stretching exercises.

STOP KICKS are probably the most effective and sophisticated kicks a fighter can use: they are the safest as they are delivered as your opponent is at his most vulnerable. ***STOP KICKS*** are delivered just as your opponent is fully committed, physically or mentally, to his own attack and as he is starting execution of his attack based on your relative position and his expectation that you can only block in place or retreat. Stop Kicks are executed when your opponent cannot change his mind any more, and they will also use to their advantage the additional power of his attacking momentum.
To paraphrase a well-known author: the most dangerous fighter, the one you should fear, is the one who waits patiently for you to make a mistake...

In this day and age of MMA, the importance of ground-fighting is clear to all Martial Artists. But kicking on and from the ground is often a neglected skill. ***GROUND KICKS*** fills that void and presents all the relevant kicking techniques with hundreds of applications. Whether you are on the ground by choice or you have been taken down, whether your opponent is standing or is on the ground with you, whether you are a good grappler or you are trying to keep a good grappler at bay, whether you were caught unawares sitting on the floor or you have evaded down on purpose, whether you are a beginner or you are an experienced Artist, ...this book has the appropriate kick for the situation. Being on the ground is certainly not being vanquished.

Other genres from Fons Sapientiae

Available in paperback and Kindle formats on Amazon

The Manual is the definitive guide to Enhanced Concentration, Super Memory, Speed Reading, Note-Taking, Rapid Mental Arithmetic, and the *Ultimate Study Method* (USM).

The techniques presented are the culmination of decades of practical experience combined with the latest scientific research and time-tested practices. The system described herewith will allow the practitioner to:

- Read faster with higher comprehension.
- Remember any type of information instantly.
- Store information in long-term memory.
- Enhance concentration and focus.
- Access deeper levels of the mind.
- Induce relaxation.
- Rapidly perform complex mental arithmetic.
- Master the Ultimate Study Method (USM).

USM is a synergistic combination of established techniques for Concentration, Long-Term Memory, Speed Reading, and Note-Taking. It involves a systematic procedure that allows the practitioner to study any topic fast, efficiently and effectively.

USM can be applied to all areas of educational study, academic research, business endeavours, as well as professional life in general.

Rain Fund: A riveting thriller

"...For the safety of the readers, this book ought to come with the disclaimer: leave this book read half-way at your own risk. Unless you are Superman, you won't be able to concentrate on much else until you have read the last page of "Rain Fund". The time has come for Patterson, Ludlum, Dan Brown et al to slide over and make space at the top for Marc Brem." - Shweta Shankar for Readers' Favorite

"...In the good tradition of Ludlum and Grisham. Five Stars" Aldo Levy

"Autistic geniuses charting financial markets; Mobster-fuelled Ponzi schemes; sophisticated hardware viruses; spies; and a rising superpower that strives for dominance – so realistic it is frightening."

COMING SOON

SACRIFICE
KICKS
Advanced Martial Arts Kicks for Realistic Airborne Attacks
Flying, Hopping, Jumping and Suicide Kicks
from Karate, Kung Fu,Krav Maga, Tae Kwon Do, MMA, Muay Thai, Capoeira and more
The 'Kicks' Series, Volume 6
by Marc De Bremaeker

Printed in Great Britain
by Amazon

63964847R00151